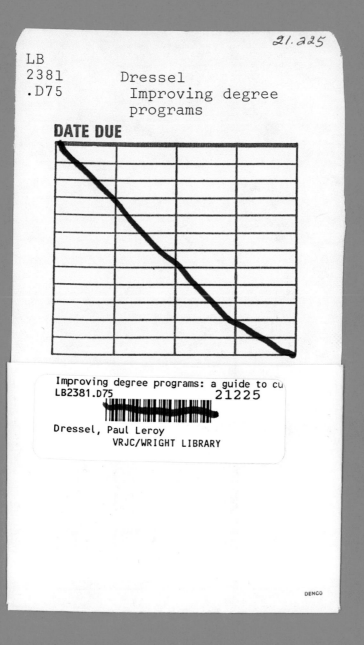

Other books by PAUL L. DRESSEL
(author, coauthor, editor)

A Degree for College Teachers: The Doctor of Arts (1977)
Handbook of Academic Evaluation (1976)
Independent Study (1973)
Return to Responsibility (1972)
The Confidence Crisis (1971)
Institutional Research in the University: A Handbook (1971)
The World of Higher Education (1971)
Undergraduate Curriculum Trends (1969)
College and University Curriculum (1968; 2nd ed., 1971)
The Undergraduate Curriculum in Higher Education (1963)
Evaluation in Higher Education (1961)
Evaluation in the Basic College at Michigan State University (1958)
Comprehensive Examinations in a Program of General Education (1949)

Improving Degree Programs

A Guide to Curriculum Development, Administration, and Review

Paul L. Dressel

∾ Improving Degree Programs

Jossey-Bass Publishers

San Francisco • Washington • London • 1980

IMPROVING DEGREE PROGRAMS
A Guide to Curriculum Development, Administration, and Review
by Paul L. Dressel

Copyright © 1980 by: Jossey-Bass Inc., Publishers
433 California Street
San Francisco, California 94104
&
Jossey-Bass Limited
28 Banner Street
London EC1Y 8QE

Library of Congress Cataloging in Publication Data

Dressel, Paul Leroy
    Improving degree programs.

    Bibliography: p. 291
    Includes index.
    1. Degrees, Academic—United States. 2. Universities and colleges—United States—Curricula.
3. Universities and colleges—United States—Graduate work. I. Title.
LB2381.D75   378'.24'0973   80-82376
ISBN 0-87589-486-0

Manufactured in the United States of America

JACKET DESIGN BY WILLI BAUM

FIRST EDITION

Code 8045

The Jossey-Bass
Series in Higher Education

⟨∿⟩ Preface

⟨∿⟩ My experience with higher education began in 1928 at Youngstown College, now Youngstown State University. With the exception of one year teaching in a secondary school immediately after graduating from Wittenberg University in 1931, I have spent all of the intervening years in higher education—almost fifty to date. Most of these years were spent at Michigan State University, an institution in which dynamic change has taken place. Much of this change has been in the development of new colleges and programs resulting from a variety of attempts to improve the curriculum and the instructional process. The experience and the studies carried on in this milieu led, over the years, to extensive writing, further research, and innumerable consultations with other colleges and universities on evaluation, instruction, and curricular problems.

I have become convinced that any attempt to specify requirements, whether in undergraduate liberal education or graduate professional education, without a clear set of principles and an adequate rationale to buttress the statement will not lead to sound education. Thus I have sought over a period of years to work out some set of concepts, objectives, and procedures that could be used by faculty members or by students of any age in developing or understanding the structure and significance of an educational program. This volume is the culmination of that effort. It is an attempt to deal with all of the sundry facets of course, curriculum, and program development in such a manner as to enable faculty members or individual students to plan and justify an educational program and to relate it to personal and career development.

This volume is based on a belief that students who have an insight into the rationale and the intended outcomes of a program will be more highly motivated, will apply themselves with greater energy, and will organize their learning in ways not possible under the usual fragmented program made up of specific required courses or some combination of required and selective opportunities. I believe that highly motivated learners ultimately teach themselves and that the development and use of that motivation are the main functions of the professional teacher.

Consistent with this view and with the view that curriculum structure and content significantly affect learning outcomes, I believe that courses and programs require better organization and structure accompanied by sufficient detail so that students and advisers can plan individualized programs. Even those who do not will benefit by increased understanding of the nature and purposes of courses and programs. The attainment of meaningful structure requires much more review and evaluation of programs than found in most institutions. It also requires understanding, acceptance, and active support by the faculty and by the students. The fate of many innovative programs in recent years demonstrates that imposed programs are of short duration and that even those programs that are accepted enthusiastically at first may soon wither as new faces appear. I believe that the sound and continually innovative maintenance of education requires much more administrative support, direction, and perhaps intervention (tactful, of course) than is usually found. In the following chapters, I offer my thoughts after fifty years of involvement in ways of achieving these ends.

Acknowledgments

This volume comes into being as a result of assistance from a wide range of experiences. For many years I taught a course or offered a seminar on college and university curriculum problems. The papers written by students in these courses and the class discussions generated many ideas that have been further pursued. I have assisted many colleges, including some on my own campus, in the process of curriculum review and change, and in these cases the interaction with faculty members and administrators has been instrumental in developing some of the points of view here presented. I have been fortunate to receive a succession of grants from the Lilly Endowment and from the Exxon Education Foundation. A number of the projects supported by these grants were essential in developing some of the materials upon which certain chapters are based. One grant from the Exxon Education Foundation supported a review of twenty-five years of change in structural organization and in curriculum which furnished the significant background for several chapters in this volume, especially Chapters Two and Three. A grant from the Lilly Endowment was especially helpful in developing the background for Chapter Five. I express particular gratitude to Laura Bornholdt, vice-president of the Lilly Endowment, and to Frederick Bolman, formerly director of the Exxon Education Foundation, for their interest, suggestions, and assistance.

I believe that I have read about all of the significant writing on curriculum in higher education that has appeared since 1900, and I am grateful to all of those who have contributed to this field. As usual, I have drawn freely upon ideas expressed by others, but I believe that I have interpreted them and interrelated them in ways that reasonably absolve me from any charge of plagiarism. In some limited sense, I have made acknowledgment to all of these persons by the extensive bibliography at the end of this volume.

Finally, I wish to express heartfelt gratitude to Ruth

Frye, who has both suffered and rejoiced with me in the many publications in which I have been involved over the years. In this particular one, many sections were retyped repeatedly, and a number of the figures and tables went through many revisions before appearing in their final form. Without her assistance, the task would not have been completed.

East Lansing, Michigan   Paul L. Dressel
October 1980

ᑐ To the Reader

ᑐ This volume is appropriately subtitled *A Guide to Curriculum Development, Administration, and Review.* I doubt that many individuals will wish to read the entire volume in a single or even in consecutive sittings. Many readers will find that their immediate interests dictate the reading of a particular chapter that appears toward the end of the book. Others will find that a search of the index for terms relevant to an immediate concern will direct their attention to pages appearing in different chapters. Perhaps a few remarks and suggestions will provide some assistance in use of the book. It is organized around the major issues that I have found repeatedly appearing in discussions of curriculum and program development and review. It is organized in what seems to me to be a logical sequence. For example, anyone concerned with program review or administration should first address the issues developed in Parts One and Two. Failure to do so will result in procedures that only reflect and solidify existing deficiencies rather than identify and correct them.

Chapter One considers some of the terminology and the varying points of view that arise in curricular and program discussions. It presents, in greatly simplified form, some contrasting philosophies of education. Individuals not previously exposed to such discussions should read this chapter prior to reading any other section of the book.

Part One discusses in four chapters some of the factors involved in program development. Chapter Two points up the importance of program structure and the necessity of considering outcomes, content, and structure in an interrelated manner if optimal impact on students is to be achieved. Chapter Three presents the various means of structuring programs that have been long used and points up some of the confusion and problems generated by ad hoc and unsound approaches that have little impact and a limited life expectancy. Chapter Four examines several approaches to structuring courses and programs that are rather more difficult to assimilate and use than those prominent in current practice. I believe that these alternatives have a sounder basis philosophically, psychologically, and programatically. Therefore, they offer a better program rationale and sounder structure having meaning to both students and faculty. Chapter Four points out specifically that the various disciplines have a structure and that this structure should be taken into account in planning programs. Especially is it emphasized that the disciplinary structure is considerably different from the ill-assorted selection of content materials frequently associated with a disciplinary-based course. Chapter Five describes four approaches to teaching. Each of these has validity in some circumstances, but each involves distinctive conceptions of educational outcomes and hence of content and of structure. I have here, as elsewhere, not hesitated to express my personal preferences among teaching styles, but my major precept here is that teaching and learning are inextricably related to each other and that the teaching-learning process is vitally interrelated with the objectives to be achieved, with the content selected, and with the structure within which learning takes place.

Part Two, on program planning and development, includes four chapters. Chapter Six discusses some of the usual approaches to the planning of courses and programs by the faculty and points up some of the deficiencies of these approaches, especially in relation to the structural and organizational problems involved in making a program out of a group of courses. Careful and conscientious faculty planning may yield a structure that is not readily understood by students. Thereby a significant opportunity to provide direction and arouse motivation is lost. Chapter Seven discusses ways in which course selection and program development can be individualized. Chapter Eight follows naturally upon this discussion of individualization in that most course and program descriptions present insufficient detail for either students or their advisers to determine the nature of the experience provided by courses or the sense in which an existing program has been structured and designed in relationship to student interests, needs, and aspirations. This chapter also has some relevance to recent concerns about truth in advertising. Chapter Nine discusses some of the possible procedures in evaluation and emphasizes that, in its initial planning, any course or program involves numerous decisions. Hence, the result constitutes a hypothesis rather than a tried and tested product.

Part Three comprises four chapters, all related, in some manner, to recurrent evaluation or review of courses and programs. Chapter Ten focuses on the purposes and content of the review process and emphasizes the importance of recurrent reviews as bases for determining program need, quality, and relationship to other curricular and program developments in the institution. Chapter Eleven points up the importance of relating the review process to possible decisions to be made at the conclusion of a review. Reviews can be overelaborate or quite perfunctory, depending to a great extent upon an initial awareness of the problems that may be found and the kinds of decisions that will have to be reached. Chapter Twelve, on the role of advising, may seem to be misplaced. It was finally placed in this section because of the conviction that the work of advisers with students in selecting courses and programs provides a highly significant feedback for evaluating how the curriculum and programs really operate in serving student interests and needs.

Chapter Thirteen emphasizes that administrative officers at various levels must be continually cognizant of program effectiveness and have feedback from various sources to detect problems before they become overly serious. This necessitates the directing and coordinating of recurrent reviews that provide the bases for evaluating quality. The review also assists in determining when programs require major revision or elimination and possible replacement.

Part Four contains two resources that may be relevant to individuals reading at various points in this volume. Resource A suggests some principles for program development that are not unlike statements that I have seen in the catalogues of a number of institutions. The appearance of these principles here is not to suggest that they represent an ideal pattern for all institutions or for all students. Rather, the principles suggest one way of structuring a program that might be as useful to an adviser or to an individual student as to an institution or department. In the main, the principles simply point to relevant considerations in achieving a meaningful program and some balance within it. Regarded as inviolable rules, they inflict an indefensible rigidity on both faculty and student program planning. Resource B suggests a way of dealing with the recurrent problem of course and section size and the sound use of instructional resources. My own experience indicates that, despite continual claims about excessive faculty load, such standards will be regularly violated by departments and faculty members unless practices are regularly reviewed and enforced. The violations are regarded as a form of self-sacrifice for the sake of a better program and are also used to document excessive teaching loads.

In addition to the comprehensive bibliography, specific references directly related to the main themes of particular chapters are presented after each of those chapters. These suggestions for further reading are also included in the bibliography.

Recognizing that readers will use this as a handbook and hence will read certain chapters without having read others, I have, in almost every chapter, at some point, injected a discussion providing clues as to how that particular chapter is interrelated with others. A significant part of the theme of this entire handbook is that program development is a complicated task, involving outcomes related to careers and to personal development, requiring relevant content from appropriate disciplines and awareness of student motivation and the learning process, and a structure and sequence that enable the student to have a cumulative, unified experience leading to an education rather than simply to the completion of specified degree requirements.

Some users of this book may be disappointed by the lack of answers to program and curriculum problems. I have not hesitated to state or imply some personal preferences but I assert that there are no answers in the sense that some persons request them. I have little patience with the individual who seeks a definite and final answer to a course or program problem. I have even less patience with those who presume to have achieved a solution of which they have become promoters. Such solutions quickly pall. As this book demonstrates, the factors involved in either a course or a program are multiple and interacting. An overly structured course or program becomes inflexible and therefore routine and boring. Dynamism in teaching and in learning require continuing and purposeful change.

Finally, I warn the reader that, here as elsewhere, I am frequently critical of faculty members and departmental structures as having primary commitments not always appropriate to planning programs that are educational in the sense of fostering in students intellectual, moral, and social development. Our concepts of institutional excellence and our administrative and management practices tend to give higher priorities to research and disciplinary competence than to intellectual abilities, value sensitivity, and a strong commitment to apply what we know and value to improving our lot. We live in a world in which irrational ideological conflict threatens momentarily to flame into an Armageddon in which intelligence and scientific knowledge are concentrated upon the destruction of all values and of man himself from whom all values (including religious ideologies) emerge.

My critical comments are directed as much to my personal deficiencies and to the errors and deficiencies of the human race as to the faculties and administrators of our colleges and universities. We are not likely to alter and improve our practices until we clarify our goals and recognize and admit the deficiencies inherent and implicit in many of our educational practices. I hold out no ready solutions to the improvement of educational programs, and I believe that any purported solution soon disappears or shortly becomes another program rigidity no more and less effective than that which it replaced. Our students must be brought to understand and share in this perplexity which is in itself the essence of education. It is the continuing search for truth that makes for education. Any administrators or faculty who believe that they have found the "truth" in program planning and curricular requirements are deluded. It is far more likely that the institution has become precious than that it is precocious.

Paul L. Dressel

 Contents

∾ The Author

∾ Paul L. Dressel is professor of university research at Michigan State University in East Lansing. He received his bachelor's degree in mathematics from Wittenberg College (1931), his master's degree in mathematics and physics from Michigan State (1934), and his doctoral degree in mathematics from the University of Michigan (1939).

Since 1932, when he first joined the mathematics faculty at Michigan State University, Dressel has served in various capacities and was often the first person assigned to a particular responsibility. In 1936 he began coordinating the orientation program for new students, which led gradually to developing a testing program, remedial services for students, and a counseling center that he directed for over a decade. For several years he was chairman of the Board of Examiners, which was empowered to grant, by any appropriate means, credit in any course offered in the institution. The Board eventually became the Office of Evaluation Services and was charged with designing and carrying out numerous studies on educational issues. From 1949 through 1952, Dressel was director of the Cooperative Study of Evaluation in General Education sponsored by the American Council on Education; results of the study were reported in *General Education: Explorations in Evaluation,* coauthored by Dressel and Lewis B. Mayhew. In subsequent years, Dressel's staff was expanded to conduct educational research and related studies at Michigan State, and in 1959 he became the first person to head the newly created Office of Institutional Research.

Dressel has served as a consultant to numerous colleges and universities. He was long active in accreditation with the North Central Association of Colleges and Universities and served on the executive board of the Commission of Institutions of Higher Education, 1966-1970. For over ten years he has been chairman of the Illinois Commission of Scholars, which reviews and recommends or denies all new doctoral proposals from Illinois state-assisted higher education institutions. He was president of the American Association of Higher Education, 1970-71, and has been involved in studying Doctor of Arts programs, resulting in the publication of *The New Colleges: Toward an Appraisal* (1971); *Blueprint for Change* (with Frances DeLisle, 1972); *College Teaching: Improvement by Degrees* (with Mary Magdala Thompson, 1974). He also was involved in critiquing nontraditional graduate programs as reported in *A Review of Nontraditional Graduate Degrees* (1978) and *Problems and Principles in the Recognition or Accreditation of Graduate Programs* (1978).

Dressel has received awards for research from the American Personnel and Guidance Association (with Ross Matteson, 1950) and from the American Educational Research Association (the E. F. Lindquist Award, 1980). He was granted an honorary Doctor of Laws degree by Wittenberg University in 1966.

∾ Improving Degree Programs

∾ *A Guide to Curriculum Development, Administration, and Review*

1

Conceptions of Educational Programs

The meanings of *curriculum* and *course* have never been standardized. Either word may be used to designate a program of study leading to a degree. A degree *program* usually refers to a fixed course of study (or curriculum), although some free electives and selectives (electives among specified options) may be permitted. In another usage, the curriculum refers to the total course offering, and perhaps other less structured educational experiences, offered by an institution. Courses are then segments or discrete units of the curriculum. A course, in this sense of a subunit of curriculum or program, may vary in length from a few weeks to a year. In the early rigid classical curriculums, courses were scheduled for the entire year and related and sequenced from one year to the next. Half-courses represented a modest breakthrough to greater flexibility prior to the introduction of options or electives. The use of credits and of variation in the credits assigned to courses in reference to number of class hours or work requirements added further flexibility.

The sequence of developments from a single completely required degree program to alternative but completely required

1

programs, half-courses, credit assignments, selectives, free electives, and individually developed programs embraces two major
shifts in view about the baccalaureate degree. The first was that
alternative programs and degrees with distinctive purposes and
character became acceptable. The second was that programs
need not be fully defined by the institution to be acceptable for
granting degrees. Individuals were permitted increasing flexibility in defining programs. Complete and rigid degree requirements gradually became more flexible both in requirements and
in degree designation. The final stage of complete individualization is still rare and is almost inevitably limited by some general
regulations or the necessity of approval by adviser, committee,
or administrator. It has always been intended that a program
involve both student progress to more complex and difficult
ideas and tasks and student integration and interrelationship of
concepts and principles across courses. In brief, undergraduate
program completion should mean something more than completing a set of courses or acquiring a specified number of
credits.

Three Aspects of the Curriculum

The preceding remarks pertain almost entirely to the formal programs or curriculums. Most formal programs and courses
have had a cognitive emphasis and have ignored or deprecated
affective factors and manipulative skills. Values are inevitably
implicit in course content and its selection and specific values
may even have become subjects of formal study. However, the
emphasis on affective outcomes in courses has always been primarily, if not solely, on knowledge and understanding of attitudes and values rather than on internalization and emulation.
Hence many educators have viewed institutionally based environmental characteristics and personal interactions as educating
and socializing agents of a significance equal to or perhaps
greater than the formal curriculum. In this conception, out-of-
class contacts with faculty, student-student interactions, social
activities, and cultural and religious programs all play a significant educational role in development of social amenities, tastes,

social responsibility, religious commitment, and personal integrity. Aspects of these features have come to be called the cocurriculum and the hidden curriculum. Some educators have regarded these features as the curriculum components that contribute uniqueness to colleges and their programs.

Before turning explicitly to these last two curriculum conceptions, it should be noted that in many discussions of the curriculum both instructors and students have been ignored. In reading such discussions, the reason for the omission becomes evident. If a curriculum is completely specified, then the instructor's obligation is to deliver and the student's responsibility is to receive the content intact. Variation in teaching style is tolerable only if it does not destroy the integrity of content. Variation in learning style is permitted only if it is unrecognized, for uniform results are expected. In recent years, because of increasing heterogeneity in courses, programs, teachers, and students, much more attention has been given to teaching and to learning. The curriculum originally was regarded as a package to be delivered intact. Today we are concerned with the delivery system, the deliverer, and the results. That system must be effective in helping the deliveree (the student) to use the package contents in a manner relevant to personal abilities and aspirations. Today no discussion of the curriculum can be complete without consideration of the teaching and learning assumptions and practices used in it. If the impacts of the cocurriculum and the hidden curriculum are to be purposive rather than random, similar consideration must be given to them.

The Cocurriculum. Faculty discussions seldom give much attention to what student personnel workers call the cocurriculum. This concept includes the opportunities and experiences provided by the institutional setting, be it rural or urban. It includes residence halls, dining halls, assemblies, chapel, athletics, student activities and organizations, fraternities, sororities, and student government. Usually these are operated quite independently of the academic program. They are advised, coordinated, or monitored by a staff that has limited or no academic stature. Although great claims have been made by student personnel staff members for the social, personal, and educational benefits of student involvement in these programs, there is evidence that, on many campuses, the number of students involved in any one activity is limited and that many students are involved in none. Living in a residence hall, for example, does not necessarily involve active participation in residence hall programming. The claimed benefits have not been demonstrated. Indeed, in many cases, some overly demanding cocurricular activities interfere with or even run counter to the efforts and intents of the academic staff.

In the present day, there is increasing attention to providing education on an intermittent (recurrent, continuing, lifelong) basis for atypical undergraduates or on a part-time basis for working adults. This calls into question, if it does not indeed deny, the contention of some persons that the four-year residence on a campus and the cocurricular campus experiences are equal to, if not more important than, the formal academic program in providing actual student development. Today many educators espouse the view that education related to and combined with "real" life experiences is more likely to be relevant and thought provoking than is an education patterned upon a period of seclusion. The expanded formal curriculum itself, by including study abroad, community service, cooperative work-study, and independent projects, takes many students away from the campus for extended periods of time. The extensive involvement of many academics in governance and business activities reflects a comparable view. Colleges and universities are no longer ivory towers. But those who would push the university into an activist stand on social issues by substituting overt action for rational analysis of controversial issues also constitute an attack on the earlier conception of the character and value formative significance of a stint of time serving on the college campus. This earlier conception was based upon the presence in the college of prestigious exemplars of the religious, moral, and ethical commitments of the day. Thus the college provided models and rules that were deemed efficacious in promoting that personal development most appropriate for service to God and man. One looks almost in vain for such models in the present-day colleges and universities simply because, in our pluralistic and generally self-seeking society, a man's stated ideal may only be viewed as "his" ideal by others. This is indeed a pluralistic society and one in which policies and practices tend to be pragmatic.

In the present day, it is probably more relevant to consider in what ways formal study in courses and programs can be related to or interact with concomitant experiences to enhance the meaning and value of both. Institutionally planned and controlled cocurricular experiences once seemed to offer the opportunity to coordinate curricular and extracurricular experiences, but the venture was never fully successful. With a new breed of student and an emerging conception of merging academic and career interests on a recurrent or continuing basis, the cocurriculum will take on a new and different meaning. The task of interrelating becomes more difficult but more realistic. Rather than developing somewhat artificial cocurricular activities, coopting students into them, and then seeking (with limited success) to relate the activities to the academic program, the task becomes that of so structuring the curriculum that individuals with advice can find courses and other educational experiences that relate to their interests, activities, and aspirations. For this to be successful, the academic sector of the institution must be involved—not simply acquiescing, but enthusiastically supporting.

In many ways, success in this respect will result in more attention being focused on the "hidden" curriculum, which will become more apparent as students find their lives less constrained by a seclusive ivory tower experience circumscribed by its own peculiar and artificial mores and folkways.

The Hidden Curriculum. The hidden curriculum justifies the description "hidden" because it is composed of many elements that are not regarded as part of the formal curriculum or even as experiences that could and should be educationally productive. The hidden curriculum includes such diverse factors as:

• rules and regulations about student behavior, automobiles, attendance, grades, and the like

- athletic program policies and fees
- scholarship awards and financial aids
- dismissal of students (grades, morals, and so on)
- faculty involvement in consultation and other off-campus activities
- treatment of students by nonacademic (business and secretarial) personnel
- use of federal and foundation grants
- discrepancies between public statements and actualities (truth in advertising)
- appeal procedures for students and faculty who believe they have been unfairly treated
- reward (or lack of it) for good teaching
- availability of faculty members

Examples of revelatory experiences regarding these factors will come to the mind of almost everyone who has long been on or near a university campus. Here are a few examples:

- A college president who is actually remote from students memorizes for a visit to a church or community the names of students and parents and fakes acquaintance and contact.
- A college is demonstrated to have misused federal funds allocated for a particular project.
- A discharged faculty member wins a court verdict for reinstatement on the grounds that he was unfairly treated.
- Of two students found guilty of collaborating in cheating, one is immediately dropped; the case of the other, a star football player, is indefinitely postponed.
- A college states that credit is granted for certain examination performance, but students seeking credit are told that the course will only be waived and another course must be taken.

The sensitive, observing student (or any other individual) readily reads into such statements and occurrences a conviction on the part of the institution and its staff that the end justifies the means, that honesty is not always the best policy, and that survival is the ultimate value. Only partly in a humorous vein, one might state that the designation "hidden" relates to those practices and policies that colleges and universities would like to hide—and often do when they can get away with it. There is an old saw to the effect that "what you are speaks so loudly that I cannot hear what you say."

It would be unfair to leave the impression that the effects of the hidden curriculum are always negative. Such episodes as those reported often receive undue publicity which magnifies their importance and impact. The availability of administrators to listen to (and act on when appropriate) student complaints, the adviser's and dean's willingness to make a program adjustment for a student, or the accommodation of examinations to student illnesses or family exigencies also constitute an aspect of the hidden curriculum. Since this aspect is individual and subjective, it is truly "hidden" except to those who experience it. The sense that a college really cares about its students and operates for their benefit is one major aspect of the hidden curriculum. Honesty, openness, and responsibility in use of resources on the part of the institution, its administrators, and its faculty bring the hidden curriculum to light and eliminate student suspicions and anger that the institution uses rather than serves them.

Academic Programs. The major focus in this volume will be on academic programs—the curriculums and the courses in which credits are granted and for which degrees are awarded. I shall ignore the cocurriculum, for I think its effect on the majority of students is negligible—especially in regard to the fundamental purposes and objectives of higher education. In contrast, I believe that the hidden curriculum has great impact on most students—much more impact than the administrators or faculty members seem to realize. This is especially so with regard to attitudes and values. The chasm between the formal or stated value commitments of institutions of higher learning and those values that actually dominate their practices is so wide that it is apparent to the public as well as to the students and faculty. Some of the insidious effects of this polarity of values applied in contrasting circumstances can be alleviated by publicly recognizing that individuals, organizations, and institutions embrace or pursue many competing values, and that priorities among these often depend upon circumstances and personalities.

It is especially true of curricular decisions that these frequently depend on factors that have little or nothing to do with student desires for a sound and useful education. Any decision regarding curriculum problems must, therefore, be concerned with delineation of a sound, rational process rather than with the sporadic and spectacular changes that seldom last or a drift over time that increases the courses offered, but not necessarily the worth of the educational experience provided for the students.

Some Views About Higher Education Programs and Curriculums

This book is not intended to present a theory of curriculum. There are several reasons for this. In a pluralistic society, differing and sometimes conflicting values, combined with the political maneuvering involved in settling educational issues, mean that no curricular theory will have much significance either in making major educational decisions or in influencing the operation of the classroom. Most studies of curriculum theory have been written in the context of the public schools where a curriculum is developed and disseminated to teachers who have limited, if any, freedom to deviate from it. This enforced necessity of coverage means that most curriculum designs are closely, even slavishly, followed, with little attention to or even awareness of the social issues, assumptions, and value commitments that presumably furnished, in one way or another, the woof and warp upon which the curriculum was woven. The circumstances existing in elementary and secondary education contrast markedly with those in higher education. In higher education, the focus has been—and is likely to remain—on the disciplines and vocational and professional programs and on the departments, schools, and colleges. The faculty in these units have the primary responsibility for curriculum development and individually they have much more autonomy in use of materials and instruction practices. So long as the disciplines or the professions remain the major focus of students and professors, it is to be expected that the cognitive outcomes of education and the superior disciplinary knowledge and experience of the professor will remain as determining factors in the undergraduate, graduate, and professional school curriculums and programs. Most of the discussions about the sources of educational objectives and goals, the statements of idealists regarding the personal and social development impacts of higher education, and the enthusiastic support for the effectiveness of some particular type of educational experience exert little effect on teaching and program development. Likewise, the analyses of higher education curriculum patterns and problems, the historical review of curricular trends and developments, the laudatory reports on various short-lived innovations, the attempts to develop an embracing curricular theory based upon a fundamental set of assumptions, concepts, and principles, although interesting and sometimes useful, seldom offer any systematic mode of curricular development and modification either acceptable to many faculty members or helpful to students and faculty in providing coherent overview of the nature and rationale of a program in relation to its purposes and objectives.

As the preceding remarks imply, there are many and contrasting views of the purposes and outcomes of college education. Equally, there are many and contrasting views about the nature of human learning and the efficacy of various teaching methods and learning experiences which expedite whatever learning is desired. These too have had remarkably little impact on curriculum and teaching except in experimental or innovative programs. And in these cases the tribulations, reversions to traditional patterns, or demise of the experiment cast doubts on both the theoretical validity of the innovative enterprise and the practicality of its operation in a society and in institutions based upon contrasting conceptions of human nature and of the nature and purpose of education. A brief review of a few conceptions of the purposes of a college education and of the means of achieving these purposes will provide some background for a subsequent discussion of the realities of college education and of the feasible, achievable, and acceptable goals and purposes that a college can and should assist its students to attain.

At times, colleges and professors in them have acted as though education were simply a matter of conveying to individuals the knowledge and the truths established by the great minds of the past. Education was revelation and the student's function was simply to learn, believe, and act in accordance with the revealed precepts. This conception immensely simplified the educational task and maintained a clear distinction between teachers and students. Thus it is not surprising that this view is still widely prevalent in practice.

Other colleges and professors have emphasized learning *for its own sake.* This contrasts with revelation in which the ultimate purpose of education was salvation. Learning for its own sake implies that knowing and learning are worthwhile, altogether apart from any significant utilization of that knowledge. The contention that learning should be valued for its own sake has always been misleading because it implies that the value of learning is intrinsic to *what* is learned rather than being a reaction of the learner. The literature professor who believes that students should study literature for its own sake may not realize that his own professional career is a result of his valuing of literature. If the value of a learning experience resides in the learner, then it is to be expected that this value will differ from individual to individual. If one values study of literature because of the insights that it provides into the mind and the values and cultures of others, it really makes no difference whether the person becomes a social worker who puts these insights into practice day by day or an accountant who also reads widely and participates in community activities in his spare time. In any case, one does not learn something for *its* own sake, but because what is being learned is interesting and *useful in some sense* to the individual.

Others, arguing either from the humanities or a personal development orientation, have argued that an education should be an esthetic expressive experience. The acquiring of any worthwhile knowledge or significant insight is, in some measure, an esthetic experience. Hence, I have always been mildly irritated by those professors in the arts and humanities who urged that study or experience in these areas was essential for an esthetic experience. Esthetic experiences are equally possible in the sciences and mathematics.

In planning a course or program with esthetic experiences in mind, there is a tendency to incorporate and analyze in detail those materials or works that have yielded significant esthetic experiences to others. With this method, the details of the analysis and the memorization of specifics may completely displace the esthetic experience desired. Moreover, there is surely some contradiction implied by the idea of providing "canned" esthetic experiences for a group. The expressive component of esthetic experience is also important. It is doubtful that anyone has fully understood or appreciated any bit of knowledge, work of art, or literary selection until the attempt has been made to express the feelings and insights generated and communicate them to others. Man differs from other animals both in being a "hole-filling animal" and in depending on words for expression of most ideas and emotions. Yet the expressive aspect can also be overdone if it is not preceded or accompanied by analysis, introspection, exploration, and tentative commitment. The phrase "pooling of ignorance" (which I first heard as a freshman in college) was a judgment made by both professor and students of the worth of the superficial discussion and quasi-therapeutic approaches utilized in some social science and education courses.

The overattention to expressiveness has resulted from the emphasis by some persons—particularly those of a therapeutic or humanistic psychology background—on openness and communal expressiveness. Their heavy stress on personal development or interpersonal and social development seems to assume that if people talk long enough they will educate themselves as well as develop fully their personal personality, character, and sociability. This emphasis has always seemed to me reminiscent of the contention that an ape using a typewriter would, in time, type every one of Shakespeare's plays. It is, of course, true that the original meaning of education was that of leading out or developing the individual. But there must at times be some surcease of outpouring in order to have some input. Thought should precede talk and be stimulated by it.

Others have contended that the college experience should be aimed at developing a radical activist who would initially undertake to change the institution and, out of this experience, undertake later to change the community and nation. What has been ignored in this view is that, at any time, only a minority of students have been concerned about the activist role and that most of them have had so little insight into the complexities of the problems with which they were concerned that they came more nearly to attain the destruction of educational institutions than to contribute to their modification and possible improvement. Action prior to reflection, understanding, and projection of possible consequences is the antithesis of those values to which higher education is committed. Education has no need to develop the radical activist, but it should provide him with an education if he will accept it, or reject him if he refuses. And that education should be, as it is with everyone else, directed to attaining knowledge, understanding, and a value orientation or perception that in a pluralistic society no one set of values can achieve support by all. Indeed, the demand, supported by radical action to achieve a particular set of values, is likely to lead to such disruption that another distinctive and more restrictive set of values will arise to restore some degree of security.

This statement about higher education purposes and goals could be expanded in respect to the very brief and contrasting views presented. However, the statement is adequate to demonstrate the existence of differing opinions that can be explored at greater length elsewhere. It also adequately conveys (both by comment and criticism) some of the author's beliefs and commitments that underlie and give rise to the views presented in subsequent chapters.

Suggestions for Further Reading

Ahearn, F. L., Bolan, R. S., and Burke, E. M. "A Social Action Approach for Planning Education." *Journal of Education for Social Work,* 1975, *11* (3), 5-10.

Bell, D. *The Reforming of General Education.* New York: Columbia University Press, 1966.

Blackburn, R., and others. *Changing Practices in Undergraduate Education.* Berkeley, Calif.: Carnegie Council on Policy Studies in Higher Education, 1976.

Brubacher, J. S., and Rudy, W. *Higher Education in Transition: A History of American Colleges, 1636-1968.* New York: Harper & Row, 1976.

Carnegie Foundation for the Advancement of Teaching. *Missions of the College Curriculum: A Contemporary Review with Suggestions.* San Francisco: Jossey-Bass, 1977.

Chickering, A. W. *Education and Identity.* San Francisco: Jossey-Bass, 1969.

Phenix, P. H. *Realms of Meaning: A Philosophy of the Curriculum for General Education.* New York: McGraw-Hill, 1964.

Rudolph, F. *Curriculum: A History of the American Undergraduate Course of Study Since 1636.* San Francisco: Jossey-Bass, 1977.

2

Integrating Program Structure, Content, and Objectives

The importance of structure and content and their interrelationships in education has, in the last decade or two, been underlined by the many educational models developed in an attempt to redirect and revitalize college and university undergraduate programs. In this country, the University of California at Santa Cruz, Evergreen State College in Washington, and the University of Wisconsin at Green Bay are examples of new state institutions in which innovation was attempted through new academic and architectural structures contrasting with the traditional patterns of long-existing state colleges and universities. A number of private colleges have developed new conceptions of undergraduate education by adding special units operating under a different set of policies and purposes than the rest of

14

the institution. The Para College at St. Olaf's and Raymond and Callison (a conjunction of two formerly separate colleges) at the University of the Pacific exemplify this pattern. Morrill, Madison, and Briggs Colleges, established as small residential colleges at Michigan State University, represent a similar development in a very large state university. Many liberal arts colleges have attempted a less radical but still major revision of the concept of liberal education through curriculum revision, including new courses, more flexible programs, use of interdisciplinary coordinating committees, or by emphasis on a divisional rather than a departmental structure as a basis for planning student programs. A few colleges have attempted to restructure themselves on the basis of a competency rather than a content basis.

Some of the new English universities, including such institutions as the University of Sussex, the University of Kent, the University of Essex, the University of East Anglia, and the University of Lancaster, undertook to organize around units (schools or colleges) focusing on themes, problems, or interdisciplinary studies as a means of bringing students and faculty together in courses and other educational interactions transcending departmental and disciplinary lines.

All of these efforts have been, to a considerable degree, stimulated by concern about the same two or three basic issues. One of these is that the departments in many colleges and universities have become so strong and autonomous that attempts to maintain a general or liberal education emphasis have been defeated by departmental insistence that their majors not be forced into irrelevant experiences and that the credit-hour output of their departments not be jeopardized by general or liberal education requirements that would cause students to avoid courses in that department. The attempts to define a meaningful distribution pattern of courses or to agree upon a common interdisciplinary required general education core for all students (long-time breadth patterns starting early in the twentieth century) have become increasingly difficult to maintain because such courses are commonly seen by students as having little relevance to their major interests and are often viewed by the instructors (especially after the second or third year of teaching them) as not only boring but also as interfering with their own career development through intensive work in the original discipline of their choice. It also became apparent that the heavy emphasis on a single discipline, complemented by an ill-assorted group of courses from other fields, has little relevance to career development except for individuals aiming toward a professional school or a graduate degree. One of the major reasons for the new developments in England arose out of the recognition that the single subject concentration did not provide the university graduate with sufficient breadth for flexible career development. Another factor involved in these attempts at radically altering undergraduate education was the spreading recognition that attempts to define a general or liberal education as the common body of knowledge possessed by every educated person, or even as a common and beneficial experience, by bringing students from all specialties together for certain aspects of their education was a delusion. It was amply clear that many of the faculty members teaching in these basic courses neither possessed nor valued either the universal knowledge or the common experience that the program presumed to provide. One result of this realization was a tendency on the part of an increasing number of educators to think of a discipline as a mode of inquiry or as a way of knowing rather than as a defined body of knowledge. Courses based upon this approach must rise above the emphasis on a predetermined set of facts to assist students in grasping the nature of a discipline and in using a discipline in acquiring and organizing knowledge. A second result is the recognition of the worth of the distinctive modes of inquiry involved in various disciplines. A third result is the realization that the basic concerns of mankind have been with the use of knowledge for the pursuit of significant values. Indeed, it is in the seemingly irresolvable disagreements about values that the major problems and the ultimate fate of mankind lie.

It is not surprising, then, that this conflict in values has been revealed in the various approaches to educational innovation. Some humanists proposed to retreat to the pattern of a completely required classical educational experience, such as was found in the early Colonial colleges and existed in some of them well into the nineteenth century. Others, starting from the same set of concerns, concluded that any requirements completely defeated the real objective of education—personal development. This objective required self-evaluation and ability to make personal decisions about needed and beneficial educational experiences. Aside from the rejection of traditional patterns of college and university education, these diverse attempts shared little in common either in defining the nature of the problem or suggesting a mode of solution. In retrospect, it appears that many of those who initiated these innovative approaches to undergraduate education were simply modeling an educational program on their own biases rather than examining in some depth the real and difficult issues of how to motivate individuals and assist them in pursuing learning immediately significant and yet also developmental and durable.

Many of these new models were in difficulty from the beginning. The announcement of new programs or new institutions with the inevitable and eulogistic claims for the benefits of the new approach, coupled with a very high degree of uncertainty as to just what would develop, inevitably attracted both faculty and students of diverse capabilities and values. Often they shared little more than their common negativism toward the status quo. Thus the new programs often immediately became embedded with contrasting and even contradictory elements which threatened the new unity before it was fully defined. In many cases, these new programs became more of a continuing confrontation about what the program should be than an education based upon a new conception. The attempt to maintain something of the original flexibility was shortly endangered or destroyed as the program was found to have developed its own set of rigidities or succumbed to some of the traditional rigidities enforced by the institution, by dominant faculty groups, or by external pressures and demands. One of the latter is exemplified by the admissions requirements of graduate and graduate-professional schools. There are also student and parental pressures that educational attainments be so defined as to be interpretable to and respected by others.

Thus, in this period of dissension about the nature of a

college education, there were marked differences in views as to the purposes of educational institutions, the learning objectives of individuals (especially as to the balance between cognitive and affective outcomes), the appropriate content or subject matter, if any, and the structures and procedures appropriate to the fostering of whatever conception of education predominated. New administrative organizations, new organizations of content, new methods of instruction, new sets of requirements, all were viewed as possible structures subject to change. Various individuals and institutions focused on one set of these while others were equally sure that the change or elimination of still another set was the real key to improvement. Thus there arises a question that can be examined, in part, out of the experiences of many faculties and institutions and, in part, on some rational or theoretical grounds. The question is: What is the relationship between structure and content? In attempting to answer this question, the meaning of the concepts *structure* and *content* must be considered in depth. Even before doing this, however, it is important to consider the nature of an educational program and determine how these two concepts and others interrelate to determine or reflect its character and purpose.

Nature of Educational Programs

An educational program brings people (students, teachers, administrators, clerks, and so on) and learning resource materials (books, exhibits, films, equipment) together in an environment. In this environment, certain processes and interactions (both planned and fortuitous) of the people with people, people with things, and people with environment take place. These interactions and processes are expected to facilitate the achievement of purposes, goals, and objectives valued both by those in the program and by society generally. Educational programs are offered by institutions (schools, colleges, universities) created and supported by society to provide the knowledge and know-how required to facilitate man's search for values through social institutions utilizing resources.

Certain words of the preceding paragraph (people, learning materials, environment, processes, interactions, purposes, goals, objectives) suggest the range of factors to be dealt with in planning an educational program. To these must be added the concepts of content, subject matter, and discipline. Courses, curriculum, and educational programs take shape out of a myriad of decisions, often unrecognized, involving assumptions and convictions about these concepts and their appropriate relationships. A course may also be determined by the selection of a textbook.

Meaning of Structure

The concept of structure has to do with organization and with form apart from whatever the content of the structure or form may be. Yet the structure or form does, in some ways, mold the content and may limit or define the content most readily admitted to the structure. The structure may be physical in nature, relating to the facilities, the site, or the environs of an institution or program. It may be human, involving the students, faculty, administration, and the immediate community. The structure may also be viewed within a context inclusive of the surroundings, whether material, mental, or social. Indeed, the word *structure* can be used in such a variety of ways that, until one defines the context in which structure is being discussed, the concept of structure is uncertain. Some writers have talked about the structure of learning, and there may indeed be a few generalizations to be made about the human learning process. Yet, recognizing the great amount of variation in individual motivation and learning, it may be more appropriate to talk about the structure of content, structure of a discipline, and structure of the process or interactions introduced to facilitate learning. Although in some cases the structure itself seems to hold major value for many people (for example, the departmental disciplinary structure), a more significant issue is that of the function served by a structure. The question might be put: Does this structure enhance motivation and increase the quality and character of the learning by individuals exposed to the structure? For some persons, learning focuses on content, and so the question would become one of whether a particular structure increases the amount of content learned. Many persons would assert that both structure and content are a means to broader learnings inclusive of competencies and values which constitute the real ends of education. Accordingly, decisions about structure should be made in reference to the content, processes, and the anticipated outcomes of education. In fact, many decisions about structure are made for a variety of reasons (convenience, faculty preference, prestige, claimed efficiency or effectiveness) that have nothing to do with what is to be learned or how learning is facilitated. Thus the structure that emerges may interfere with, rather than expedite, motivation and learning.

Meaning of Content

Content, as used in connection with a curriculum or course, has widely differing meanings. For some persons, content means little more than those aspects or segments of a discipline covered by a particular course. Used in this manner, content refers to the facts, principles, modes of inquiry, and skills that are dealt with in the course. Mastery of this content, then, constitutes the objective of the course. Thus content may be regarded as an end in itself. Content may also be regarded as that field or base of concepts, principles, and ideas selected to assist students in understanding the nature of a particular mode of inquiry and the breadth of its applicability. In this latter sense, content is arbitrary and chosen largely because of convenience, interest, or special relevance to the pursuit of more pervasive and significant objectives. Similarly, content may be defined in terms of certain themes or significant concepts. In this case, the concepts, principles, or themes may themselves be regarded as the content. These concepts (with the understanding and ability to use them) can also be regarded as being (or implying) objectives. The specific course materials (books, paintings, audio and videotapes, and the like) constitute the resource materials through which the objectives (concepts, values, themes) are brought into focus for study and understanding.

The language pertaining to content, regarded as both means and ends, differs from the language pertaining to content as means to more pervasive ends. For example, the commonly used phrase *content coverage* often implies or expressly indicates that particular topics, authors, or works have been selected because of their own importance and significance and that the essential content of the course lies in covering these items and becoming familiar with them in detail. Consistent with this meaning, courses, classes, modes of teaching, educational technology, and scheduled interactions of students with teachers and of students with students may be regarded as a delivery system. The obvious and rather distasteful implication of this phraseology is that the content has been selected and, by one means or another, is delivered to the student. But whereas many delivery systems involve delivery of a product in usable form to the purchaser, the traditional academic delivery system delivers knowledge at the convenience of the institution and the teacher and depends upon an elaborate scheduling process to bring the student to the delivery point. The student picks up the package of learning but, lacking the opportunity to assimilate or to use that learning at the delivery point, must take that package elsewhere and assimilate its contents under circumstances neither specifically structured for nor entirely suitable to the learning task. If the content is an end in itself, this delivery system may be appropriate. The matter delivered is the content and it is the student's job to assimilate it.

When the content, on the contrary, is means to an end, the situation becomes more complicated. The criteria for selecting the content generally repose in the teacher or the manager of the delivery system. If every student is exposed to precisely the same content, this enforced uniformity seems both to the student and to the instructor to underline the significance of that content rather than the ends to be attained through that content. The organization or structure of the content becomes the structure of the course. However, if content be regarded as means to certain ends, the content is always somewhat arbitrary. It may even, if common for all students, be varied from term to term and year to year to accommodate the interests of varying groups of students and instructors. It may, if emphasis is on individualization, be varied from one individual to another with the rationale that that content most interesting for a given individual may provide superior means to achieve the common set of ends than any uniform content requirement. It is also possible to take the view that the content of a course and its objectives are determined and conjoined by the people involved and by the interactions among them that take place in a course. In this circumstance, content really arises out of the interests and interactions of students with a teacher or therapist and the only additional objective is that of providing opportunity for the interactions leading to the fullest development of the individual. Content, in this case, might be regarded as almost pure affect. Some structure is required to promote affective expressions and interactions, but this structure may be regarded as introduced to ward off an unsympathetic world as much as it is to define the nature of the experience. Thus a room with no furniture in which individuals recline on the floor (or on each other) may be adequate to an educational experience (if it be that) in which experience becomes the content.

There is one other extreme position that should be noted. If the disciplines be regarded as determining content—that is to say, the aims of education are to master aspects of a discipline, and if that discipline is, in turn, regarded as having a unique structure determined by its concepts, modes of investigation, principles, values, and the foci of concern—then structure and content, both emerging from a discipline, are determined by the teacher who is also the immediate model of disciplinary mastery to be emulated by the students. In this traditional conception of education, little attention is given to the individual student. Some sequence may be determined by difficulty or by the historical development of a discipline and students are expected to take courses and learn in that sequence. Attention to the students is then given only in the sense that difficulty may refer as much to that which the novice experiences in trying to learn certain aspects of a discipline as to a difficulty intrinsic to the discipline itself.

The centrality of our concepts of structure and content

emerge from the preceding discussion. Structure is generally introduced because it facilitates the interaction of people, materials, and content to achieve educational objectives. But in the extreme, content can become regarded as both ends and means and as determinative of structure. This is obviously one reason why the traditional departmental disciplinary orientation to the development of education has made it very difficult to establish new structures and to relate structure, content, and the interactions involved among these to their effectiveness in producing or stimulating growth toward broader and more enduring behavioral objectives. This also suggests why it is that those innovators who have studiously ignored the content and structure of disciplines and the relationship of disciplinary experiences to the educational growth and development of individuals have been no more successful than traditionalists in educating people to take a significant role in society. One may attribute this either to the fact that society really does not value a high degree of idiosyncrasy in individuals or to the existence of a basic inconsistency between the fullest development of the individual and of society. Although some educators would argue that the fullest development of an individual must always be in the context of some social order, this in itself assumes that *all* individuals in the society accept that view. There is an inconsistency between fullest development of the individual as desired by that individual and of the society in which the individual exists. A successful, viable society requires the existence of order and therefore of cooperation and of some communal value commitments which inevitably impose restrictions on individual freedoms. If these restrictions are understood and accepted as reasonable and acceptable for the common good, and as providing optimal freedom for individuals consonant with optimal opportunity and equity for all, then group and individual needs can be balanced to the satisfaction of all. But note that there are some problems with definitions and underlying assumptions. Reasonable, common good, and optimal freedom are highly subjective and are variable in interpretation in time and circumstance. Inevitably, then, the desired outcomes of higher education also vary with time and circumstance and thereby the purposes and the priorities, if not the essential character and objectives, of education are subject to change. The selection of appropriate content for programs and courses depends, in some part, on the expansion and reorganization of knowledge, but it also depends upon social concerns and individual aspirations and upon faculty competency and commitment. Like it or not, the specific outcomes desired and sought at a particular time and place depend, in large part, upon social context. They must, at the least, be seen as relevant by the society supporting higher education and by the students seeking the education provided by it.

The essential nature of education involves the assumption —even the expectation—that individuals will not acquire through educational experiences knowledge, intellectual abilities, and values unless they attach some importance and significance to them. Thus the success of education in helping individuals to attain significant educational outcomes depends upon developing a conception of educational objectives that interpret the desired outcomes in reference to educational experiences and resultant learning. These, in turn, must have implications for the selection of content and for appropriately structuring experiences and interactions of individuals, ideas, and materials to assist students in achieving the educational objectives and thereby the desired individual and social outcomes. In this view of education, content is not an end in itself. It may become a significant end for individuals because of the enjoyment or satisfaction they take in assimilation and interrelationship of ideas, but it is the satisfaction of the individual that justifies the content, not simply the content itself. For others, the content assumes meaning as they are enabled to achieve new levels of understanding and to deal more insightfully with their own problems and those of society. And since the individual and society are interdependent and interrelated, there is at least a suggestion that the individual who moves beyond the acquiring of knowledge would somehow denigrate its significance.

If educational objectives are viewed as attempts to interpret desired social and individual outcomes in the context of a process for achieving these, the objectives must have implications for the selection of content and also for appropriately structuring a sequence of experiences and interactions of individuals, ideas, and materials so as to assist individuals in achieving the educational objectives and thereby the desired individual and social outcomes. Education is, in part, a socializing process and, to be successful as such, the educational process itself must include, at least in some part, interaction of individuals in a variety of contexts involving people and personal and social problems. Accordingly, both structure and content become of vital importance in the achievement of objectives and outcomes. The role of the teacher must be seen in the context of the structure and processes as well as the content and the objectives. No course and no program of courses can attain optimal impact until the interrelationships of the structure including experiences, content, and materials with the activities and interactions of students and teachers have been clarified and exploited in reference to the achievement of program objectives and the social outcomes upon which these are based. For most individuals, content becomes meaningful only as it is presented through meaningful and relevant structures.

Suggestions for Further Reading

Anderson, O. R. "The Effects of Varying Structure in Science Content on the Acquisition of Science Knowledge." *Journal of Research in Science Teaching,* 1968, *5,* 361-364.

Axelrod, J., and others. *Search for Relevance: The Campus in Crisis.* San Francisco: Jossey-Bass, 1969.

Belknap, R. L., and Kuhns, R. *Tradition and Innovation: General Education and the Reintegration of the University.* New York: Columbia University Press, 1977.

Dressel, P. L. *The Undergraduate Curriculum in Higher Education.* Washington, D.C.: Center for Applied Research in Education, 1963.

Dressel, P. L. *College and University Curriculum.* (2nd Ed.) Berkeley, Calif.: McCutchan, 1971.

Feldman, K. A., and Newcomb, T. M. *The Impact of College on Students.* San Francisco: Jossey-Bass, 1969.

3

Conventional Approaches to Program Structuring

There are many different and distinctive ways of structuring an educational program. At one extreme, a student (perhaps with the help of a faculty adviser or counselor) may develop an individualized program based on personal interests, aspirations, and abilities. In using this approach, some students might take only courses or experiences that are enjoyable and require no demanding work. Such a loosely structured or unstructured program might yield a sound education, but many educators (including the author) are highly skeptical. Course requirements or program specifications and a set of procedures for approving programs are introduced to structure and restrain this highly individualized approach. Carried to the opposite extreme, this results in completely required programs, but this rigidity is usually modified to allow for some electives or alternatives to accommodate individual differences in interests and backgrounds, to permit choice among subspecialties of the field, or simply to provide some degree of flexibility.

The policies or recommendations of the program rationale may be directed to the student, the adviser, or both. The statements deal with such matters as majors, minors, concentrations, electives, and breadth or general education recommendations or requirements. Directed to students, the statements may originally have been intended as suggestions or models, but their specificity and the reluctance of some advisers to approve alternatives soon transform them into virtual requirements. Addressed to advisers, the statements may appear as general principles relating to the planning of student programs. However, faculty members do not altogether trust themselves acting as advisers to resist unsound student requests. Neither do they have confidence in the ability of advisers to critique and approve sound student programs that depart from traditional patterns. Accordingly, an adviser's handbook may spell out alternatives in such detail that student and adviser flexibility becomes limited to a choice among these alternatives.

Departmental interests and emphases usually generate rules designed both to forward and restrain departmental policies. These rules deal with such matters as: maximum number of departmental courses permitted in a departmental major, maximum and minimum number of hours required for a major, minor, or concentration, procedures for approval of interdepartmental programs, and definition of the courses acceptable for general education or distribution requirements. Some of these rules are directed to limiting major requirements, some to establishing controls over deviations desired by students, and some to meeting graduate school, professional school, or accrediting agency specifications.

Other rules are imposed because many faculty members feel that even the individual student who develops on paper a strong program may not find the will to cope with it unless various regulations and rules with regard to time, effort, credits, and grades are imposed and enforced. Some faculty members view the disciplinary departmental structure as transcending any concern about human interests and weaknesses. The task of the student is to master a discipline. But only in mathematics and the natural sciences is there a clear enough structure to disciplines to accept this as a dominating force in structuring educational programs. In the humanities and social sciences, the structure that emerges in a faculty-dominated development is more likely to be based upon graduate school specializations, commonly accepted patterns of courses existing in other colleges and universities, or on a significant disciplinary-related committee report that has sufficient prestige to focus general attention of people in the discipline on the committee recommendations.

In occupational and professionally related programs, the role and the competencies required of a profession serving certain needs of society are generally regarded as the dominating factor in developing the sequence and organization of programs. Yet the complex combination of basic knowledge from several contributory disciplines, specific applied courses dealing with facets of the professional performance, historical, philosophical, and ethical considerations related to the profession, and a practical experience (practicum, internship) under the control of the professional program bring into any professional program a mixture of courses taught by varied specialists, many of whom are neither experienced in nor knowledgeable about the profession. Hence, the structure and content of professional programs are continually subjected to local and national studies and always in flux. There are disagreements as to exactly what a profession is and should be doing and how it is related to other professions. Even the conception of a profession may change. For example, many health specialists believe that medicine should move from treating illness to maintaining health. It is not surprising that professional programs have varied over the years from completely required to heavily elective, from highly theoretical to heavily practitioner, from separate disciplinary-based courses to a variety of attempts to develop integrated courses bringing together several aspects of a profession in a more realistic way than can be done with single-discipline offerings. Environmental considerations have also weighed heavily in decisions about such programs. Since the Flexner report in 1910, the emphasis has been on the development of professional schools in a university context where the related fields of study are strong and the theoretical research aspects of the program are well supported. There are, however, those who would still argue that a medical school interrelated with a number of hospitals and using active professional practitioners as the staff will provide a better educational experience than a campus-based program.

These remarks provide some insight into the various factors and pressures involved in structuring the curriculum. The following sections discuss these in greater detail.

New Organizational Units

A possible point of attack for any institution rethinking its educational program is a review and alteration of its organizational and administrative structures. It is tempting to assume that a carefully calculated change in the organizational structure (buttressed by one or two new appointments) will materially change the activities, goals, processes, objectives, and ultimately the educational programs of the institution. In reading college catalogues and related materials over a period of time, it becomes evident that when an administrator (usually a new one) believes that departmental interests dominate the curriculum, a weakening of the departments by a division or other structure is contemplated.

Many new institutions have totally avoided departmental structures or have made them subsidiary to colleges or schools so designated as to imply interdisciplinary study of a theme, problem, or geographic area. These new models soon drift toward departmentalization and traditional majors. The reasons for this are apparent. It is easier to designate a theme or problem than to find professors interested in and qualified to deal with it. The departmental disciplinary structure is very strong. It is sanctioned by tradition, by graduate school admission and program requirements, and, to a considerable extent, by society. The career of an academic depends greatly on disciplinary contacts and scholarship.

Science faculties requiring laboratory and research facilities can usually maintain an independence of interdisciplinary academic units. The student demands placed on faculty housed in a special college or school virtually eliminate research and lead to a diminished status and a faculty caste system. Prospective employers who have a degree of understanding of traditional structures and terminology are often dubious of credentials reflecting marked departures therefrom. Thus the careers of students and of faculty members are jeopardized by nontraditional structures and by programs that deviate from traditional patterns. Extensive reorganization within an institution is also difficult because it threatens the identity and status of each faculty member, student, and alumnus. Reorganization thus raises issues far from the curriculum. Indeed, the curricular concerns may be lost both in the process and in the accomplishment of reorganization. Major reorganization usually requires a moratorium on all other change—a cooling-off and settling-down period.

Major reorganization in an existing institution of the college, departmental, and institute structure is a complex, time-consuming, and morale-destroying task. Usually an add-on is easier to accomplish, for it threatens no established unit and offers opportunities for recognition of existing special interests. If the departmental major dominates the undergraduate program, perhaps a center for coordinated studies involving a director and some sympathetic staff members can provide a place for students who want a different approach. If departments are placing unreasonable demands on students or holding all (able, average, and marginal) students to the same rigid programs, a center for self-paced learning (perhaps including some independent study possibilities) may provide some options to students. If moves to self-paced learning or independent study result in numerous students doing a limited amount of work, partially because of lack of direction from faculty members, a center for contract learning may promote a trend toward specifying in detail exactly what is expected of the student. These details and expectations may also be related to the final grade or other evaluation. If there are complaints from many sources that students do not read, write, or speak adequately well, a program or a center for the development of reading and writing may be introduced. If students complain, as they usually and rightfully do, about the quality of faculty advising, putting forward such criticisms as unavailability, lack of knowledge, indifference, over-promotion of their own discipline, and so on, then a program for training of faculty members as advisers, additional rewards for work as advisers, or the introduction of a counseling center may be proposed as the solution to the problem. In many cases, additional administrators with particular charges are seen as the best solution. Deans of freshman studies, assistant deans for undergraduate lower-division offerings, divisional directors, or the delegation of advising responsibility and authority to deans of students or residence hall personnel have been suggested in many colleges as ways to deal more effectively with undergraduate education and move it toward a more stimulating integrated experience related to each individual's life and work beyond the college.

A review of the various new units and administrators suggested thus far indicates—as may not have been apparent on first reading—that they are aimed at such different factors that all could be incorporated in a program simultaneously. The divisional organization inserts between a college dean an administrator who seeks cooperation of several departments and disciplines in thinking about common solutions to their common problems. The division director can be either an extension of the dean's office (an associate dean, perhaps) or a representative of a group of departments facing central administration with a statement of conjoint needs. The appointment of divisional directors is dealt with in various ways. Appointed from the hierarchy above, the individual may be a long-time prestigious faculty member who is expected to emphasize and promote the concerns of the dean or president. Selected by the departments, the director may well be a junior member of one of the departments and pretty much subject to the beck and call of the several department heads or chairmen who use the division for their own purposes. In one college, the departments in the science and mathematics areas said the division was a useful unit for planning with regard to joint needs and for organizing seminars and bringing in outside speakers on topics involving the

several sciences composing the division. If a division serves as a
budgetary unit—with the departments included being dependent
upon the division for funding and recommendations with regard
to salary and promotions—and if the director has some definite
educational goals and is willing to drive toward these regardless
of faculty reactions, the division, over time, may have significant consequences in changing programs. However, in our observations, a budgeted divisional unit is rare when a *formal* departmental organization exists. Equally rare is the divisional unit
that administers interdisciplinary programs, concentrations, or
general education courses. Most divisions involve several disciplines with quite different orientations and needs. No director
can be equally adept in all of the disciplines represented, and
the director who admits this and leaves to the department chairmen the major authority on curricular matters thereby endears
himself to the departments. If the divisional structure is developed around career-related programs, the coherence and
strength of the division as a program development unit may be
enhanced, but such conceptions as European studies or area
studies remain so loosely defined that a division, school, or college based upon such concerns may have no more unity than a
division based upon department disciplinary lines. A key factor
is the authority and budgetary control of such a unit in appoint-
ing and rewarding faculty independent of a department connection.

Another type of divisional unit involves separating the
first two years (the lower division) from the last two years (the
upper division). The origin of the lower-division conception apparently lies in the feeling that juniors and seniors have made
choices of majors or programs and that their educational program is best placed directly in the hands of the department or
other unit concerned with that particular program. Students in
the first two years frequently have yet to determine a prospective major; they have numerous problems in completing general
requirements and adapting to the college situation. It follows,
then, that a unit dealing specifically with freshmen and sophomores is likely to maintain a greater realization of the problems
of that level and a greater degree of flexibility in providing

assistance in these strategic years of meeting requirements and making choices. It is also obvious that this separation creates some problems in that students who are reasonably certain of their majors are somewhat separated from the units providing them. General requirements too are viewed in isolation from the particular interests that students have or develop. Thus general requirements become distractions to be gotten out of the way rather than a significant aspect of education buttressing and leading into a degree of specialization.

In a sense, the lower-division concept shares the origin and weaknesses associated with the development of centers such as those mentioned earlier: coordinated study, self-paced learning, and the like. In each case, a decision has been made that the existing educational program, as based upon departments and the teaching faculty, has not served *all* students well, and is not likely to take on the responsibilities for doing something about the improvement of reading and writing, providing for more specific self-paced or contract learning, or encouraging the development of individualized integrated programs. Thus these centers arise out of a sense of futility with the existing structure and a conviction that, if any significant change can be made, it will be only by adding to that structure. This addition may be effective in some respects, although it has limited impact on what still remains the central structure of the institution: the department. These add-on special mission units are likely also to require additional faculty and equipment, add to the budget, and complicate the faculty governance practices, though sometimes by bypassing them completely. Foundation or government funds may be obtained to cover the initial stages of these programs, but ultimately they must be assimilated into the general fund budget of the institution, at which point they become direct competitors for the funds previously allocated to the traditional academic unit. Thus the attitudes of the faculty toward these add-on units become some composite of irritation and suspicion which, in turn, raises problems with regard to the quality of staff involved, the prospects for tenure and career development, and the compartmentalization of these units within the institution. All of these interact, making it difficult for them to function effectively. Moreover, as they are add-ons to the institution, they frequently turn out also to be add-ons to the work required of students who utilize these services. In an attempt to avoid some of the difficulties arising when these add-on units deal directly with students, an alternative approach has been to add a variety of centers promoted as serving departmental and faculty needs in developing teaching materials, methods, and improved evaluation. In the nature of these units, they must usually work with individuals or small groups of faculty members, and they are forced generally to deal with specific teaching or learning issues rather than with the total problem of educational philosophy and learning objectives. Thus such units may help individual faculty members to write better objective test items, even though these may still focus on recall of educational specifics of short-term significance and dubious value. Faculty members, like students, finding that these services add to their work with limited benefits resulting, are inclined to retire to their disciplinary tower once again or, if they have achieved enough stature by their extracurricular activities, may move into administrative positions with the attendant hope that, having seen the light, they may be able to focus it beneficially on their former associates.

The preceding comments on new organizational units that serve as environmental structures presumably favoring certain kinds of educational processes and emphases suggest that they are not uniformly successful in bringing about the desired benefits. In fact, they are peripheral to the central structure of the institution, they tend to increase costs, and the many centers (such as those suggested) tend to be operated with what departmental faculties regard as second-rate individuals. The success of these add-on units depends heavily on the personalities of the individuals involved, their dynamism in working with faculty, and the availability of sufficient funding to encourage and provide support for innovative thinking within the departmental units. Those new structures that are set up to deal directly with students seem usually to be of benefit to some students but, at the same time, they set up a competition with the departmental units for program control and for resources. In the long run, tight budgets, new administrators who would ease existing strains in order to forward their own educational goals, and the interpretations of these new s.ructures given to students by faculty raise doubts about the success of organizational units per se in changing the traditional character of a college education. Special facilities or campus layouts based upon an organizational structure have frequently contributed to high costs and have posed later an inflexibility in environment and structure difficult to overcome when some alternative organization becomes desirable.

Depth and Breadth

Depth and breadth, despite the seeming implication of opposites, are interrelated concepts that have been used for eighty to ninety years to describe and judge curriculum requirements. Despite the extensive usage, the terms are a result of twentieth-century curriculum developments rather than of any earlier period. The required classical curriculum had no need of these terms since it was viewed as providing all of the knowledge required to become an educated man. As knowledge rapidly accumulated and became so structured into an increasing number of disciplines, few persons could attain any significant level of ability in more than one or two disciplines. The drift was then toward an education in which one emphasized one or two closely related fields of knowledge and either buttressed these with selected studies in other disciplines or maintained a fiction of broad mastery of knowledge by a breadth requirement. Both breadth and depth are relative terms. In the extreme, breadth becomes superficiality, depth becomes overspecialization.

There can be breadth in depth, as many graduate programs demonstrate. The relatively new Doctor of Arts degree was, in part, introduced because of the high specialization required, encouraged, or permitted in some Ph.D. programs. At the undergraduate level, some history departments offer majors in American history, English history, European history, or some other segment of the field. One can be either broadly or narrowly based in a discipline. Although doctoral work has often taken on a very narrow focus, justified and supported by a narrowing perception of the discipline as more advanced work is taken, it is still possible for individuals with a broad background of experience and familiarity with several languages to acquire a broad education possessing sufficient depth that it becomes, at times, difficult to determine whether they are specialists or generalists. Archeology, for example, in embracing the total cultural development of past eras, can involve such a range of knowledge and skills crossing a number of disciplines that some persons in this field could be reasonably described as specialists in breadth.

In practice, depth and breadth are processes defined by rules or requirements which, in part, define the nature of the educational process. Thus depth is readily interpreted by stating the requirements of various types of majors and concentrations. Breadth is readily interpreted by distribution requirements, core requirements, or core interdisciplinary courses or experiences that provide knowledge and insights into a number of disciplines. But these definitions are oversimplified. They exemplify the concept but lose its meaning.

The concepts of breadth and depth go well beyond the formal curriculum. In the academic arena, breadth and depth usually refer to courses, classes, and the interactions of students and faculty in these formal settings. But breadth and depth can also be interpreted by nonacademic involvements in social and group activities, including governance, fraternities and sororities, community activities, and athletics. Indeed, traditionally, a great deal of emphasis has been put on this aspect of educational experience which has been regarded by some educators as of equal importance with the strictly academic. External and nontraditional degrees emphasizing real-life experiences currently cast some shadows on this idealistic conception. Depth and breadth conceptions can also be related to life and work experiences, internships, and study abroad. In substance, breadth and depth, like liberal education, must be defined in reference to individuals rather than by imposing specific experiences on all students. The attempt at solving the interrelated issues of breadth and depth independently of each other fore-dooms the effort. Breadth unrelated to depth is dilettantism, and depth unrelated to breadth is overspecialization. Balance and interaction of breadth and depth are essential to either a liberal or professional education. Both breadth and depth, and especially their interaction, involve more than knowledge of content.

Services such as counseling and advising and the sensitive use of developmental services for reading, arithmetical, or writing deficiencies not only can provide the skills required to advance the educational progress of the individual but also, in the nature of the experiences offered, can be significant in personal development because they embody the values and the communication accomplishments of human society. At a later point in this discussion, a further range of developmental or integrative experiences will be examined, pointing out that they can be process or environmental in nature or a combination of the two. The relationship of these experiences with more formal aspects of the student's education determines whether these non-academic experiences contribute to breadth, to depth, or, most probably, to both.

Various Conceptions of Breadth

In recent years, some colleges have offered students the possibility of double, triple, or combined majors. The value of this variance from the typical single departmental major is that it permits an individual to develop a program that has more of a personal or career focus than is usually possible with a single discipline. It accommodates individuals who find that they have equal interest in several fields or who visualize a career requiring facility in all of them. Among these students, there will be a few whose particular goals involve an unusual combination. I recall an actual case in which a young woman requested permission to waive general education requirements in order to take three majors in biology, journalism, and art. The waiver was denied. Yet this example illustrates how breadth and depth can be defined in a combination far transcending in educational impact

the usual disjointed and ill-conceived attempts at ensuring depth
and breadth. Double and triple majors have hard going in many
colleges, if one can judge by the relatively small number enrolled in such programs. The reasons are not far to seek. Department faculty members possessively count the number of majors.
Thus they tend (so students say) to suggest that the single major
would be better understood and that the individual would avoid
the perils of satisfying two or more different departments.
There is some truth in this, for in colleges requiring comprehensive examinations or special projects for majors, the student
caught up in two or three majors could face an excessively demanding composite made up of three isolated experiences that
would detract from the student's aim of integration. However,
the advice to take a single major and elect courses from the
other desired department may not be practicable in that nonmajors frequently experience difficulty in gaining access to advanced courses reserved for majors. The *combined major* (as
defined in some colleges) represents an alternative to the double
or triple major wherein two or more departments agree on a
program cutting across the departments. If required, a single
composite comprehensive examination can be given. The combined major is likely to become highly structured and rigidified
because the several departments must all be satisfied.

In some cases, *minors* are used as depth. Minors closely
associated with a major can greatly strengthen the major without imposing any of the specific major requirements of a second
department. Yet our review of practices indicated that, in some
colleges, the formal specification of a minor must be approved
by the minor as well as by the major department. The minor
may even be defined by the department as a specific set of
courses. For example, in one college, a department chairman remarked that the department had specified those courses that a
student must take for a minor. When the chairman was asked
about possible variations for individuals, the retort was to the
effect that no other set of courses would constitute sufficient
insight into the field to justify it being called a minor. When it
was further suggested that students, without declaring a minor,
might take courses equal in credit hours to a minor, the re-

sponse was that this would not be permitted without approval from the department. Although the concerns exhibited by these restrictions may have some slight justification in some conception of rigor, the apparent effect is an irrational rigidity.

Several chairmen and two registrars suggested that a major must be precisely defined in a catalogue; otherwise, graduate schools to which a student might apply would have no idea what a major really meant. Two persons in the records area confessed some dissatisfaction with the idea of double, combined, and triple majors because they were cumbersome in the records and were hard to define. Only if particular double or triple majors were specified and named in the catalogue could the bookkeeping be handled satisfactorily—as a single composite major, of course. Thus it is no wonder, in such circumstances, that students are discouraged from enrolling in these innovative combinations. Even when described in the catalogue, such programs are seldom presented in orientation or suggested by advisers. Thus in many institutions offering alternatives to the traditional major, it is the rare student who learns about them, and only the most persistent of those overcome the red tape and the hurdles imposed by traditional interests.

There are several administrative approaches other than catalogue listing to approval of these innovative concentrations. One is to offer to the students the possibility of developing a program and of finding an adviser who will approve and support it before some committee or administrator to achieve approval. The detailed procedures may discourage students. In some institutions, it is difficult to find a faculty adviser who will support an individualized program because of fear of jeopardizing status with colleagues. In other institutions, the authorization of an interdepartmental type of program requires departmental collaboration in approving a "joint program." When this is done in advance, the concentration title and course requirements are presented much like that of a departmental major. Joint majors or concentrations are likely to have a far heavier course and credit requirement than the typical departmental major. If the student is still required to complete distribution or general education requirements, the total credit specification may be diffi-

cult to meet. It should be possible to develop a set of policies
covering all or a range of interdepartmental composite programs, but no such statement was found in any of the institutions reviewed, apparently because departments cannot agree on
such a statement.

The respective roles of the student, adviser, departments,
and college in defining or approving programs and requirements
become a highly significant factor in encouraging or discouraging flexibility. If a group of faculty members develop interdisciplinary (or interdepartmental) options, they will usually seek to
do so through identifying several points at which two or three
disciplines are interrelated or support each other. Concepts,
values, or themes usually provide the structure. Alternatively, a
conjoint program may be developed in relation to professional
or job specializations that apparently demand people with
depth in several disciplines. Thus a combination of business,
mathematics, and statistics or computer science is one of obvious merit and can usually receive support in a college. However, a student concerned with modern business practices and
values who proposed a conjoint program in philosophy and
business might run into serious difficulties in finding a sponsor
because no one in either of these areas would feel sufficient
competency to direct the student's work. A significant gift con-
tingent upon starting such a program would quickly overcome
such reluctance. The success of any innovation depends upon
the existence of conditions making the innovation attractive to
both students and faculty. Interdepartmental or interdisciplinary majors centering on themes or special interests will cover
most ad hoc majors developed by individuals. Once authorized
for several students, the programs soon are incorporated into a
list of concentrations or are adopted as a major by a department. Future students can select the program but not have the
experience of developing it. Programs without some such formal
status tend to become lost because they and the students enrolled lack identification and support.

Terminology

It is difficult to determine just what distinctions are in
the minds of colleges and of faculty members when they use

various terms. A *concentration* seems, in most cases, to be a collection of courses that focus on a particular theme, problem, or skill. Thus one can imagine a student successfully building a concentration in the social sciences along with work in journalism as a preparation for writing, reporting, or editorial activities. Indeed, many programs in journalism are essentially this. A concept of *coordinated studies* suggests a pattern in which faculty members from several disciplines develop a group of courses and maintain sufficient cooperation and communication that these courses are not only in themselves somewhat related but are also so taught as to bring certain ideas or concepts into more meaningful focus. In some cases, a student entering a coordinated studies program is expected to do a certain amount of *individualized work* or *independent study*. *Area studies* hark back to World War II in which there was a need for individuals with a strong background in the language and culture of particular geographical areas. Popular for a period of time, these programs are much less so in the present day because faculty members became concerned that studies related only by their basis in a culture or geographical region might supply breadth at the expense of depth. Such programs as continue in colleges today are usually directed to specific cultures in which the faculty has already some strengths and can propose a program that might be characterized as coordinated studies rather than options from a number of disciplines. Today the emphasis is on use of the methodology and content from several disciplines in exploring the culture and religious, economic, social, and language characteristics of broad geographic regions.

Some institutions emphasize offering *individualized programs*. In some cases, this term is used to cover the situation in which a student is able to work out a completely unique program fitting idiosyncratic interests and background. This can even include waiver of general education or distribution requirements. In others, actual individualization of program begins only after certain basic requirements have been satisfied. Another conception of individualization refers to independent study and contract learning. In this context, contract learning seems to be little more than a formal agreement by the instructor and student as to what the student must do. The use of contracts in independent study is an interesting idea but hardly consonant with a more significant approach to independent study in which what the student does is, in great part, determined by interests that emerge as the independent study develops.

The term *integrated studies* has been used in a number of colleges with such varying descriptive phrases that some doubt exists as to the precise intent. In contrast with independent study, however, where integration is one of the obligations placed upon the student, a program of integrated studies apparently requires careful planning by faculty members so that interrelationships among courses at a period in time and sequential continuing relationships as the student moves through the program are built in. Instead of depending on the student to integrate experiences, the emphasis seems to be on defining a program of studies with obvious integrative threads in it. The phrase *synoptic major* has also been used to designate integrated study in two or more departments.

This confusion of terminology reflects faculty concerns, objections, and criticisms of deviation from tradition. There is a tendency to introduce new designations for various conceptions of depth even though the distinctiveness of that title from others is not always clear in the minds of those who propose it. Viewed in this way, it is understandable that when in college catalogues one finds two or three different types of nondepartmental concentrations (individualized programs, independent study, and honors programs), students and faculty express ignorance or confusion about the differences. Usually, an honors program must be within a single department, and the student must have an excellent record generally and specifically in the department. The student may be required to take a comprehensive examination or produce some culminating piece of work to satisfy the honors requirement. Is this an individualized program? Well, perhaps, but an individualized program need not be an honors program.

Problems with Individualized Programs

Although many colleges now provide the opportunity for students to develop an individualized program, relatively few students do so. Departmental offerings are elaborately displayed, and it is natural that students' attention is focused on them. The flexibility of individualized programs makes it difficult to say much in detail about their nature. Unless advisers or other faculty members encourage students to think about such possibilities, it is entirely likely that only the unusual student (both in intelligence and in maturity) will raise questions about such possibilities. Furthermore, there is little real interest on the part of most advisers in such programs and no motivation to push them because they run counter to the interests of departments and also, in many respects, counter to the interests of administrators and record keepers who find that the individualized programs require both undue attention and variation from typical record-keeping processes.

There are other problems involved in individualized programs. The selection of an approved program outlined in detail provides a degree of security in attaching one to a traditional unit in the university and securing an association with faculty members and students who have some common interests. The development of an individualized program may bring students under a continuing critical examination from a variety of sources. The success of an individualized program is endangered because the various courses selected provide little help to the student in relating them to the goals upon which the individualized program was based. The student and the adviser must develop the bridging experiences among courses taught from entirely different points of view.

One attempt to deal with this problem is evident in the extent to which interdisciplinary programs, joint and triple majors, individualized programs, and others of the innovative pattern are formalized and introduced as alternatives within the traditional structure by associating them with one or more departments or with some special center or institute. This tends to give such programs somewhat more stature but also destroys their individual nature. The student is encouraged to choose a program by selecting a catalogue option rather than by, in part, becoming a master of his or her own destiny.

The preceding discussion of individualized programs has concentrated almost entirely on building an individual program out of existing courses rounded out with independent study and special projects. *Fully* individualized programs permit determination of program structure by: (1) individualizing educational objectives; (2) individually developing criteria of successful performance; (3) varying the amount of formal instruction required; (4) selecting learning experiences considered appropriate; and (5) varying the amount of time and the pace at which learning proceeds. Few colleges are prepared to handle this flexibility.

Core Course Problems

As the discussion of depth has indicated, breadth can be either associated or contrasted with depth. In fact, most of the departures from departmental majors increase the breadth of the major. However, breadth is commonly regarded by administrators and faculty members as relating to distribution requirements (course options or credit requirements) spread across three to five groups of disciplines, to especially designed general education (usually interdisciplinary) courses, or to a required set of core or basic studies courses. Included in these latter or supplemental to them may be several skills courses such as reading, writing, computation, and how to study. Again, the precise meaning of these various breadth conceptions is variable. Distribution requirements (fifteen credits in the social sciences) exhibit concern for breadth and provide some flexibility in student programs while maintaining departmental course enrollments. Basic or core course requirements may be rigidly defined and regarded as providing a *common* background for further study. A set of required core courses could be interrelated and sequenced, but they seldom are. If acquiring sufficient mastery of related fields is exhausting for the faculty, it is even more exhausting for students to cover in each of several courses the substance of two or three courses in various disciplines. Understandably, superficiality in these courses becomes commonplace.

Core courses designed to bring together ideas related in some manner pose many problems. A core course can be based on one or a combination of such diverse themes as ideologies, regions, cultural stereotypes, nationalism, imperialism, or religion. Alternatively, the focus of a course may be on forms and varieties of esthetic expression or on problems such as disease and equality of opportunity, or on change and change agents. Personal and social values and modes of inquiry are still others. Some core courses become little more than an ill-assorted collection of facts, concepts, and generalizations selected from diverse disciplines. Such courses tend to be compromises, covering all too much material for any satisfying degree of mastery. Sequence and integration become major problems. The courses are most effective and most likely to survive when one or two able and enthusiastic professors accept long-term continuing responsibility for maintaining, revising, and teaching the courses.

What proportion of the total program should be given over to core courses? The answer to this question depends upon how tightly a core is defined and what range of specialty programs is offered in the institution. A core program could run as high as 50 or 60 percent of the total degree requirements if all programs were liberal education in emphasis. The addition of business, education, health fields, and others almost immediately places some limitation upon the proportion of work that can be specified in a general education or liberal education core.

Although the concept of a core program that provides a common background for students and faculty and thereby generates a dialogue and a community of scholarship is attractive, that result is seldom, if ever, achieved. The usual experience is that each core course stands in isolation from the others and the entire set of core courses is equally isolated from that program substance that is of primmary interest to the students and the vast majority of the faculty. The time and effort required in developing core programs have rarely been justified by the results. They are usually brief and disconcerting breaks in programs that were, and soon return to, a departmental disciplinary emphasis.

If required core courses are, in part, departmental offerings or if they draw upon particular departments for staffing, then the core course requirements may become major factors in determining departmental size and ultimately the richness and range of offerings offered in particular departmental majors. This one factor has become, in many institutions, a major point of concern in defining the nature of core courses and the extent of requirements of core courses.

Skills Courses

Student deficiencies in communication and arithmetical skills are continuing concerns in most colleges. Faculty members prefer to assume that students can read, write, speak, listen, and calculate effectively at entrance. Concentration can then be placed on coverage of disciplinary content, ignoring the obvious fact that knowledge can neither be effectively assimilated nor used unless communication skills of adequate level are already present and are continually developed. In the past, English departments have been assigned responsibility for reading and writing. Occasionally, speech departments have provided a required course in public speaking. These attempted solutions never solve the basic problem, for when the faculty rejects responsibility for basic communication skills, requirement of a few courses will not resolve the deficiency. Single departments or services assigned responsibility for teaching skills find no great challenge in it. Those persons assigned the task are almost automatically second-rate faculty members. Deficiencies in communication skills and faculty reluctance to accept responsibility in all courses is at the core of our difficulties with liberal education. Communication skills, broadly interpreted, are the most significant educational outcome to be attained by a college education. There is no merit in memorizing material unless the ability to master additional materials as need or interest dictates and the ability to communicate about the acquired insights are also achieved. If departments and individual faculty members assume no obligation for this area, college students, whatever their grades and later success, have not achieved a liberal education, and they have been deprived of the fullest opportunity for personal development. In a college where these skills are seriously regarded by faculty members, breadth and depth become matters of less concern. Majors, minors, and distribution requirements are relatively unimportant. Education emerges through the continuing interaction of faculty members and students and the continuing challenge to students to accumulate significant insights and sophistication in using the insights.

Developmental and Integrative Experiences

Developmental and integrative experiences include such educational experiences as individualized studies, independent study, cooperative work experience, study abroad, community or public service, internships, and planned realistic life experiences. Typically, the last five of this list are add-ons to or interruptions of the campus academic experience. The coordination of education with full-time work is another such experience in which education becomes an add-on or an interruption of full-time work. The ideal of an interrelated and continuing work-education experience is difficult to achieve. Developmental and integrative experiences can be regarded as either depth or breadth, depending upon the perceptions of the faculty and the individual. Study abroad is, in most cases, regarded as breadth but, if study abroad is a required and advanced component of a language major, it is obviously a depth experience. Cooperative work experience, if related to the student's on-campus concentration, may be regarded as depth, although the possible contribution of work experience to breadth and to integration is also evident. Generally, these developmental and integrative experiences involve a realistic (nonacademic) environment and a distinctive set of processes. These experiences may be regarded as either for credit or as noncourse practical experiences required for a degree. The experiences are characterized as developmental and integrative because they involve cognitive, affective, and psychomotor-oriented experiences and outcomes. The student is expected to apply formal campus learning but is also expected to learn through observation, organization, and integration of insights and experiences unique to the particular pattern of experiences.

Individualized studies require an individual to plan a program based upon personal interests and goals. The planning itself is a developmental and integrating experience. Here *integrating* must be regarded as distinct from *integrated*. Faculty-produced integrated courses promote acceptance by the student of another person's integration. An integrating experience places the responsibility on the student to develop a personal, unique, and meaningful integration across disciplines, content, problems, and objectives.

Cooperative work experience, by bringing a student into a new and often disconcerting environment, may make the environment so significant that coping with it requires most of the student's time and energy. This need not be of concern if one views cooperative work experiences as opportunities to develop the ability to analyze and adjust to an environment in a limited space of time. For example, the round of clerkship experiences in medical specialties may involve experiences in six or eight different hospitals with different instructors and different emphases. While the change of environment is a distraction, the development of ability to adapt and operate within varying environmental patterns is essential to success in the profession.

Foreign language deficiencies and a tourist orientation may weaken some of the anticipated academic benefits of study abroad. The task of interrelating the environment and formal study requires considerable planning, but that planning itself may lead to overstructuring and sacrifice of opportunity. Only individuals who have had extensive experience in planning and carrying through study abroad can plan so as simultaneously to assure adequate structure and maintain flexibility. Unfortunately, involvement in a study abroad program is an opportunity that many faculty members prize. Hence there is a tendency to pass the prize around even though faculty experience and competence are sacrificed thereby. One may wonder at times whether the purpose of study abroad is an experience for students, a paid vacation for faculty members, or an opportunity for the president and spouse to travel abroad each summer at the institution's expense. The desired and realized objectives of study abroad are not always the stated ones.

If students are not prepared in advance for off-campus experiences, the frustrations of dealing with a new environment and requirements may completely obscure the benefits presumed to be implicit in that off-campus experience. If a student is specializing in French literature, history, and government, it is difficult to imagine how a period of study in France could avoid fostering an integration of on-campus and off-campus experience. Even so, courses and experiences preceding the travel abroad could be planned in such a way as to encourage expectation that certain things studied in the class can be pursued at a later date. There is, likewise, a problem after students return from such off-campus experiences. Students, enthusiastic and desirous of reflecting upon their recent experiences, may be discouraged if their instructors are uninterested. Thus an off-campus experience can, if not carefully planned and interrelated with on-campus experience, be simply a major discontinuity in the student's program and even result in the withdrawal of some students from school because they are not able to bridge the gap that has been introduced into their program. Quite commonly in the sciences and mathematics, which are highly structured disciplines offered through a rather tightly organized sequence of courses, faculty members are not only completely uninterested in these off-campus discontinuities but also actively antagonistic to them as disrupting what should be a continuous sequential experience. Despite these recurrent problems, developmental and integrative educational experiences offer the possibility of relating study, personal development, and career preparation.

Modes of Teaching and Learning

The various modes of teaching and learning involve a composite of process and environment. The phrase *modes of teaching and learning* suggests that one view the classroom environment and processes in terms of either teacher activity or student learning. Most faculty members view teaching as referring to their own classroom activities. This is reflected in the terminology of lectures, recitations, discussions, and tutorials. In fact, individual teacher classroom behavior is seldom as distinctive as these terms imply. Discussions often become informal lectures with limited active student involvement. Many lecturers encourage student comments or questions or achieve a depth of student involvement characteristic of discussions or seminars. Various instructional modes imply somewhat different types of environments. A tutor's office or sitting room is also his or her classroom. A lecture hall or recitation and discussion classrooms present quite different environments. Facilities of the same type vary markedly in visibility, audibility, student comfort, and other such factors. Many lecture-demonstration halls of an earlier year involved very steep high-rise seating to maintain a minimal distance between students and the demonstration table. In the present day, television, monitors, and other devices provide visibility and audibility in less formal situations or even in separated facilities. Thus environmental circumstances may be greatly modified from past traditions by the effective use of modern technology. That same technology may be effectively used to repeat filmed or videotaped demonstrations or significant aspects of a field trip, thus permitting the coordinated planning of processes and environment so as to foster certain insights and skills on the part of the students.

If one views *teach* as a transitive verb, it follows that teacher activity is teaching only if someone learns something as a result of it. Teaching is effective if the actual learning is, in amount and character, in accord with the purposes and learning objectives the program was designed to meet. Teaching facilitates the process of learning by setting up appropriate circumstances and conditions that facilitate learning. It does not require the physical presence of the teacher. In fact, the physical presence of the teacher is, for many students, less important than circumstances, materials, and conditions that facilitate learning. Our heavily teacher-structured modes of learning tend to assume the existence of a body of content that all persons should experience, although the sheer mass of that body of content ensures that mastery by many students is unlikely. Indeed, by insisting upon such extensive coverage, teachers commit themselves to accepting casual familiarity with materials as a basis for a passing grade. If one assumes that all learning ultimately is individually accomplished, attention naturally turns to the possibility that there may be modes of self-teaching or learning and associated processes and environments that permit individualizing the learning process while simultaneously developing the capacities of self-confidence, self-direction, and continuing commitment to self-education. Every college and every teacher has a few self-directed students quite capable of acquiring on their own a more significant depth and integration of education than the usual courses provide. But the rigidity of our patterns, segmenting knowledge into courses, and conforming evaluation specifically to course coverage have the result that many of the so-called student-dominated modes of learning are quite different from the typical description. Self-paced instruction is often regarded as individualized. In fact, the materials to be covered and the facts or concepts to be learned are generally even more specific than in traditional courses. The individual does have an opportunity to move at a self-determined pace. In theory, this approach is excellent; in practice, it turns out to be entirely unsatisfactory to most teachers and students. There are several problems with self-paced learning. It is likely to be overly structured, it is easily postponed by students, and it proves embarrassing to some teachers when a few students complete requirements very quickly while many others never do.

There is, furthermore, a basic inconsistency in structure between a self-paced program and the division of the academic year into segments of various lengths with fees being collected at the beginning of each segment. What does one do with a student who, at the end of a term or even two or three terms, has not completed a self-paced program with specific due dates and a downward adjustment of grades for people who do not meet them? It is evident in colleges such as Hampshire and Evergreen that students in programs that are highly flexible with regard to what the student does are delightful in prospect, but many, finding that they are not able to impose discipline upon themselves, drop out or transfer to other institutions where more pressure and rigidity of structure exist. There they may attain a greater sense of progress and accomplishment.

So-called life experience education, based upon the expectation that individuals in the normal course of living may attain a depth and breadth of education worthy of recognition in courses and degree credits, perhaps represents the ultimate in acceptance of a concept of self-directed education. Only two structures are applied in these circumstances: one specifying the knowledge or skills to be assessed and the other defining the means and criteria of assessment. Difficult and irresolvable problems arise here. Does one simply accept the statement of life experiences by individuals and their interpretation of what they gained thereby and then attempt to interpret this in standard course and credit patterns? Is an individual's word to be accepted with regard to the amount and quality of what has been learned through life experience? Can ability to deal with content materials be assessed independently of knowledge of a *specific* body of content?

Even more extreme student-oriented modes of learning are found in T-groups or encounter groups. These experiences can be productive of insight and learning, and they have been successful with some individuals as a therapeutic procedure. For those who believe that education is primarily personal development, it is easy to confuse therapy with cognitive learning. I met once with students in an unstructured new college who demanded degree credits for undergoing psychological and psychiatric counseling. Many of the faculty supported their demand.

It becomes apparent in discussing these various modes of teaching and learning that they involve varying degrees and conceptions of structure, that these conceptions are interrelated with process and environment, and that, ultimately, the particular conjunction of structure, process, and environment is based implicitly or explicitly on a conception of the nature of education and content and the objectives toward which students should move or be moved to be characterized as educated. Observation of the various patterns of affectively oriented, loosely structured, highly individualized, or group patterns of learning indicate that there is a relationship between the existence of generalizable and structured knowledge in a discipline and the attractiveness and relevance of these various approaches to practitioners of the discipline.

Curriculum and Progress Units

The curriculum, regarded as a set of courses and required experiences for a degree program, is an aspect of the environment. Reading of curricular statements and course descriptions generates an impression of institutional and departmental philosophies of education and of the nature and worth of knowledge. The curriculum also implies or involves a set of processes. Education is structured not only by the nature of the curriculum but also by the way in which student progress is measured and recorded. In the days of the fully prescribed and rigid classical curriculum, there was little need to be concerned about units of progress. Everyone took the same thing, and the progress was readily determined by current enrollment status. The original program was simple, but highly structured, emphasizing commonality of experience, continuity and sequence in learning, integration of knowledge, and—through required chapel, philosophy, and a senior presidential seminar—a concern for morals, ethics, and religion. This composite was thought to produce a strong character essential for a satisfying and productive earthly life and also for assuring the life in the hereafter.

As that common rigidly required program disappeared, more attention was necessarily focused on courses. Many courses initially were full-year courses and a terminology of half-course or part-course was introduced for one-semester courses. The course had become the unit. As knowledge further proliferated and new disciplines emerged, further compartmentalization of content was introduced, leading to a finer unit—the "credit hour." Programs under this new system of credits tended toward fragmentation. Students were exposed to an increasingly large number of unrelated courses, with insufficient time allocated to any one of them to acquire any significant knowledge or competency. The actual amount of work required of students for a course might be completely out of proportion to the credit granted for it. A two-credit course in mathematics might, for many students, require many more hours than a five-credit course in history or the social sciences. These inequities encouraged students to search for courses requiring little time or effort to bolster their point averages. As always, changing structures and practices induce unanticipated and often undesirable behavior.

Gradually, most institutions developed a rationale for assigning credits in relation to time requirements, classroom, laboratory, and field study. Generally, this system operated on the basis that the teacher talking for one hour generated one credit for the students, but the students had to work two, three, or more hours in a laboratory or in field study to acquire a unit credit. These practices not only provided a structure for education but also implied a philosophy of education and generated a set of attitudes toward it hardly consonant with sound educational purposes and objectives. In particular, the meaning of the credit hour and its significance relative to various forms of educational experience became a continuing and distracting concern. One university, in an attempt to solve the dilemma, had in its rules and regulations for many years a statement that "The student shall receive one credit for three hours of effort, however expended."

˙ Modules

The term *module* has become prominent in some curriculum discussions. It appears in various contexts and with uncertain meaning. A *course* module is generally a unitary or coherent segment or part of a course. The intent is to divide a course into parts, each part so defined as to emphasize in detail just what is to be learned (mastered) in the segment, and to indicate the means of evaluation to be used. The module statement may involve specific tasks to be completed and a specified level of performance. Time for completion may be a variable factor, so that modules are especially appropriate when the academic year is divided into a number of periods, each only a few weeks in length. If a course is composed of several independent or sequentially related units or topics, the module may be a useful means of clarifying the appropriate time and importance of each. It permits differential rates of progress and also defines the extent of progress. If, however, the entire course is regarded as a unit, cumulative and developmental in nature, the use of modules may seriously disrupt that unity.

A *program* module is usually a structured segment of a program composed of two or more interrelated or sequential courses. Here the designation *module* points up the relationship and makes evident the expectation that all parts of the module are to be completed. In one sense, this does little more than underline the complete sequence as a requirement or recommendation. In still another use of module, it indicates a group of interrelated courses that are to be taken simultaneously. An example in an area study program would be the requirement that a foreign literature course be accompanied by a history course and a geography course devoted to the country or area where the language is used. Such a specification has significant educational impact in focusing most or all of a student's work in a term on interrelated materials. Unfortunately, such a combination of courses severely limits the number of students who can take the entire block.

The curriculum is, in many respects, the central feature of a college program. The nature of the curriculum and of its content and methods goes far to determine both the learning environment of a campus and the processes that go on in it. It would seem, then, that the curriculum might become the major means for solving the problems with respect to structure and content. In only a very limited sense is this true. The domination of the department and the disciplines is focused on content and a content primarily designed for majors. The structure of the discipline itself and the discipline-related structural and process preferences of the faculty determine structures and processes within courses and whatever relationships exist among them. It is unfortunate that concerns about the major have determined curriculum structure within departments, for majors typically constitute only about one-third of the undergraduate degree requirements.

The curriculum usually follows the administrative and academic structure of the institution. If, as is usually the case, the chief administrative unit is the department, then the curriculum is little more than the sum total of all of the departmental offerings plus some rules, regulations, or policies for solving the curriculum maze. Supradisciplinary schools or colleges with curriculums based upon problems or themes of sig-

nificance have been introduced in some new institutions—
usually where an administrator was able to formulate a curriculum plan and administrative structure before any significant
number of faculty members were hired. The identification and
building of separate college facilities and the assignment of faculty members from various disciplines to the same college have
provided, in many institutions in England and in this country,
the opportunity to break through the departmental structure to
an interdisciplinary college structure. This history of a number
of universities organized on interdisciplinary theme patterns
indicates that, although this pattern may work reasonably well
in the early years of a new institution, the tendency over time is
for members of the same discipline to seek association with
each other in research, in seminars, and ultimately in the resur-
rection of departments and use of standard graduate and undergraduate majors. The structure of the disciplines is very strong
and, in the long run, innovative curricular considerations are not
likely to stand against it, except as the disciplines are forced to
a minor role by becoming contributors to a vocational or professional program. Even then, the definition of disciplinary content relevant to professional needs is a continuing problem.

Evaluation

The use of evaluation as a major structural feature of a
program has long been recognized. The role of comprehensive
examinations in encouraging both faculty and students to regard education as a cumulative, integrative process has been
widely though seldom successfully exploited. A similar use of
divisional examinations, forcing majors in particular disciplines
to demonstrate some capability in immediately related disciplines, also indicates that a formal evaluation structure can have
significant impact on course organization and on the orientation
of students and faculty. Some culminating type of performance
—a recital, a paper, a work of art—can also play something of
the same role as a comprehensive examination. Institutions
making extensive use of such culminating unifying experiences
have generally found it necessary either to point courses on a

cumulative basis toward this examination or to provide some type of integrative seminar for students to both motivate them and force them to do some thinking and integrating prior to the examination. However, as with other possible structuring elements, the disciplinary and content focus within departmental courses can undermine the intentions. Many patterns of cumulative or comprehensive examinations have disappeared over time because faculty members resented the time requirement and students felt themselves ill-used by examinations forcing them to an integration for which the faculty had not prepared them. When such views exist, the red tape and costs of such examinations will come to be viewed as unreasonable in relation to their benefits.

The types of examinations used in courses and the nature of the questions in these examinations reflect the organization and emphasis of the course as well as structuring the education of students. Students preparing for a factual objective examination tend to prepare differently from those taking oral or written examinations. Some type of performance activity that demonstrates the assimilation of knowledge as well as its application demands more of both students and faculty than does a formal examination. Rating or grading the results requires time and concentration to achieve reliable and value indexes of student performance. As teacher time so spent yields little recognition, evaluation in courses tends to be a personal affair and is done as expeditiously as possible.

In contrast, an ongoing program evaluation that transcends courses should attempt to find out what students have gained from a course or program, what elements of the program have been successful or unsuccessful in promoting this development, and what aspects of the course, content, resource materials, and experiences need be revised to maintain vigor and enthusiasm. This form of evaluation produces information that tends to modify instructional materials and processes and also the manner in which they are conjoined into courses. In an integrated, cumulative curricular experience, evaluation must be a major structural component, but it cannot be the sole instrument for developing or maintaining such a program.

Sequence

The sequencing of courses within a department or program is a difficult curricular problem, but it is often ignored by
recourse to tradition, personal preference, or recommendation
of a professional disciplinary society or association. The failures
to deal effectively with problems of sequence in the development of curricula are of several different sorts. One is that,
being divided into departments and disciplines, the faculty tend
to think about sequence within a discipline rather than as a sequence of courses pursued by students through the entire curriculum. Further, there are various ways to conceive of
sequence, and some sequential bases are more appropriate to
certain disciplines than to others. The problem of sequence in
mathematics or physics may be decided on entirely different
grounds from that of sequence in literature. Sequence within a
total curriculum becomes difficult unless there is general agreement on certain principles among those persons planning the
courses intended to be sequential. But the planning of such
courses poses another difficulty. It is easier to plan a sequence
when all students take exactly the same courses at the same
time. If there are many elective opportunities, so that students
either do not take a large number of common courses or take
them at different times in their program, sequencing becomes
virtually impossible. Another problem is whether sequencing
should be based on characteristics intrinsic to the materials to
be included or on the ability, experience, motivation, and past
education of individual students. What may seem to be a logical
sequence for the materials may not be so if one looks at differences in preparation, motivation, and rate of growth of the students.

Some disciplines have an inherent sequence. In the very
nature of history, it is expected that there will be a strong
chronological component. In cumulative fields, such as mathematics and the hard sciences, the learning of some topics requires prior knowledge and understanding of prerequisite materials. To some extent, one can modify sequence even in
cumulative disciplines by dealing with certain content materials

in a different way than is ordinarily done or by accepting a lower level of insight and understanding. The physical and mental development of individuals, combined with interest in and sensitivity to materials and ideas, provides a somewhat different basis for sequencing. Breadth or general education is commonly regarded as something that should precede concentration or specialization. Thus it appears that most academics accept that a broad overview is useful as a background for dealing with specifics, and they also assume that the broad overview is less demanding and less difficult and therefore should precede the more intensive material. A case could readily be made for the opposite point of view—that the specific and concrete is far easier to assimilate than is the broad sweep involved in the breadth component of education. Others have made a case for a sequence in which depth and breadth are interrelated throughout the program, arguing that this contributes to greater perception in both areas. From these comments, it is readily seen that sequence can be based on chronology, on human development, or on a number of concepts having to do with difficulty and dependence of one concept or principle upon others which must therefore precede in the program. This discussion will be resumed in the next chapter.

Physical Environment

The physical surroundings of a college, including grounds, facilities, equipment, and the upkeep of these physical facilities, have a significant role both in attracting students and in generating an attitude toward learning. The two aspects may be at odds in that some environments attract students who are not motivated to learn. Although it is true that human beings are highly adaptable as to the circumstances in which they learn, motivation can be undermined by environmental circumstances and both learning and motivation can be curtailed when excessive noise, poor visibility, and bad acoustics get between the student and the material being presented. Possession of the most recent audiovisual equipment is not necessarily conducive to learning. Highly sophisticated scientific equipment may permit students to get answers without understanding just what is involved. Overuse of learning aids and teaching resources may well cause wonderment as to why it is necessary to bring students and teacher to a campus and classroom at specific scheduled times. Comfort and privacy for both the instructor and the students are not to be disdained in classrooms or offices. There is certainly no unique answer and no infallible set of steps whereby an environment may be planned to facilitate learning; but lack of sensitivity or apparent indifference to the physical environment imposes conditions that the teacher will be hard put to overcome. One must beware equally of architects who would build monuments for themselves and the idiosyncrasies of faculty members and administrators whose overly specific and personal demands lead to excessive remodeling costs rather than to enhanced motivation and learning by students.

Purposes, Goals, Objectives, and Outcomes

It would seem that the development and evaluation of a program must be dependent upon commitments to institutional purposes and goals and to educational objectives and outcomes. Yet these considerations are rather less important than might be expected because so many program decisions are made in reference to the purposes or goals of departmental units where courses are offered. Broader institutional concerns and stated educational objectives of students are remote and are ignored or regarded as too general and vague to be useful at a course level. Furthermore, courses tend to place emphasis on content coverage rather than on more pervasive cognitive, affective, and psychomotor objectives and outcomes. Many disciplinary content-oriented teachers understandably feel that the presentation of a discipline involves an obligation not to be compromised by differences in institutional purposes or goals.

The purposes of an institution are related to the accepted mission of the institution, but that mission may itself be under almost continuous discussion and subject to change. An undergraduate program in an institution committed to prepare young people for responsible jobs may have wisely avoided a department of classical studies, but that does not ensure that some segment of the faculty or a donor may not, at a later date, push for (and succeed in) the addition of a department of classical languages. In short, institutional purposes are determined by people, and the people involved range from board members through faculty, students, donors, and many others who take an interest in the institution and regard it as a means for promoting their own purposes.

The meanings of the words *purposes, goals, objectives,* and *outcomes* vary so much in educational writing that I shall not attempt to give a standard definition. Rather, acknowledging that there are significantly different implications in these words, I shall, in a sense, impose upon them my own definition. Institutional purposes are written to impress and inspire but not to restrain. Resources rather than purposes impose restraints on institutional expansion. Goals are different from purposes in the sense that they specify particular steps or stages of progress that an institution or its adherents hope to achieve within a specified period of time. Goals may deal with program range, endowment, facilities, student body, size, or any other matter that may be of concern to an educational institution. It is usually more difficult to achieve unanimity on goals than on purposes, for the former tend to be more specific and more immediately attainable. Departments and faculty members have goals of their own which, in substance or in priority, may differ significantly from others. In thinking about curriculum problems, it is necessary to review institutional purposes and specific goals and the views of the many people in setting and changing these. These, in turn, may involve eliminating programs, adding new programs, or combining or modifying existing ones.

The immediate attention in developing a program ought to be focused on the objectives of that program and the outcomes (a specific statement of the level to be achieved with regard to the objectives). Those will be dealt with in Chapter Eight. However, there is always (implicit or explicit) a philosophical framework within which purposes are determined and educational objectives are written. As indicated in Chapter One, there are many different frameworks for discussion of this matter. Educators collectively offer a wide range of educational objectives. The education of an individual is seen as serving social goals, providing useful knowledge, developing value and moral commitments, fostering creativity, developing tolerance, and encouraging appreciation and respect for cultural and individual variations. Citizenship in a democratic society has frequently been suggested as another specific objective of undergraduate education.

Objectives may be implicit in a statement of the purposes of higher education. These purposes may then be stated in such terms as humanizing the individual, or as creating a community of interaction and commitment within the college situation that in and of itself socializes the individual to take a significant role in community, state, and national matters after leaving the institution. *Humanizing* largely refers to making the individuals aware of their heritage from prior cultures. Many faculty members would regard the humanizing aspect of education as the liberal education component, arguing that it has been largely through the arts, literature, philosophy, and other humanities that the essential nature of man has been made apparent. It can also be argued that mankind's attempts to understand the physical world and to understand the nature of the human biological organism has led to insights and findings that are as much distinctive of human potential as any artistic or literary production. Indeed, science and mathematics are, in somewhat different ways, as much a creation of humans as anything in the humanities area.

The *socializing* aspect of education probably has less significance than it once did. Modern communication technology has brought to many people new insights into the world and its cultures. Thus education in the present day probably has its major socializing aspect through studies that give insight into the nature of society, its problems and modes of resolving them, and through bringing together students of markedly different cultures and heritages. Where once the socializing aspect of education was thought of as socializing in the context of a liberal education, a current concern must be that there are many other cultural strains than the Greco-Roman and that an experience that causes an individual to define, reconsider, contrast, compare, and ultimately resolve personal values in the light of an insight into alternative sets of values is an important aspect of socialization.

The third broad area of purposes is that of *individualization*. This can be dealt with from an internal orientation, developing the individual's interests, capabilities, and aspirations in such a manner that he or she can find a significant role in society and attain personal satisfaction while contributing usefully to that of others. The fourth broad area of purposes deals with *community* and refers to the way in which the humanization, socialization, and individualization of people are brought together in achieving a common community of interests and means of resolving issues to optimize the satisfactions of all.

Ideally, in a social order in which there is a common commitment to a set of values, all of these areas of development would be interrelated and encouraged so as to result in a harmonious whole combining fullest development of the individual and of society. In fact, because of the many and contrasting values in our culture, any attempt to lay out such broad areas of purposes and objectives immediately raises issues. Should education primarily develop individualism or collectivism? Should education focus on bringing about educational change or educational stability? Should education focus on development of the intellect or of affect? These are profound questions that are essentially unanswerable except as individuals achieve answers satisfactory to themselves. And generally these answers will be personal compromises between extremes and compromises predicated upon such a wide range of considerations that commitments may vary from one unrealistic extreme to the other in reference to particular issues. The result is that faculties find great difficulty in achieving an acceptable unambiguous statement of educational objectives.

The Structure of "No Structure"

Various discussions of the problems and deficiencies of higher education have led some persons, in organizing a new education program, to look at all of the traditional accoutrements of education with suspicion and disdain. Out of this comes what might be regarded as a completely negative approach, a denial of structure. Thus a few new institutions have started with the commitment that there would be no departments, no formal courses, and no repetition of any learning experience. This approach has been extended by abolishing faculty rank, eliminating permanent administrators, discarding specific calendar units, such as terms or semesters, and avoiding a definitive statement of degree requirements. A few colleges have avoided permanent private offices by using movable head-high partitions or even by assigning desks in large open areas. Elimination of the traditional classes (freshman, sophomore, junior, or senior) and perhaps even an attempt to abolish the distinction between students and faculty have been tried. A few institutions have eliminated tests and grades, arguing that they are serious deterrents to learning. Others have put the emphasis on evaluation, attempting to so define evaluation practices as to emphasize that abilities or competencies transcend specific course content.

Elimination of traditional structure, however, does not eliminate structure; it only focuses attention on the need for some structuring and generates another kind. The apocryphal question of the young student in an elementary classroom some years ago—"Teacher, do I have to do what I want to do today?" —indicates that even a structure that supposedly turns education back to the individual can be seen by the individual as unduly rigid. One institution that foreswore standard courses, departments, and the like emerged with a pattern in which four or five instructors would develop in a prospectus an array of content and experiences for a total year of work. This was regarded as a fifteen-credit block and was expected to occupy the full time of the faculty and students for a year. Concerns about a unified experience, opportunity to pursue significant ideas in some depth, combination of travel and education, practical experiences related to classroom discussion and theory, all were evident in this revolt. Yet, in many respects, this program became one of the most rigid programs in modern American higher education. Students had to commit a full year to an ill-defined program and to association with the same group of students and faculty. Ultimately, continuing low enrollment forced a regression to a more traditional structure.

What seems to happen as an institution strives to develop a new structure is that it tends to do so by addressing the actual or imagined evils of existing structures. Depending upon the person's value system, various factors will be seen as crucial ones, and the attempt to remodel is likely to overemphasize a particular set of concerns and result in an innovative pattern that is either not internally consistent or is so much at odds with the prior experiences and the expectations of students that it falls of its own weight. Many of these innovative programs place severe burdens on faculty so that they are not able to engage in the developmental activities necessary for maintenance and growth in scholarship. Furthermore, those disciplines that have a well-elaborated structure of their own are not readily accommodated in this denial of all traditional structure. Some new institutions have been built around an idealized concept of novel and/or flexible learning structures as releasing and challenging the motivation for learning that presumably exists in every student. These idealists ultimately learn the hard way and change or leave, but the approach has been unduly expensive and the returns no better and perhaps worse than in more traditional institutions when costs and withdrawals are taken into account.

Radical innovations are difficult to maintain. The chief difficulty for the faculty, having been conditioned by their own prior learning and environment to aspire to achieving stature in a discipline, is that their ultimate future is under a shadow, especially when tenure is also nonexistent. In addition, students are not so uniformly and enthusiastically committed to learning on an intensive basis as some idealistic planners would like to assume. And almost invariably there are many more complications and consequent unanticipated and often undesirable outcomes in any major change of structure than the planners foresaw. It is not surprising that extreme innovations inevitably regress toward the norm.

Summary

In this chapter, the various means of structuring an educational program, including organizational units, course organizational characteristics, modes of teaching, curriculum patterns,

sequence, evaluation practices, objectives, and the physical environment have been examined. The attempt to eliminate all traditional structure has also been noted, with the accompanying
caution that such attempts actually result in the adaptation of
new structures with unpredictable effects. Indeed, the problem
may be due less to the structures than to the rigidity that tends
to take over in such structures. Structuring arises out of assumptions and predictions about people and circumstance. The
chances are good that no completely new structure is going to
be satisfying to all persons concerned any more than the traditional structure has been. Both faculty members and administrators involved in program planning are all too likely to impose
their own preferences and prejudices in various structural forms
and also to make some idealistic assumptions about students—
perhaps viewing them as much like themselves. Another and
perhaps the central major problem in curricular planning is that
those who engage in it do so without recognizing the full and
complicated range and interaction of decisions that need to be
made. One decision may negate or neutralize another. In the
next chapter, the task undertaken is that of pointing up the
various types of structural and content decisions to be made
and the procedures and problems involved in making them.

Suggestions for Further Reading

Astin, A. W. *The College Environment.* Washington, D.C.:
American Council on Education, 1968.
Astin, A. W. *Four Critical Years: Effects of College on Beliefs,
Attitudes, and Knowledge.* San Francisco: Jossey-Bass, 1977.
Bruner, J. S. *The Process of Education.* Cambridge, Mass.: Har-
vard University Press, 1961.
Committee on the University Calendar. *The University Calen-
dar.* American Association of Collegiate Registrars and Ad-
missions Officers. Washington, D.C.: American Council on
Education, 1961.
Elam, S. (Ed.). *Education and the Structure of Knowledge.* Chi-
cago: Rand McNally, 1964.
Ford, G. W., and Pugno, L. (Eds.). *The Structure of Knowledge
and the Curriculum.* Chicago: Rand McNally, 1964.

4

Alternative Means of Program Structuring

In the previous chapter, most of the common means of structuring courses and programs have been mentioned. The use of these structures is determined by convenience, tradition, or cost rather than by considerations intrinsic to the learning process or to what is to be learned. This chapter presents a number of continuums and basic pervasive concepts that are derived out of consideration of motivation, learning, and the desired results of an educative-learning procedure.

Although the disciplines and the departments in which they are embedded have, to too great an extent, dominated college curriculum development, the more serious aspect of this domination lies in the limited understanding of the disciplines upon which it has been based. Since a proper understanding of the nature of the disciplines and of their relationship to education, life, and work is essential to resolution of structural issues raised by the several continuums and concepts, this discussion begins with consideration of the disciplines.

There are certain structures inherent in the disciplines and their interrelationships with each other. Most disciplines have arisen out of attention to an aspect of the real world or of man and his interactions with it. To move from the highly subjective observation of that reality to some depth of objectivity and understanding, a set of conceptions, interrelationships, and operations are defined. These lead to development of a theoretical construct having many points in common with the reality that generated it. Thus the development of a discipline has implicit in it a set of *substantive structures* that include some assumptions about the particular variables of interest to a discipline, and these, in turn, control the questions asked and the inquiries undertaken. Once the substantive structures are determined, the development of the discipline may proceed with limited attention to that part of reality and the components of it that generated the discipline. But if reasonably well modeled after the nature of the reality, the development of the discipline may reveal new concepts and principles that are found to be applicable to the understanding of the generating reality. The use of mathematical models in the natural and social sciences well illustrates the process.

There is also in the development of the discipline a set of *organizational structures.* These spell out a set of principles relating a discipline to other disciplines. The organizational structure should locate the discipline in the context of all of organized knowledge. There then emerges a structure of the disciplines enabling one to see a discipline or group of disciplines in relationship to a problem or a reality that is to be understood or resolved. The substantive and organizational structures of knowledge have little meaning until a third structure, the syntactical, is added. The *syntactical structure* of a discipline is a system for collecting and organizing data, posing and testing hypotheses or assertions, and relating justified assertions to the broader generalizations and exploratory schemes of the discipline. The substantive structures include assumptions, variables, concepts, and principles and relationships among these at some relatively simple, perhaps observational, or other verifiable levels. The organizational structure—that is, the relationship to other disciplines—is determined, in part, out of the substantive structure but, in part also, out of the syntactical structure. The disciplines grouped in the arts and humanities have substantive structures different from the sciences, but they also have different syntactical structures and therefore the two groups tend to be clearly separated when one thinks of the organizational structures of the disciplines. Even when distinctly different disciplines are used to study the same entity, they tend to focus on distinctive aspects of that entity. Thus a human being can be viewed as a biological organism, an illustration of the principles of chemistry and physics, a creative individual, or a computer. The study of mankind falls in no one discipline, and the attempt at understanding calls for a composite integrated effort that must at least be interdisciplinary and may actually emerge as transdisciplinary in the sense that, although each discipline studies a part of man, the whole man is greater than the sum of these parts.

Nature of the Disciplines

A discipline can be viewed in many different ways: a field of study, a mode of inquiry, an organized body of knowledge, an interrelated set of interests and value commitments, or a set of objects or phenomena that man* has attempted to explain. Since a discipline is an artifact of man's thinking and has no existence or significance in the absence of man, a discipline may also be identified as a group of individuals sharing common concerns and interests in attempting to understand man, his world, his origins, his failures and successes, and his future.

There are, among these alternative conceptions of a discipline, four distinct structural elements. Perhaps the most generally recognized conception of a discipline (based on the substantive structure) is that of a body of organized knowledge including observable or verifiable facts and a set of concepts. These concepts may have been developed out of idealization or generalization over many observations, but most of them also have an objective physical reference and pragmatic significance.

*The use of the word *man* in this book is generic, referring to all humans.

Some concepts may be abstractions regarded as useful in imposing a structure on reality. That imposed structure may be hypothetical—that is, independent of the overtly perceived character of the reality. This conceptual or substantive aspect includes the major ideas to which the discipline is addressed and the categories for organizing these ideas in meaningful and interrelated ways. The substantive structure of a discipline also includes the principles, concepts, propositions, hypotheses, rules, theories, and laws that provide the dimensions within which the disciplinary knowledge can be applied and expanded.

Second, a discipline may also be regarded as a mode of inquiry (syntactical structure), an array of methodologies, or a structure involving assumptions, values, and means of collecting, organizing, analyzing, synthesizing, and evaluating the significance of data. The term *syntax* is frequently used to connote the structure of the discipline and the means used to expand that structure. The mode of inquiry includes the kinds of admissible evidence, availability of data, quality of the data, and criteria for testing and validating data. The mode of inquiry also involves the procedures in progressing from data to conclusions. The syntactical structure, then, constitutes a kind of grammar or a form of discourse characteristic of the discipline. There is implicit here also a value commitment in the sense of a rhetoric involving esthetic considerations, elegance, style, and beauty.

The third structural element (organizational structure) of a discipline is a *specialized language,* a *system of symbols,* or a *technical terminology* that is interrelated with both the mode of inquiry and the rhetoric of that syntactical structure. This specialized language (perhaps most evident in mathematics and logic) permits the scholar to develop a language intrinsically related to the discipline and its foci of operations that is independent of the ambiguities and emotions of ordinary language. To some extent also, the use of this specialized language and system of symbols allows exchange among scholars at a level transcending existing cultural and language boundaries. This language enhances the theoretical development of the discipline but it may separate the discipline from the practical problems or concerns that originally gave rise to it. This separation results both from the language and from idealization of a set of problems into an abstraction.

There is also a fourth structural component in every discipline. This is a set of values related to both the substantive and the syntactical structures. These values involve such considerations as taste, style, simplicity, and appropriateness. As the discipline is used to provide explanations or solutions to problems, characteristics such as the adequacy and universality of these solutions add a further dimension. In a sense, all disciplines are attempts to establish *order* and *understanding,* and these two concepts are themselves values of high significance, particularly when further explicated by taste, style, simplicity, appropriateness, and universality.

No one can fully understand or apply a discipline without some grasp of these four structures (substantive, syntactical, linguistic, and value) which are embedded in each discipline and markedly influence its nature and further development. The disciplines vary, however, in the extent to which these four structural components are present and rigorously utilized, and scholars within a discipline may differ on these matters. The introduction of quantitative methods (mathematics, statistics, computer science) into a discipline can almost completely change its character with respect to subject matter, syntax, language, and values. By elaboration of these structural elements (and perhaps others), it might be possible to define a discipline rigorously, but it is uncertain that this would be a significant accomplishment. Is mathematics a discipline? Few persons would deny it. Is history a discipline? If not, what is it? Is journalism a discipline or a profession? What can be said of engineering, law, medicine? At what point does a subfield of a discipline (biochemistry, for example) become a discipline? Obviously, these are issues of some interest, but attempts to provide widely acceptable answers other than pragmatic ones in particular circumstances are not likely to be possible or profitable because of the existing differences in conception and practice of disciplines.

It is useful to be aware of some of the associations made among disciplines. Thus the disciplines have been variously grouped in terms of their major contributions to the development and expansion of human capability. These contributions are suggested by the following groups:

* communication skills: language, literature, art, music, drama, logic, mathematics, statistics
* accurate inquiry: natural sciences, social sciences, mathematics, statistics
* valid reasoning: logic, science, mathematics, statistics
* synoptic understanding: history, philosophy, theology, metaphysics
* sensitivity to human values: art, music, literature, language
* wisdom in evaluation: ethics, esthetics, literature

Implicit in these groupings are judgments of the extent to which individual disciplines involve the characteristics or abilities expressed in the first column. Obviously, these, in turn, are interrelated with the four structural components just specified. Note that these groups differ from the curriculum distribution categories commonly listed as science and mathematics, humanities, social sciences, and fine arts.

    Another conception of the disciplines emerges from their historical development and the insights into the intellectual and affective capabilities and sensitivities of the human mind that this development provides. It becomes obvious that disciplines developed out of man's efforts to understand himself, the world about him, and the origin, role, and ultimate destiny of mankind. Thus the disciplines were all intensely practical in their initial stages. Their structure and their modes of inquiry were intertwined with the objects, phenomena, problems, and realities that man was trying to understand or explain. As the disciplines have become more complex and more esoteric in concepts, inquiry modes, and use of abstractions, their relationships with specific problems, phenomena, real objectives, and actual behaviors have become less apparent both to the practitioners of the disciplines and to the public which supports disciplinary study and research in the hope that human ills will be ameliorated and that some steps toward human and social perfectability will be achieved.

Thus every discipline has a *subject matter*—a group of interrelated problems, ideas, and phenomena—of which some aspects can be analyzed and therefore better understood by use of the concepts and modes of inquiry of that discipline. It is likely that several other disciplines might be equally understood by use of the concepts and modes of inquiry of that discipline. It is likely that several other disciplines might be equally applicable, although possibly directed to other facets of the problem or phenomenon. The fact is that as disciplines have become better defined, their purview has also been narrowed so that "real" problems of people and society cannot be understood or resolved by recourse to a single discipline. Since study in depth of a number of disciplines is time consuming, courses drawing upon two or more disciplines have become popular. These courses, for various but usually not clearly defined and consistent reasons, have been labeled as interdisciplinary, intradisciplinary, transdisciplinary, and supradisciplinary. A course developed to explore the broader meaning and significance of concepts, principles, or research techniques common to several disciplines is interdisciplinary and is useful in pursuing the study of a discipline as a mode of inquiry. Courses that deal with an identifiable subset of topics or ideas within a discipline chosen because of relevance to some subject matter concern might, by analogy, be regarded as intradisciplinary, although that term is seldom used. Courses drawing upon many disciplines developed to examine a problem may well be described as transdisciplinary. Courses dealing with concepts, such as truth and beauty, that have some significance in all disciplines can be labeled as supradisciplinary (above the disciplines).

Courses that cross or ignore disciplinary fences may arise out of specific problems (minorities, regions), particular themes, or conjunctions of materials, concepts, and ideas regarded by some persons as interrelated and therefore justifying a course in which these interconnections, advantages, and limitations can be studied. By this pattern of thought, Black Studies, Area

Studies, Women's Studies, Urban Studies, and others have come into being. Separated from the disciplines that provide a measure of rigor and objectivity, and dealing with issues of great complexity and emotional involvement, such courses run always the risk of superficiality in coverage, limited requirements, and low standards. Whereas interdisciplinary core programs have often contained an excess of factual knowledge, this second approach to courses that draw on several disciplines has often been focused more on emotion and affect. Identification of a problem and a "catchy" or attractive course title does not ensure that an educational experience of substance will result. In avoiding the courses, students frequently seem to have been wiser than the faculty and administrators who rushed to approve them. Nevertheless, courses that transcend traditional disciplinary boundaries are essential in that their existence arises out of a recognition that formal disciplines are complexly related in the realities with which mankind is concerned.

The fatal defect of the disciplinary approach to phenomena is that the disparate separate facts and principles accumulated through the independent application of several disciplines to a problem or phenomenon cannot easily be conjoined into a coherent picture of the totality. This is particularly true as one moves into the study of biological organisms and of the social groups that they form. Thus with the expansion of the social sciences and the behavioral sciences in the use of scientific methods to study mankind and society, the interdisciplinary mode has become essential. Some of the initial interdisciplinary attempts in the colleges were to be seen in the broad-gauge general education courses, or what are now more commonly called core courses and core course programs. The difficulty is that deciding to offer an interdisciplinary course is far easier than developing and maintaining one. In the first place, there are numerous ways of cutting across disciplines. One may look at a diamond in terms of its beauty, the problem of diamond cutting, the physical principles of light reflection, the chemical composition of the diamond, the economics and business aspects of production of diamonds and controlling the oversupply, or the study of why diamonds and other jewels have become so highly valued by individuals. The diamond conjures up all of these issues. Each, to a considerable extent, could be studied separately, but the last question raised is one that could be answered only by some consideration of all of the preceding issues, and then only if those preceding issues had been examined in the context of the broader question.

A second way to become interdisciplinary is through the concepts and methodologies used in a number of different disciplines. Thus a statistician might become interdisciplinary simply by pursuing the various uses and implications of statistics across all disciplines. Undoubtedly, in this process the statistician would arrive at some generalizations about how probability operates in similar and contrasting ways with varying kinds of objects, materials, and phenomena. In some cases, interdisciplinarity means nothing more than dealing with certain problems that cut across two disciplines. The long-existent course title of physical chemistry and the more recent one of chemical physics suggest something of this emphasis. Social psychology and psychology of social groups—the first offered in sociology departments, the second in psychology departments—indicate another common focus of two different disciplines.

From the viewpoint of the departments, interdisciplinarity comes most readily if a group of departments or faculty members simply designate those disciplinary courses in the several departments that may be taken by a student to satisfy an interdepartmental or interdisciplinary major. Thus the integration, if such there is, across these courses is left to the student. The courses enroll other students and devote little attention to integrating the disciplines, either for their own sake or for understanding some externality. Such a program ought to be designated as interdepartmental rather than as interdisciplinary. The student may become interdisciplinary, but neither the department nor the instructors have done much more than to make that possibility slightly more feasible.

A second possibility is that in which a course is organized around a theme or problem and faculty members from various disciplines are brought together to offer the course. Thus a course in history and civilization may draw upon professors from art, sociology, history, and science. By acceding to join together to offer a course, the instructors take on some obligation for interrelating, if not fully integrating, the diverse parts of the course for which they are responsible. The effectiveness of this approach obviously depends upon the individuals involved and their willingness to take on the obligations of learning what is done in other parts of the course. It also depends, in great part, upon the way in which the course is offered. If the course is built around a significant era in history (such as Florence 1500) and each member of the instructional team coordinates his or her phase of the course with that of others to enable the student to get a coherent, unified view of how Florence 1500 came about, what the nature of the flowering of many disciplines at that time really was, and what the impact of Florence 1500 was on subsequent developments, then the course may indeed become integrated, both from the professorial and the student sides. But the faculty depth in their respective fields may mean that their individual integrations differ from each other as well as from those of the students. The student in such a course may direct attention to those aspects of greatest personal relevance and achieve a coherence and unity of great personal significance. Whether or not this is acceptable to the instructor would be a difficult issue to resolve. The initial form of such a course as Florence 1500 would probably be characterized as interdisciplinary or multidisciplinary (preferably the latter because of the sheer number of disciplines involved). A possible later development of a course taught by a single professor may well become transdisciplinary in the sense that the professor has reached the point of dealing with ideas and issues at a sophisticated scholarly level without recourse to particular disciplines for justifying his or her terminology, analysis, or conclusions. It is also possible to rise to a supradisciplinary level by identifying concepts or principles useful in almost every discipline but having a depth of meaning that can be effectively dealt with only as one seeks for an ultimate unity and insight well above and beyond the disciplines. The disciplines, properly placed in a superstructure of disciplines, should make possible a unity enabling one to look at ultimate concerns (truth, beauty, equality, and the like) in the fullness of their meaning and implication without the limitations imposed by a disciplinary structure. Ideally, every undergraduate should, sometime before receiving a degree, rise for a moment or two to the supradisciplinary level.

In the preceding discussions of the disciplines, their components, and their impact on the curriculum, additional concepts have appeared. A discipline involves a body of knowledge in reference to some subject matter. It includes procedures (mode of inquiry) for collecting and organizing data. Value concerns and commitments are implicit in these considerations and are even, at times, made explicit by the rhetoric, the special language or symbols or inquiry modes. These aspects of a discipline imply some flexibility in the manner in which it is presented by a teacher and learned by a student. Thus the commitment to a disciplinary structure as the resolution of curricular problems does not provide a unique answer to curriculum and course development. There remain questions of sequence, of emphasis on content or inquiry of values, of adjustments of content to practical concerns that must be resolved by reference to institutional purposes and educational goals. As attempts at interdisciplinary programs indicate, the addressing of some of these concerns may result in modifications of the traditional disciplinary structure. It may become apparent that the traditional structure is less effective than sometimes assumed, and that traditional conceptions of a disciplinary-based curriculum may lead to overemphasis on content and theory and to a rigidity and compartmentalization that fragment the educational experience and thereby deny to the student any sense of coherence or progress.

The disciplinary structure imparted to the curriculum by departmentally based courses and programs and by the rules regarding majors and distribution requirements that determine the curriculums of students overshadows all other structural considerations in most colleges. This structure has a pragmatic justification based upon the way in which knowledge is organized and colleges are organized and administered. This "disciplinary" structure became embedded in the early years of the twentieth century and has successfully withstood attacks launched under the banners of general education, personal and social maturation, individualization, social and economic reform, and career development. Yet this structure is an outgrowth of the way in which knowledge has been sought and organized rather than one that is firmly grounded in a theory of knowledge, a sound conception of reality, or an understanding of how individuals learn. These very deficiencies have been viewed, at times, as virtues, thus making the disciplinary structure almost invulnerable to attack or alteration. In the rigid disciplinary structure, objectives are unimportant because they are implicit in mastery of content covered in courses. Understanding of the essential nature of a discipline (concepts, modes of inquiry, structure) is reserved to those who pursue study of a discipline at length and in a depth justifying induction into its mysteries. To those espousing this view, the learning idiosyncrasies of individuals (interests, motivations, competencies, and cognitive styles) are irrelevant. A discipline must be understood and mastered in its own terms. Some persons can and will; some can but won't; and some can't. Only those who can and will are the concern of the college and its faculty.

There exist scholars committed to this view, although some of them would object to the brevity and crudity of the presentation. Even so, it is an attractive view in many respects. It eliminates arguments about the relative importance of research and teaching. It would eliminate many of the costly services and activities now deemed essential to attract and retain students. It would eliminate the necessity for courses, credits, grades, and other paraphernalia that are incidental or even inimical to learning. It would also eliminate most of our colleges, for, in the present day, the individual is seen as more important than the disciplines; solution or alleviation of social and economic problems is of more concern than knowledge for its own sake; and the college exists to serve society. Structuring on more than disciplinary grounds (although not entirely excluded) is essential if program objectives and outcomes are to be made clear and functional, students are to be motivated to learn, and departments and disciplines are to be harnessed and directed in the service of society.

Once the commitment is made that structuring solely by disciplines is unsound, it becomes necessary to find other criteria for structuring and devise means for using them. In seeking them, one learns that the disciplinary mode of curriculum structuring has led to policies and processes that result from and support the disciplinary structure. Hence additional criteria for curricular structuring can be derived out of identifying and clarifying the factors involved in the extension of the disciplinary structuring, although they are not inevitable results of it. In fact, in developing a curriculum, there is no single comprehensive set of criteria that can be applied to ensure that all relevant factors are taken into account. Rather, what happens is that various decisions are made in isolation from each other and with very limited awareness of the actual impact of the requirements on students and their education. What seems to be needed to overcome these deficiencies in curricular planning is a recognition of the major decisions that are involved in the process and a definition of them that provides a number of dimensions for structuring the curriculum in a manner more clearly related to the students to be educated and the ends to be achieved than to departmental and faculty concerns and fears.

Continuums Underlying Program Development

A review of curricular practices and problems suggests that, with varying emphases, six continuums underlie program decisions. After a discussion of these continuums, we shall consider a set of assumptions and principles which, added to the continuums, provide both a rational and a necessary series of steps to arrive at a sound program, and then see how this model for developing program structure actually works.

The six continuums that will be explored as a basis for program development are as follows:

teacher . . . . discipline
student(s) . . . . .content
practical . . . . theoretical
flexibility . . . . .rigidity
unity and coherence . . . . compartmentalization
continuity, sequence, integration . . . . .fragmentation

These six continuums are not entirely independent of each other. Neither are the extremes of the continuums necessarily mutually inconsistent emphases, but they can be so. Certainly, neither extreme is to be regarded as the ideal, with the other regarded as completely inappropriate. It is true that traditional undergraduate education has been close to the right-hand extreme of each of the six continuums. Much of the emphasis in recent years has been on movement toward the left-hand end of the continuums. My contention is that the extreme positions on each of these six continuums should be considered so as to achieve a balance at some intermediate position, depending upon the desired structure, content, and objectives to be achieved by those admitted to the college. There may be conditions under which a particular course or educational experience will be at the extremes in one or more curriculums, but that should be a conscious decision based on sound grounds. That decision should also be based on the program considerations rather than the bias or preference of the disciplinary department responsible for the course and the teacher assigned to it.

Teacher-Discipline. The first continuum suggests that a decision need be made about the role of the teacher and the nature of the discipline. In a sense, this is a matter of establishing priorities. Those who view the discipline as a well-organized body of knowledge, including basic concepts, modes of inquiry, and well-defined structure, may regard the teaching act as simply purveying the nature and content of the discipline in its purest possible form. The course structure and content are then a discipline or departmental commitment that the teacher is obligated to accept. This pattern defines many undergraduate lower-division multiple-section courses. This orientation is also characteristic of some graduate courses. However, the graduate professor who offers a course based upon his or her own research exemplifies a situation in which teacher and discipline may merge. But the teacher who, in effect, dominates the discipline through personal contributions to it, while presenting a model for some students, may ignore students except as they furnish an audience for a display of his or her mastery. Relatively few graduate professors fit this mode. Hence, graduate programs tend to be on the discipline end of the continuum, and research-oriented professors who teach graduate seminars and direct dissertations for doctoral students might reasonably regard this end of the continuum as the ideal.

There are, however, relatively few professors who completely subjugate their own personalities, judgments, and interest in students to a course outline or textbook. The teacher who accepts an obligation for student learning becomes a mediator of learning or an interpreter of the discipline to the student and recognizes that the interest, capability, and possible area of application of a discipline by each individual may be far more significant educationally than pedantic knowledge of facts, concepts, or structural characteristics of the discipline.

The character of this initial continuum can be summarized as follows: When the disciplinary emphasis is decisive in a course or program, attention is directed to such factors as specific knowledge, means of problem solving, modes of inquiry, mental discipline, and intellectual development. All students are expected to assimilate knowledge in its organized form. Teachers are virtually interchangeable units in such courses. If the teacher is the key element, the teacher's role can be regarded as that of taskmaster, model, interpreter, mediator, motivator, or adviser. Student learning about the discipline is the responsibility of both teacher and students.

Student-Content. The second continuum places the student or students as a focus of emphasis against content. In some respects, this continuum is closely related to the first, but there are differences of major importance. In the first place, the content of a course may be drawn from several disciplines. Interdisciplinary courses of various types and for various reasons are offered in many colleges and universities. Generally, these have been derived out of an attempt to draw together from several disciplines relevant materials (concepts, principles, modes of analysis) that can be so organized, presented, and learned as to give an individual insight into a race, a culture, or a particular problem of major immediate concern, such as ecology. Usually this involves also the specification of some combination of learning experiences or processes. This emphasis can become a structure just as rigid as the disciplinary structure. However, students who come to such a program largely because it is a new one and not fully defined come with varied interests and differing objectives. Thus emphasis on the student clientele would tend to give more attention to student interests, student differences, and the expectations that the students have for utilizing the content of the course in the future. Many interdisciplinary courses, initially successful because the students expected a treatment of the issues of the day today and mastery of ways to resolve them by tomorrow, became more overburdened with content than the traditional disciplinary-based courses. In still another sense, the difference between the two extremes is a matter of whether the emphasis is on a purely intellectual treatment of content materials or on the creation of affective states and outcomes in the students. Finally, the focus may be on student or on students. When a course or curriculum is planned specifically for an identified group of students, it is tempting to make advance commitments based upon assumed characteristics of this group. Often the plans formulated on the basis of some hypothetical averages or norms turn out to be inappropriate. Undue flexibility for adaptation can be unsatisfactory both to the students and to those who are concerned with their achievement. Thus this continuum suggests that rather than designing a course solely on the basis of content coverage and appropriate processes for acquiring the knowledge and skills, attention should be given to the students served by the course. Adaptation to that group and further flexibility to provide for subgroups or for individualization may be more important than extensive content coverage. On this second continuum, content emphasis tends to be on a present or past orientation, with the course experiences and content defined by knowledge, skills, processes, problems, and themes that the students are expected to know and understand. Emphasis on the student is made evident by statements of individualized learning and objectives, career development concerns, attention to individual interests and aspirations, evaluation of student progress, encouragement of student self-evaluation, and stimulation of individual and group interaction.

Practical-Theoretical. The third continuum places practicality or life-related educational experiences on the left and theoretical or academic experiences on the right. Again, this pairing is not intended to indicate that one extreme is more desirable and therefore should completely displace the other. Einstein's theory of relativity was a major breakthrough leading to many insights of practical importance. Theories, abstractions, and broad generalizations are useful in organizing and thinking about problems, but strict adherence to theory without regard for any possible application is unfulfilling for most students and is almost sure to fail in developing their expectation that increasing knowledge will have utility in dealing with practical life-related problems. The understanding of theory should reach the point where one can take account of its assumptions and limitations and develop from it some models for increased insight into reality as a major outcome of education. Just as sole emphasis on theory results in inability to apply the theory, overemphasis on practical matters at each stage results in the inability to deal with underlying and clarifying abstractions and with generalizations of broad applicability.

The practical-theoretical continuum also involves an examination of the balance between acquiring greater knowledge and the obligation of the college or university to develop people who are able to apply their knowledge to the betterment of society. The right-hand end of the continuum could, in some respects, be regarded as an ivory tower conception of education completely detached from the workaday world. The left-hand end of the continuum emphasizes the responsibility of the college or university to attempt to meet the needs of society through research and service and specifically through educating people to perform well the essential roles required in society. However, unless this activist orientation is balanced by relevant knowledge and sound judgment, attempts at change are not likely to be understood or accepted or successful if accepted. To summarize, the theoretical end of this third continuum moves beyond the content end of the second continuum by attending to concepts, theories, principles, generalizations, and forms of inquiry rather than to isolated facts and skills. The emphasis is on assimilating an integrated understanding of a discipline by acquiring sufficient mastery of unifying theories, general principles, and concepts so that the discipline becomes unified and coherent.

Flexibility-Rigidity. The fourth continuum involves flexibility on one end and rigidity on the other. Obviously, in many respects, this continuum relates to the preceding three, but it should be pointed out that emphasis on either of the extremes of the preceding three would, in itself, be a form of rigidity. Programs that have attempted to focus on affect and individual development and permitted content to be generated out of the needs and interests of individuals have been just as rigid, in many cases, as educators who emphasize the priority of an organized body of content above the interests and needs of the individuals and circumstances. Since individualization is important, counseling is likely to be a significant aspect of a flexible program as against traditional advising that provides only limited assistance to students in selecting among the restricted number of options available. Rigidity, the other extreme, implies the existence of rules, requirements, and standards. Basically, the existence of these rigidities reflects a conviction on the part of many administrators and faculty members that college students (even graduate students) are not to be trusted with the planning of their own education, partly because they have inadequate knowledge of the field, partly because they may try to find the easiest route to a degree, and, most of all, because there is generally a great desire on the part of faculty members, departments, and colleges to lay out specific programs from which students can choose. Most colleges offer some flexibility because there are many alternative programs among which to choose. But, once the student has made a particular program choice, requirements or advising may take over and determine all the rest. A fundamental weakness with the rigidity position is that program suggestions or recommendations too readily become requirements as soon as they appear in printed form. This relieves the adviser of many hours spent assisting the student in a choice among electives. It also relieves a number of departments of the need to revise their courses and programs in order to attract students. The major difficulty is that it relieves students of any serious responsibility for the planning of their own programs. Indeed, it encourages them not to think much ahead of the immediate term's enrollment because there are no significant choices to be made by the student. The program structure is specified by the faculty, and the students must perforce go through it. Even in those cases where some element of flexibility is suggested in a program (for example, the individualized major in a number of colleges), the student must jump through so many hoops to get the program approved that it becomes easier to follow docilely the standard pattern. A major contribution to rigidity is often found in the multiple-section, large-enrollment courses offered within the freshman and sophomore years of college. Typically, syllabuses are developed for such courses that specify each day what pages or materials are to be covered, what books or references are to be used, and what examination practices should be followed. The rigidity imposed on both teachers and students in these circumstances points to an emphasis on covering and learning specific content materials rather than on educational objectives that could be readily attained by use of a wide selection of materials. This rigidity also reflects doubts on the part of faculty members that their associates—particularly junior faculty members—can be trusted to develop and present a course on their own. The argument that this rigid pattern provides equity in the treatment of students regardless of sections raises some questions about what is meant by equity. Is this achieved by requiring everyone to do the same thing, or by some modification of materials and tasks in relationship to interests, aspirations, and capabilities of individuals?

It should also be pointed out that the demand for flexibility can be carried entirely too far. When the first meeting of a course is started with a question by the professor as to what the students would like to do in this course, flexibility has become excessive. It is akin to a theater owner's indicating the hours at which films will be shown and then asking the assembled audience to decide what film will be used at that time. Extreme flexibility is simply chaotic. Rigidity arises out of imposition of standards, rules, and requirements that are uniformly and rigorously applied to everyone. Modifications or waivers are obtainable only by procedures that are themselves exemplifications of rigidity. Flexibility does not require forgoing standards, but it does permit individualization, adaptation to circumstance, counseling, and the encouragement of self-evaluation and self-motivation.

Unity-Compartmentalization. The fifth continuum ranges from unity and coherence on one end to compartmentalization on the other. Within the first year or two of college, students are likely to be enrolled in anywhere from three to six or even seven courses, including something in composition, science, mathematics, history, psychology, and physical education. The student is not expected to perceive any relationship among these courses, and any overt attempt to do so is likely to be discouraged by pressure to cover all of the course materials. Thus the student is faced, in the early years of college, with a rigid compartmentalization of courses and disciplines and adjusts learning patterns and thoughts accordingly. Rigidity in disciplinary lines certainly contributes to this, but so also does flexibility. Flexibility is, to some extent, revealed by the wide range of offerings in various departments and the lack of specific requirements or sequences. Thus the students, in any particular classroom, have diverse backgrounds, and the instructor who would attempt to create some sense of unity and coherence by referring to ideas, concepts, and modes of inquiry characteristic of other disciplines finds no opportunity to do so because of the diversity of background. The enthusiasm for a required core of courses for all students evident in the general education movement of the 1940-1960 era was an attempt to deal with this problem. But with the variation in student background and the diverse competencies and breadth of knowledge required of teachers, these core programs in themselves became a rigid pattern rejected by faculty and students alike.

The search for unity, coherence, and meaning is, after all, an individual search. It can be motivated and expedited through teaching, through some curricular planning across courses, and through evaluation. It is too important to leave to students, who can hardly be expected to develop unity and coherence when the faculty involved in teaching them apparently has been unable to do so. Only continuing and constant administrative efforts and pressures will keep faculty attention on this concern. This continuum emphasizes the interrelationship and interaction among courses and learning experiences within a specific period of time. The major concern implied by this fifth continuum is that an ill-assorted array of courses across a number of disciplines can cause students to perceive disciplines as organized and unrelated bodies of knowledge which, in turn, have very little relevance to the real problems of individuals in society simply because they are compartmentalized. Compartmentalization supports specialization, isolation, and ignorance about and indifference to what is happening in other fields. Unity and coherence imply that, in the short term, students are encouraged to select courses having some perceived relationship and to seek interrelations and connections within and across courses and disciplines.

Continuity-Fragmentation. The sixth continuum, involving continuity, sequence, and integration on one extreme, and fragmentation on the other, extends the concept of unity and coherence to concern about the relationship within and among disciplines and courses over time. Continuity refers to the awareness and use of principles, ideas, and values of such broad significance that they transcend courses and can therefore be used as threads that help students relate knowledge as they pursue study within a discipline or across several disciplines. The spiral curriculum conception implies this intent. One could imagine an agreement (highly arbitrary, of course) on 100 major concepts which would be touched upon in various ways in increasing depth (sequence) over time. Truth, beauty, equality could be examples; at a more specific and functional level, the concept of symmetry, in one form or another, is significant in all disciplines.

The conception of sequence has almost disappeared in curricular planning in higher education. The tendency in some beginning courses is to introduce principles or concepts in the most rigorous form, involving distinctions and subtleties beyond the comprehension of the students at that stage. The textbook

writer who would avoid this is concerned that colleagues reviewing the text will criticize both the book and its display of scholarship because of what will be labeled as errors or inaccuracies.
One of the major reasons for lack of sequence has been the
tendency to increase greatly the number of courses offered in
departments, coupled with a demand that courses be kept flex-
ibly open to all students by removing prerequisites. This had led
to scheduling of offerings in such manner that even students
who desire to plan a meaningful sequence of courses have difficulty in so doing. Discontinuities in student attendance further
complicate that problem.

Integration includes unity and coherence but speaks to
this across time and involves also a relationship with issues and
problems extending beyond the college program. No doubt all
faculty members expect, in some sense, that the student completing the baccalaureate degree has achieved a breadth of
knowledge, a sense of values, and the ability to relate these to
the complex problems of life. Yet, generally, little is done to
encourage integration, and when concrete action is taken, it is
likely to be in the form of a course—a senior seminar that can
be successful only with extraordinarily capable professors who
are likely to find the task so burdensome that they seek freedom from it after a few years. This approach is typical of the
attempted solutions to many problems in higher education. Students cannot do arithmetic, so we require that they take a
remedial course. Students cannot write, so we require a composition course at the beginning of college. Students do not
know how to study, so we insert a course. Thus we attempt to
alleviate basic deficiencies in programs by inserting more
courses that contribute to the fragmentation, the other extreme
of our sixth continuum. And to further reinforce that fragmentation, students are given degrees based upon courses taken and
credits amassed rather than on what they have actually acquired
from the educational process. Fragmentation results from the
lack of attempts in curriculum planning to recognize an effective program as an integrated whole fully understood by all faculty members who, in turn, motivate students by continually
pointing out relevance, sequence, and progress.

The virtue of these six continuums lies in the emphasis placed on the total curricular experience of students. It is unnecessary, and probably impossible, for every course offered in a department or college to strike a happy balance between the extremes of each of the continuums. Every course can be improved if the instructor reflects upon the continuums and consciously seeks to expand its cumulative impact on the total curricular experience. Balance across the continuums ultimately depends upon advising or counseling that makes students aware of the significance of these elements in their education and places more responsibility on them to plan a balanced program enabling them to achieve educational outcomes that transcend courses and other discrete educational experiences. Courses are means not ends, but courses can and should be so planned and offered that ultimate curricular ends are explicit in courses and in day-to-day activities in these courses. Thus these ultimate ends become visible and motivational goals for students.

Interrelationships and Implications. The six continuums are interrelated, yet each can be addressed somewhat independently of the others. The interrelationships become more apparent when the objectives implied by views on the curriculum are identified. The extreme right of the six continuums (discipline, content, theoretical, rigidity, compartmentalization, and fragmentation) hardly calls for a statement of objectives, for they are both implicit and explicit in the discipline-content emphasis. The left extreme (teacher, students, practical, flexibility, unity and coherence, continuity, sequence, and integration) is rather more ambiguous in its relation to objectives. The first two, teacher and student(s), present a human focus that may be either on individuals or on the composite group. The third, practical, clearly indicates that the knowledge acquired should have some relevance to external realities and be so presented that students assimilate this relevance and practicability. The necessity in applications of being sensitive to assumptions and limitations implies an awareness and sensitivity to values and a concern for the long-term implications of immediate decisions. Flexibility, in the context here presented, connotes adaptation to individual interests and learning patterns and the fostering of self-evaluation and self-motivation, assisted by personal counseling. Likewise, both unity and coherence *and* continuity, sequence, and integration involve recognition that these qualities and their attainment require individual effort and are not intrinsic to the disciplines. Thus the left extreme of the continuums is associated with objectives directed to personal and social development which, when overemphasized, constitute a denial of intellectual and content emphases of the right-hand continuum extremes. Therefore, it is my personal conviction—and I believe that of the vast majority of the college and university faculty members—that some intermediate position that balances the intellectual and affective and the personal development and content emphases is desirable. This position still admits that some courses and programs may justifiably move toward the extreme positions on one or all six continuums.

Additional Pervasive Concepts. There are numerous additional concepts that may be introduced into the discussions of curriculum planning. A review of the discussion of the six continuums and the relationship between the continuums and objectives quickly brings the realization that nothing has been said explicitly about educational typologies, such as general, liberal, vocational, and professional. Environmental factors, noted in the preceding chapter as one of the means of structuring an educational program, are completely ignored. The social responsibilities and obligations that an educational institution and its faculty assume have been touched on only relatively lightly in the continuum extending from practical to theoretical. Although this continuum is worded in terms of practicality or relevance for the individual, the individual as a member of society must apply his knowledge in that context. The left extreme involves a humanistic orientation, and the concepts of continuity, sequence, and integration are interpreted as individual goals rather than as characteristics of the discipline. This implies that these qualities must be regarded as both personal and social. In short, the perception of relevance, the recognition of a sequence, or the accomplishment of an integration is always personal and always takes place in a physical and social context. The more realistic this environment context is, the easier is the transferral of the behavior to life situations.

In these continuums, learning and teaching have not been explicitly introduced. Although consideration was given to promoting this dichotomy of learning and teaching to a continuum status, close analysis indicated that this could not be justified. The difficulty revolves around the conceptions of teaching and of learning and the fact that these conceptions are closely interrelated with individual motivation and educational objectives. An advanced undergraduate or graduate course in physics or mathematics, for example, may hew closely to the right-hand end of the six continuums, using experiences satisfying to both the teacher and the students and resulting in an intellectual grasp of the disciplinary content and modes of inquiry. Thus the selection of the instructional practices and learning experiences has profound implications with regard to the placement of a course on each of the continuums. Indeed, the teaching modes and the learning experiences of a given course or program provide the key variables for defining varied intermediate positions on the six continuums. These positions, in turn, imply something about the appropriate learning materials and the nature of the environment in which these are used.

The six continuums appear to touch only lightly on the matter of values. However, the decision with regard to the desired position on the several continuums is, in itself, a commitment to certain values or to a balancing or ordering of values. The decisions involved are essentially philosophical, for they depend upon views or commitments as to the nature and purposes of educational institutions and their roles in determining educational processes. One extreme implies assimilation of organized knowledge in an objective manner uncolored by affect, in a highly structured environment, and using rather rigidly defined procedures. The other extreme clearly indicates that the development of individuals is the major purpose of education and that this development is fostered by the elimination of confining structures and the provision of an environment in which each person is free to grow as personal interests and aspirations dictate. The several educational typologies of general, liberal, vocational, and professional, in themselves, involve philosophical commitments. Although liberal education and professional education have sometimes been contrasted in a manner that would suggest that liberal-professional might also constitute a continuum, my view is that liberal education and other typologies involve value commitments that, in turn, help to define the nature of learning and teaching and the qualities of the environment appropriate to the educational objectives chosen. Thus, in this discussion of pervasive concepts, I have pointed to a number of concepts so intimately related with objectives and outcomes that their definitions and interpretations become means for defining the positions to be sought in regard to the six continuums. Further discussion of some of these pervasive concepts will make clearer their role in this regard.

The Individual and the Environment

Every human being is embedded in some near environment composed of three interrelated environments. The individual and these several environments are constantly engaged in interactions or transactions that affect the individual, those around the individual, and also the environments. The first of these environments is what might be described as the *natural environment*—the physical and biological world and the space and time in which these environments are bound up. The individual's and the group's interaction with the natural environment leads to a *constructed environment* with three parts. One is a *social-cultural* environment made up of cultural factors, value commitments, and social institutions and laws. Another aspect of the constructed environment is the *sociophysical,* also subject to human alterations. The third is the *sociobiological* aspect of the biological world. The physical and biological environments may be exploited or wisely used in achieving human goals. These environments are subject to change. The individual interacting with these environments is likewise subject to change. As the emerging artifactual or constructed environment eases certain problems and needs, the priorities of the individual and society may change. Thus the interaction of society with the biological and physical factors in an environment, and the further interaction between these environmental factors and the culture itself, may lead to further reconstruction of the environment.

There is also a *behavioral environment* in which the wants and needs of individuals and social groups interact to change factors in the near environment of individuals and to set up aspirations, goals, and stresses that generate interactions with and perhaps manipulation of other aspects of the environment. I have found that almost every document dealing with undergraduate education expresses, at some point, the pervasive concern that individuals have some sense of progress toward an overall unity not only in the educational process itself but also in the organization of knowledge, insights, and personal commitments resulting from that education. The range of words used to deal with this conception of unity provokes some thought. Integration can be defined as the process of making something whole or entire out of parts or ideas presented or dealt with separately. Much of the discussion about integration implies that the student is to assimilate an integration already existing. It seems at times to be assumed that the integration of ideas is explicit in the ideas themselves or in the physical objects or problems to which they have reference. Thus an automobile is an integrated operation of many parts, of diverse physical and chemical knowledge, and the development of a functioning interrelationship among these various elements. At a second level, there is the possibility that a professor has developed a personal integration of many ideas with the intent that the students assimilate the integration the professor has already made. At a third level, there may be a concern that students make their own integration—that is, the student becomes an integrating individual. Not uncommonly, faculties engaging in the discussion of educational problems will ultimately take the position that the integration of materials and ideas across disciplines and over four years is a task that the individual must do for himself. This is true, but it also is obviously a way of ignoring the problem. Ultimately, every individual must also learn for himself or herself. Effective teachers not only demonstrate their own integrative efforts but also encourage and facilitate the integrative efforts of students.

Connectedness is closely related to integration. Connectedness is the quality of being joined or hooked together. It is related to the overused word *relevant*. The meaning of "being joined together" depends upon individuals and circumstances. The links of a chain are joined together in a real and functional relationship. A connection between symmetry in works of art and symmetry as used in mathematics might very likely be a personal imposition of connectedness upon what, to many people, would appear to be unrelated matters. In the steps of a proof or a demonstration, connectedness may be a logical and sequential relationship. Clearly, connectedness involves an association of one thing with another, and it could be a step in the integration process. Explicitly, though, connectedness does not involve the extent of interrelatedness implied by an integration. The word *relatedness* also is used in curricular discussions, usually in specification of some particular manner of being related. In most cases, it seems to involve an intrinsic connection between two or more ideas or concepts that the student should learn. Thus relatedness is very close to connectedness but, as used, seems to be at a more abstract level. Obviously, relatedness could be seen as something produced by the student and imposed upon his or her observations rather than as a principle or proposition to be learned.

The word *synoptic* is frequently used, often in speaking of disciplines like history or philosophy that attempt to give a comprehensive overview of a set of interrelated concepts or problems. The characterization of a discipline as synoptic indicates that one of the major purposes of that discipline is to give a unified interrelated picture of a complex and multipartite entity. In order to develop a synoptic experience, somebody must engage in the task of bringing materials together. Once again, then, it becomes important that the student not simply be asked to master the work of others, but that part of the learning experience be that of achieving a synopsis. There is one other aspect of synopsis that is significant in the learning process. A synopsis implies a relatively brief concise overview of a complexity and may be less concerned with demonstrating interrelationships or achieving an integration than with presenting the major facets, say, of some historical era in some coherent organized way.

The word *synthesis,* implying the combination of parts to

form a whole, is also frequently used in curricular discussions. The opposite of synthesis is analysis, and discussions frequently imply either that there is too much analysis and not enough synthesis or that there are attempts to provide a synthesis at too early a date before one fully understands the essential nature and interrelationships of the components to be synthesized. There is also in the word synthesis some suggestion of synthetic or artificial. A concern about this is implied in some discussions by phrases discounting or discrediting the synthesis made by a student and emphasizing or demanding that the program itself provide the synthesis. Comprehensive examinations, senior seminars, and other specific curricular components have often been introduced to promote in the senior year a synthesis carefully avoided at all earlier stages. The words *unified, unity,* and *whole* are also used, and the combination, *unified whole,* is not uncommon. Unified, of course, refers to a merger or consolidation of ideas; but more than that, it implies that these merge to form a unity. This is apparently possible only if there existed a whole that has somehow been fractured and must be put together. Most frequently, again it seems to be implied by the context that there is a unity or a whole that should become apparent to the individual, although the very inability of the faculty to make this specific suggests that either many of them have not found this possible or that they have differed in the concept that they have developed.

The *form* of a course includes its desired outcomes, instructional model, dominant processes, accounting and evaluation processes (course, student, faculty). The *context* refers to the social, cultural, and organizational climate providing the filtering and interpretative influences as a program is developed and made operative.

The *content* of a course draws both upon the available and relevant knowledge and upon what is known about human motivation and the learning process. The content is drawn from whatever resources are available to the course designer. The designer fits all of these materials and ideas together into a structure that includes the mode of presentation to students. Design involves creativity or inventiveness in putting all of these elements together so as to attain a new structure (sequence, organization, form) that is a clear response to the function of the course in fostering student development in regard to avowed objectives and outcomes that will enable students to reshape the world about them.

My personal view is that most of these discussions would be markedly improved if they started with a conviction that the purpose of education is not to provide a unified educational experience that develops a   holistic and integrated view of everything in man's experience. Rather, the aim in education should be to examine some forms of integration so challenging that students are encouraged to search for integrations. No doubt one must start with the integrations achieved by others, but the ultimate goal should be that students arrive at their own conceptions of connectedness, relatedness, synthesis, and integration. This view adds greater meaning to another term that has occurred in curriculum developments in recent years, perhaps largely because of its use in the Krathwohl (1964) affective taxonomy. The term is *internalization*. Internalization implies commitment—at least sufficient commitment to the worth of an idea or concept that it is included in one's own thought and valuing processes. This acceptance also gives a subjective character to whatever is internalized. One can memorize something in the exact words of others and repeat it by rote when that behavior is demanded. That is not internalization. Internalization involves not only the adoption of an idea as one's own but also the adaptation of that idea to one's own preconceptions and assumptions. This is surely one of the major objectives of higher education. Awareness and continuous concern about internalization would make a great deal of difference in the curricular experience and the learning of undergraduate students.

Sequence and Integration

The organization of a sequence of experiences on the basis of difficulty may seem to offer a relatively clear solution to the curricular problems implied by the several concepts just discussed. A number of problems immediately arise. One of them is the question of what is meant by difficulty. Lifting a two-pound weight requires more energy output than lifting a one-pound weight. The two-pound lift can be said to be more difficult than the one-pound lift because it requires a greater energy output. If one moves into the weight-lifting competition, it becomes evident that weight is a factor in difficulty. One might say that the difficulty in this sense is intrinsic to the task, but in other circumstances the difficulty is imposed by surrounding limitations or conditions. The conditioned weight lifter has developed particular skills and techniques; hence, even for a moderate weight, the uninitiate may find more difficulty than does the well-trained weight lifter. If, however, we furnish each of them with a derrick operated by pressing buttons, neither the amateur nor the professional will experience any difficulty. Running backward is, for most people, a rather more difficult task than running forward, but by sufficient practice individuals may become reasonably proficient, though hardly ever graceful, at it. Cutting an oak board with a dull handsaw is a more difficult task than cutting the same board with a sharp power saw. Thus it appears that the difficulty of a task is seldom entirely intrinsic to the task itself but depends upon the resources and the methods used in attacking it.

The quality of the product desired may be regarded as relating to difficulty; yet the exercise of fine discrimination or measurement with accuracy and precision may be more a matter of practice, ability, or available technology than of any actual difficulty in the moment at which the task is done. Relatively simple tasks requiring much time and perseverance are sometimes regarded as difficult. The material that is available for the execution of a task may contribute to difficulty. As a naive person in the field of sculpture, I would regard the sculpturing of a marble figure as considerably more difficult than creating the same figure out of soap.

Difficulty can, in a certain sense, be related to the number of obstructions that have to be overcome. Making a new garden in an area in which there are many rocks and weeds certainly would be regarded by most people as more difficult than making one in an area lacking these obstructions. Complexity is another factor related to difficulty. The performance by an ice skater or gymnast calls for careful and graceful coordination. In a sense, the effectiveness of the performance is determined by the ease and elegance with which the task is completed. The difficulty of a task may also be related to the level of understanding or of generalization required. In the spiral concept of curriculum, this element particularly is realized because the curriculum, although arranged on a sequential basis, is also organized to return to basic principles and concepts from time to time, each time at a higher level of understanding and ability to use the concept. The difficulty of some tasks is directly related to the words or symbols used. One has only to try to multiply or divide using Roman numerals to realize that the Arabic numerals and the introduction of zero and place value made relatively easy what was previously a difficult task.

In analyzing test questions, difficulty is often imputed to the test question in terms of how many persons are unable to answer it correctly. In this sense, a question asking the birthdate of Julius Caesar's grandfather would be difficult simply because few people would know it, even supposing the date is a matter of record somewhere. Obscurity, the specificity of detail, or unnecessary or irrelevant precision make for extrinsic difficulty when there is nothing necessarily difficult about the question asked. Differences in individual interests and skill are also factors in difficulty. For the beginning violin student, difficulty means something very different from the conception of the violin virtuoso. Time is a consideration often related to difficulty but, in fact, the task that takes more time may be far easier than prestidigitation done with a flip of a finger. Knowing when and where and how much force to use to get the specified results may have required extensive practice, whereas a longer task may only be a matter of doing a number of easy tasks in succession. One cannot do very much with physics or engineering without some background in mathematics. Hence there is implied a sequence requiring students to take some mathematics before they move into physics or engineering courses, but this sequence, based upon dependence, in itself depends, to a considerable extent, on how various materials are approached.

Perhaps ideally, as it becomes clear that the performance of biological organisms is based upon physical principles that, in turn, are based on mathematical concepts, anyone wishing to study biology should be required to take mathematics and physical science before enrolling in biological science courses. In the humanities and the social sciences, sequences are much less clear. One can base a sequence of courses in American history upon chronology and argue that no particular period in American history can be understood until a great deal is known about previous eras. Application of this in the extreme would require that all study of history begin with ancient history and proceed to the present. However, the development of significant ideas is often not pursued in the most meaningful way on a chronological basis.

Obviously, it is much easier to organize a sequence of tasks in terms of the expenditure of physical strength than it is in terms of mental effort. In both cases, factors with regard to skill, practice, and motivation are involved, but the working of an individual's mind is much less open to scrutiny than is physical activity. Intuition, for example, is beyond explanation. In some ways, however, quantitative factors are involved in mental as well as physical activity. Personal risk is also a factor. A difficult physical task may, for the person executing it, involve a high degree of risk; but careful and controlled practice can reduce that risk.

Contiguity and remoteness have sometimes been used as a basis for sequence. It may seem to be easier to start with the immediate environment and with the social institutions and people there and then move to the more remote which, by their differences, may be more difficult to assimilate. It is equally true, however, that lack of contact with contrasting cultures may make it difficult for individuals to perceive the essential characteristics of their own. Thus sequence in sociology or psychology could well be built upon a succession of experiences moving to and from one's own culture to attain perspective. This, in a sense, is an artificial or contrived sequence—an extrinsic one—that can, nevertheless, have a very significant impact upon student motivation and learning.

One of the more important reasons for developing meaningful sequence in a program is that students have some sense of progress. The emphasis in recent years upon offering a wide range of courses with minimal prerequisites causes many students to see each term of college as completely independent of all others. It may be an advantage to organize a program that permits people to enroll for a while, drop out, and return at their convenience. At the same time, a program built on that basis offers no continuing and cumulative challenge to a student and arouses no great motivation in terms of maintaining college attendance to achieve a well-defined goal. In professional programs in which there is relatively little choice—as, for example, in medicine—the sequence of courses is a factor of greater concern than in liberal education. The medical student must take a significant amount of basic science before moving into clinical courses, but an exposure limited entirely to the basic sciences may generate so much dissatisfaction on the part of the student anxious to come to grips with medical problems that attendance and performance will suffer. Yet, the student cannot do much with the clinical area—particularly in work with patients—until a significant background of knowledge and capability in using it has been developed. There is a further problem of sequence that becomes evident in this context. Presumably, all required experiences in a medical program are ultimately interrelated in the task of diagnosing health problems and prescribing treatments. At the same time, there are problems in the interconnections and relevance of the several courses taken by a student in one term. It is desirable that there be some interconnectedness between these so that the student becomes aware of any relationships and of the ultimate unity in practicing the medical profession. Even here, differences in views and training of basic science and clinical faculties and the marked differences in the prior experiences of students make resolution of the problems of sequence a matter of compromise subject to alteration with advancing knowledge and change in personnel.

Despite the fact that development of a sequence is at times arbitrary and even artificial, it is a concept of great significance in curriculum development. However, it can be effective only if instruction capitalizes on it by developing expectations and habits of interrelating ideas, concepts, and principles from various sources to enhance understanding and arrive at new levels of generalization and application. A well-developed and logically sound sequence may be sensed by some students without faculty direction, but a well-planned sequence is often wasted because the faculty does not use it. Almost any course organization can, in some sense, become sequential if all instructors are aware of what is done in other courses and direct their efforts to taking full advantage of interrelationships. Sequence and integration as educational concepts imply objectives involving personal habits and expectations rather than a mere structuring or ordering of content materials. Our ineffectiveness in the present day in providing a liberal education results, in large part, from our inability to agree on liberal outcomes and define a sequence of educational experiences that would foster their development.

Posner and Strike (1976) have developed an outline of principles for sequencing content that includes many of the prior considerations and adds one or two more. Somewhat paraphrased, here is their useful checklist for thinking about problems of sequencing content and courses:

1. Sequence the content in a course so that the course organization corresponds to or is apparently consistent with the way in which the world (space, physical attributes) is or is perceived. (empirically verifiable relationship)
2. Sequence content so as to be logically consistent with the organization of the concepts used (class relations, propositional relations, sophistication level, logical prerequisites, and the like). (conceptual properties of knowledge)
3. Sequence content to be consistent with process of inquiry. (logic, empirics, sequence of inquiry)
4. Sequence content in relation to student. (interest, familiarity, difficulty in the learning process, processes of internalization, personal development)
5. How can (will) the student utilize the content after he or she has learned it? (frequency of utilization, circumstances, procedures in utilization)

The first of these principles bases sequence upon the perception of reality. The second bases sequence upon the conceptual system imposed upon that perception. The third would use the logic, mode, and sequence of inquiry to determine content sequence. The fourth draws upon student interest and other personal traits and abilities. The fifth would base sequence on the extent and manner of utilization. Each has obvious benefits, and they are not necessarily incompatible.

Liberal Education Outcomes

The number of books and essays that have been written about liberal education reflect, in great part, an idealistic point of view and rise out of a concern that the nature and objectives of liberal education are not widely understood, especially by the faculties in our colleges and universities. It is, I believe, the idealistic nature of the discussions of liberal education that causes faculty members to reject any serious effort to define or operationalize liberal education in their own institutions and specifically in their own teaching. A composite of liberal education outcomes in an abbreviated fashion generally includes a knowledge of the cultural heritage, often phrased in terms of understanding of some of the great literary, scientific, and artistic works of man. The body of knowledge associated with liberal education is usually defined also to include some chronological grasp of the major events in one's own nation and culture and in those nations and cultures from which that one is derived. A third facet of knowledge is that of knowing and perhaps being able to use, to some extent, the modes of inquiry that have arisen in the development of the various disciplines.

Another outcome of liberal education involves understanding and the knowledge and appreciation of the behavior of individuals and groups and the comparative and contrasting values of one's own and other cultures, both current and past. The choice of terms in this statement is of particular interest. Knowing, understanding, and appreciating carry somewhat distinctive overtones. Generally underlying the statement of this objective is a concern about personal, social, and religious values and the awareness of the differing emphases and contrasting priorities across cultures and individuals. This area furnishes an example of the difficulties of defining a liberal education. For many persons, there are certain values inherent in the development of Western civilization, and these values are promoted to the level of absolutes to be assimilated, accepted, and applied. Others see this as the antithesis of liberal education and move to almost a complete relativism, insisting that apparently similar situations often involve such complications and subtle distinctions that rigid commitment and consistent application of values are impossible. Others would relate this understanding of behavioral differences in individuals and groups to the development of effectiveness in communicating and interacting with groups. Here again, there are marked differences of view. Some adherents or proponents of liberal education would argue that the increased knowledge and insights into concepts and values should aid individuals to interact with others in group situations, but they would tend to deny that this is a necessary outcome of liberal education. One reason for this denial is that there exist among scholars some who are so committed to their particular interests in pursuit of knowledge and insight that they disdain and avoid interaction with others, except as that interaction is directly related to primary interests and concerns.

Another group of concerns regarding liberal education outcomes may be put under the heading of understanding of self, personal development, self-actualization, or any one of a number of such phrases. The difficulty comes when liberal education outcomes dealing with communication, knowledge, and methodology are regarded as aspects of self-understanding and development, but with manifestations so highly idiosyncratic as to be beyond faculty direction or intervention. A few academics would promote self-development or self-actualization to a major outcome, apparently committed to the belief that maximal individual self-development not only yields increased personal satisfaction and happiness but also leads to the best possible society.

It is apparent, in these various statements about liberal education outcomes, that there are a number of different continuums involved. These are directly related to the continuums discussed earlier. Variations in the conception of liberal education, then, include extreme positions on each of these continuums. In my judgment, rather than attempting to reach an institutional position on liberal education, it would be better to concentrate on taking a position on the several continuums and relating this position to what can reasonably be expected of an individual performing in a democratic society.

Implicit both in the continuums and in these contrasting views of liberal education is the two-culture phenomenon: the humanities and the sciences. Many humanists tend to emphasize knowledge of particular authors and works and seem generally to feel that literature, fine arts, philosophy, and history constitute the areas where the essential nature of man and especially his creativity are evident. Curiously enough, these are areas in which the works of human beings seem to be more objectively appraised after a lapse of time. Thus there is always something of a past orientation. There is also a lack of cumulative impact in this arena of humanities, evidenced in those programs based upon a "great books" pattern. In contrast to this, as Bruner (1966, p. 75) has pointed out, the five great humanizing forces are toolmaking, language, social organization, the management of man's prolonged childhood, and man's urge to explain his world. It is important to note that Bruner calls these the *humanizing forces,* and they all represent, in some way, man's ability to accumulate and organize knowledge and bring about changes through it. It is notable too that in these accumulative fields there is much less emphasis on knowing what a specific person did at a particular point in time and much more emphasis on the current and prospective future stages of development in which that and other discoveries are integrated. There is much more emphasis on the individual's ability to assimilate and apply what he has learned than on simply knowing who did or said what and when.

The vast range of views existent under the banner of liberal education is also evident when one turns to psychomotor outcomes. Performance in this area involves some knowledge, it certainly involves some affective considerations, but it implies always some physical involvement, some directed movement calculated to attain certain ends. The divergent views on this category of educational outcomes divide even the humanities. Some regard the humanities as in one-to-one correspondence with liberal education and would deny the validity of the performing arts as an aspect of liberal education. And some who might accept performance or composition so long as the result has no utilitarian value reject the applied arts as part of liberal education. The extent to which time has been wasted in discussions and confrontations among faculties concerned with curriculum reorganization raises serious doubts as to whether any really significant agreement about the nature and purpose of undergraduate education is to be achieved unless a dictatorial position is taken and faculty and students carefully screened to assure acceptance of that position. It is a vain effort to attempt to agree on what a liberal education is so long as the focus is placed on what this means with regard to materials and specific knowledge. The only possible resolution is to discuss and agree upon certain types of behavior and views and values that characterize what may be called a liberally educated individual. And even in this circumstance, a great deal of restraint must be exercised to keep that statement to a minimal set of specifications acceptable to almost everyone in a faculty as describing aspects of the liberally educated individual, whether or not that list is accepted as a complete characterization. The attempts to elaborate such a statement to include long lists of values and attitudes, exceeded in length only by the list of specific items of knowledge, inevitably throws such discussions back into the content (materials and processes) pattern of thought, which is completely unproductive.

A structure of the disciplines approach to definition of educational objectives and of liberal education has great value, even though the extreme disciplinary emphasis constitutes a denial of liberal education. First of all, the understanding and ability to use a mode of inquiry characteristic of one or more disciplines permit an individual to achieve greater insight into the knowledge that has been accumulated by the application of that discipline to particular phenomena or subject matter. One who understands the methodology used in acquiring knowledge has a greater insight into the validity of that knowledge and the range of applicability possible. A second consideration is that the mastery of the mode of inquiry of a discipline provides a more sophisticated and more effective way of dealing with problems to which that discipline has relevance than would be possible for individuals lacking a systematized and organized way of dealing effectively with new situations. Disciplinary modes of inquiry have been developed by many excellent minds over many years. They furnish an economic way of dealing with problems because they eliminate the necessity of developing a procedure specific to the particular case. This is an economy in that one can use a set of existing tools rather than manufacturing a new set for a specific purpose. Further, the mode of inquiry approach provides greater power. It does so in two ways. First of all, the ability to apply a common and powerful methodology to a whole group of problems makes it possible to see interrelationships not otherwise observable and makes available a capacity for generalizations otherwise both impossible and meaningless. The second consideration is that, in liberal education, knowledge of a discipline is relevant only if (1) the significance of that discipline is made apparent by having acquired some knowledge of the development of the discipline and of its role in promoting and reflecting human and social growth; (2) its characteristics and concerns are understood both in regard to closely related and greatly contrasting disciplines; and (3) the relevance and use of the discipline in addressing a variety of subject matters and problems are understood.

Mastery of a discipline is simply specialization unless that mastery is carried to the point where one can see the significance of the discipline in understanding and addressing the problems and aspirations of humankind. This means also that any discipline assumes its full significance in liberal education only as it is viewed in the context of its interrelationships with other disciplines. Some disciplines contribute significantly to the understanding and application of other disciplines. Thus mathematics contributes significantly to many other fields but draws relatively little from them. Communication skills, while an essential component of being human, are most significant in the fact that they are basically contributory and essential in all other disciplines. Some fields, particularly applied ones, can hardly be called disciplines in their own right but draw widely upon relevant disciplines by incorporating these into a mode of thinking about a particular class of problems. In brief, I assert that emphasis on a discipline is specialized education. It becomes liberal education only when the disciplinary insights and ways of developing them become part and parcel of an individual's values and modes of thought and, perhaps more than anything else, make it apparent to the individual that, to function satisfactorily and productively, he or she must also incorporate the knowledge and insights of other disciplines into his or her bag of competencies.

In this view, liberal education is not separable from career or professional education. Rather, since every individual has a career or practices a profession, liberal education is a part of all education. It includes perception of one's career in relation to society and of one's practice as an interaction with others in ways mutually beneficial. In this view, general education is inconsequential because it constitutes an excuse for ignoring liberal education. In emphasizing some common body of knowledge, general education would force everyone into a common experience, denying the great variability in background and goals already existing in individuals. By emphasizing knowledge, general education permits and encourages the grasp of inquiry modes, the development of judgment, and the sensitivity to values. By separating general education from both liberal education and professional education, proponents of general education thereby promote some minimal level of skills and knowledge as essential and common possessions of all. When the focus is on general education, the more significant concepts of liberal education and their integration with career education are not simply ignored—they are, in fact, denied.

Summary

The discussion in this chapter has pointed up a set of six continuums, extremes of which define very contrasting points of view about education. These continuums have been suggested as a vehicle for thinking about a course or program, with the implication that the decision made will vary somewhat in terms of the discipline, the students, and the teacher, as well as the educational objectives involved. The discussion has also pointed to a series of additional concepts that are frequently involved in decisions about education, but which are so variously interpreted that they do not, in themselves, determine a position on a continuum. However, the interpretation made of these concepts is one of the factors in determining the actual position of a course or program with regard to the six continuums. It is my conviction that a forthright consideration of these matters implicitly determines the educational objectives that an individual accepts, whether or not these are ever made definitive by lengthy statements. Whether or not one wishes to state educational objectives, the decisions with regard to the conduct of a course in reference to the six continuums will enable a teacher to maintain some consistency in emphasis from day to day and will also, if this pattern is interpreted to students, give them some understanding of the mode of operation and the emphasis in the course. There are teachers who believe that the contact with a teacher or with certain work—that is, the experience—is the important consideration and that what results is unpredictable because it is individual. Thus education, to a great extent, becomes an experience in contact with selected great works or ideas, contacts with originals rather than with copies, contacts with a variety of interpretations, and ultimately (one hopes) the development of individual interpretations based on some personal rationale. But even in this view, which denies the validity of educational objectives, some commitments must be made with regard to how a course is run. It should be evident that the development of the individual to the achievement of capability and confidence in making judgments has implications for teaching.

Implicit in this chapter and explicitly stated in various ways are two markedly contrasting philosophies of education. The teacher who views his or her assignment as that of adhering strictly to the disciplinary emphasis and the delivery of a body of accumulative knowledge in rigorous manner to a group of students will find no significant idea in this chapter. At the same time, this chapter conveys no criticism of that approach, except as the attendant circumstances are analyzed in some detail to determine whether that view is justifiable in context. In contrast, if one accepts that education is the opportunity to help individuals to attain personal and social values through work and use of social institutions which, in themselves, are seeking values and utilizing physical and biological resources to do so, then knowledge becomes means to transcendental ends, and education that does not carry an individual some steps along that path toward application of knowledge and value attainment is unworthy of its designation as education. People interact with each other and use the environment, materials obtained from the environment, and processes developed to use those materials to produce outcomes. The outcomes may have desirable or undesirable effects, intended, unintended, and sometimes unrecognized, so that continual evaluation is essential, both of the outcomes themselves and of the nature of the environment and the processes and materials used. Education worthy of that designation must recognize this. The purpose of this chapter has been to lay out an approach by which a faculty member and students can see the relationship between educational experiences and ultimate goals and objectives. Later chapters will expand upon how this is to be accomplished.

Suggestions for Further Reading

Bellack, A. A. "The Structure of Knowledge and the Structure of the Curriculum." In D. Huebner (Ed.), *A Reassessment of the Curriculum.* New York: Bureau of Publications, Teachers College, Columbia University, 1964.

Chickering, A., and others. *Developing the College Curriculum: A Handbook for Faculty and Administrators.* Washington, D.C.: Council for the Advancement of Small Colleges, 1977.

King, A., and Brownell, J. *The Curriculum and the Disciplines of Knowledge.* New York: Wiley, 1966.

Mattfeld, J. A. "Toward a New Synthesis in Curricular Patterns of Undergraduate Education." *Liberal Education,* 1975, *61* (4), 531-547.

Morrisett, I. (Ed.). *Concepts and Structure in the New Social Science Curricula.* West Lafayette, Ind.: Social Science Education Consortium, 1966.

∾ 5

Relating Teaching to Structure, Content, and Objectives

∾ A program of educational experiences is planned to foster achievement of certain educational objectives on the part of those participating in the program. These objectives may be overt or covert, explicit or implicit. The objectives will be determined by some combination of the views of the following:

- the individual student
- students collectively
- the teacher
- teachers collectively

- the department or college faculty
- administrators
- academic traditions

Note: The assistance of Nellie Hardy in the exploration and development of the ideas presented in this chapter is gratefully acknowledged.

- textbook and other learning materials
- professional societies
- educational philosophies
- societal needs and expectations
- prospective employers
- political actions
- law
- accrediting agencies
- governing and coordinating boards

The objectives that direct the learning of students are frequently compromised or destroyed by the purposes or goals of the units offering a program. A few examples will make the point. A course prescribed early in a program (for example, mathematics for business students) as a weeding-out mechanism can be unnecessarily difficult, poorly taught, and irrelevant to major programs so long as it eliminates weak students. A course developed by a department to bolster fading enrollments and maintain existing staff may be made attractive, easy, and superficial in the process of attaining that purpose. Because of this interaction of purposes, goals, and objectives, I prefer to make the following distinctions:

- Purposes are those institutional (or unit) commitments or intents that constitute the *raison d'être* of the institution. These may emerge from a variety of statements, from legislation, or from state-planning authority designations of the role, scope, and level of institutions.
- Goals are statements of specific intended accomplishments by some future date; they may relate either to purposes or objectives.
- Objectives indicate expectations in the learning accomplishments of students as a result of being enrolled in the program.
- Outcomes are the actual accomplishments after a span of time with regard to purposes, objectives, or goal attainment.

The educational objectives of an institution are not limited to those supported by the academic aspects of a program (courses and instruction). They may include objectives thought to be forwarded by cocurricular, social, religious, and esthetic experiences that *some* students indulge in while in college. I believe that, in our multiple and conflicting society, an educational institution that purports to inculcate or even to support actively certain attitudes or values should so state and should limit its clientele to individuals already espousing or desiring to explore and possibly adopt these values. This does not rule out affect, but does suggest that affective objectives should be subsidiary to cognitive objectives and be assimilated only by a conscious personal commitment of each individual.

The nature of the educational objectives accepted and pursued by a teacher should markedly affect the learning and instructional materials used, the in-class teaching and learning procedures, the out-of-class assignments, the nature and extent of interpersonal relationships, and the evaluation practices. Thus there can be an almost infinite variety in teaching practices. Nevertheless, there are certain apparent typologies that are reasonably distinctive and therefore useful in talking about teaching or in advising teachers on self-analysis and self-improvement.

Terminology

The verb *teach* is both transitive and intransitive, but the intransitive usage (to give instruction or act as a teacher) provides little insight into the nature of teaching. To state that "Jones teaches" is only to say that Jones engages in activities designated as teaching—whether as a self-characterization or the pronouncement of another. The statement conveys little information about what Jones does and nothing about the results of his actions. In its transitive form, *teach* implies that someone learns something as a result of the activities of the teacher. To say that "Jones teaches history" is no improvement over stating that "Jones teaches." Indeed, it is a misstatement intended to mean that "Jones gives instruction in history." A disciplinary attachment is indicated, but the audience (the object of the teaching activity) is not. Worse yet, the sentence states that Jones does something to history, although history is not changed because of Jones's teaching. In reality, Jones teaches students about history rather than teaching history to students.

The success of teaching must then be determined by what the student learns, not by what the teacher does or insists that the students do—and most certainly not solely by the scholarly precision and verve with which Jones presents the historical materials. This is not to say that the materials, content, and forms of presentation are unimportant or irrelevant. Rather, it emphasizes that these are subject to choice by the teacher, who selects them for their effectiveness in promoting learning. There is no teaching unless someone learns. One who learns on his or her own is self-taught.

Content evokes such words as disciplines, knowledge, subject matter, values, abilities, and skills. But closer examination reveals that these are by no means equivalent terms. A discipline is both an organized body of knowledge and an organized mode of accumulating and ordering knowledge. As such, it includes disciplinary methods, skills, strategies, concepts, principles, structural elements, value commitments, and analytic and synthesizing modes of thought. Knowledge, understanding, and mastery of the methods, skills, and strategies are not taught so much as they are exemplified by the teacher and the materials used, and then imitated and learned by students. Students emulate, assimilate, and learn in individual modes and often in ways not well understood by either the teachers or the students.

Course content connotes what is in or what is covered by a course. It is used in much the same sense as in the contents of a book to indicate the substantive material of the course without any implication of how, why, or where the material will be presented. The interchangeable use of content and subject matter misses an important distinction. I prefer to regard *subject matter* as external to the disciplines and as referring to the problems, concerns, issues, phenomena, or aspects of reality around which the discipline developed or to which its methods are being applied. The introduction of subject matter implies an application of knowledge to understand, explain, predict, or control some aspect of that subject matter. For example, the disciplines of physics and mathematics can be directed to making musical instruments, to bridge construction, or to analysis of aspects of human behavior. The application of a discipline to distinctive subject matters involves assumptions, values, abilities, and skills that are often ignored when a discipline is regarded solely as an organized body of knowledge.

Disciplines developed out of the attempt to understand, predict, and control. In order to separate the essential from the incidental, disciplines introduced abstractions corresponding to the real or imagined components of reality. These include undefined terms, assumptions, hypotheses, pursuit of logical implications, and the development of models. The lack of correspondence between disciplines and reality has been recognized in the curriculum by introducing concentrations, including interdisciplinary, transdisciplinary, and supradisciplinary majors.

To the extent that knowledge, values, abilities, and skills are acquired by students as intended consequences (objectives) of teaching, these outcomes justify the costs of education. These outcomes have personal, esthetic, social, economic, and political implications. The individual who acquires knowledge, abilities, skills, and values achieves some immediate personal satisfaction and develops the capacity for a more pleasurable and productive life. Society benefits both qualitatively and quantitatively by the presence and contributions of these educated individuals. The nation also benefits from the contributions of these persons to goal setting and political decision making. Teaching is provided because of these benefits, and these same benefits provide much of the satisfaction of those teachers whose vision of their role extends beyond their interest in and commitment to their disciplines and coverage in their courses or segments of it.

"Jones teaches students about history" resolves some of the ambiguities about the teaching task. However, teachers are generally well trained in their disciplines but are relatively uncertain about appraising and adjusting to differences in students. The scholarly readers of a definitive research report at that moment become students of the writer, but at a very different level than found in the typical college freshman course in history. Sensitive teaching must recognize and adjust to this audience difference. The concept *student* must be qualified as to graduate, undergraduate, major, or service status. Each of these groups has distinctive reasons for taking a course. The part-time adult student of age thirty to forty and the full-time freshman of seventeen or eighteen bring quite different backgrounds and purposes to the learning situation. If the teacher accepts any responsibility for student learning, these differences among students need to be taken into account. Learning objectives, instructional materials, and teaching methods need to be adapted to individual differences in motivations and goals. Even if the teacher does accept this responsibility, this role as motivator and director of learning may not be fully realized. It is not a simple task.

In contrast, many professors perceive teaching in a very limited intransitive sense as descriptive of their activities as they appear before groups of students in a structured classroom or laboratory situation for a specified period of time and at specified intervals to present a carefully predetermined segment of knowledge to a highly selected and relatively homogeneous audience. With such an audience, this conception of teaching may produce learning, but it is not a model likely to be effective with most undergraduates.

Teacher Prototypes

Many writers on college teaching have attempted to define distinctive prototypes, typologies, or categories of college teachers. Among these we find the efforts of Axelrod (1973) especially insightful. Axelrod defined two broad types as didactic and evocative. He dismissed the didactic mode by defining it as solely cognitive in intent and as stressing memorization and skill mastery through repetition and practice. Evocative teaching was further divided into discipline-oriented (emphasizing principles and facts, but accepting some responsibility for motivating and evaluating student learning); instructor-centered (involving a strong ego orientation and domination of the classroom); the student-as-mind (focusing on the student, but solely on cognitive outcomes, including the ability to engage in discipline inquiry); and the student-as-person (which accepts a broader set of objectives inclusive of affective outcomes and the active participation of students in their education with extensive individualization of goals and experiences). Most teachers will reject the imposition of any one of these prototypes, and reasonably so, for it is unlikely that any one teacher will fall entirely into any one category. In some disciplines (mathematics and natural sciences), emphasis on affective development would be regarded as irrelevant and inappropriate, although the extra-class interactions of professors and students may contain potent affective elements. Although such prototype categories are understandably distasteful to many people, they do have two highly practical benefits: First, they can be useful in clarifying different assumptions or values that teachers appear to accept; and second, they provide a set of alternative conceptions of teaching for the teacher to use in thoughtful engagement with the task of defining a preferred teaching style and the planning of a program to develop it.

As we reflected upon the Axelrod categories and related them to our own experiences and observations, we arrived at a somewhat different typology. The *discipline orientation* appeared useful and valid, but it seemed to include two subdivisions: the discipline as a body of organized knowledge and the discipline as a mode of inquiry. Likewise, the *instructor* or *self-orientation* also included two subdivisions: the Renaissance mind at work and the dominating personality, whether egoistic or humanistic. A *student orientation* might emphasize either the student as mind or the student as person, with the latter including both cognitive and affective concerns. To these three orientations stemming directly from Axelrod's discussions, we added *social orientation* as a fourth possibility. The social orientation involved overt acceptance by the teacher of the responsibility that an educational institution (and therefore each teacher) contribute, through the education of individuals, to resolution of social problems. Socially oriented teaching would point out social issues and problems and aim to produce a better society through the agency of well-educated and concerned students. In this form, it would be primarily cognitive in nature. An activist social orientation would move toward immediate attempts to change society by encouraging immediate faculty and student action and intervention.

These four (or eight, including the two variants of each major type) teacher "types" struck us as possibly useful in pointing out differing conceptions or approaches to teaching. However, since our interest in developing a typology of teaching was directed to improving the teaching process, we reviewed and discussed this four-part categorization with individuals and groups of faculty members and graduate students. Initially, we did not undertake to define the categories rigorously because we were interested in finding out whether others would find meaning and utility in the approach. Generally—indeed, almost unanimously, after initial suspicions and antagonisms were released—the reactions were that the categories were useful in stimulating conversations about teaching and in clarifying distinctive views of it. However, there was a remarkable consensus that the categories, as defined, would not help individuals to clarify their attitudes or select a model to emulate. The reasons given were of several kinds. With regard to the disciplinary orientation, the distinction between knowledge and mode of inquiry was recognized as valid, but the view was expressed that most disciplinary-oriented teachers have a commitment to both. The mode of inquiry emphasis is found by both teacher and students to be difficult, requires time, and cannot proceed until some common background of knowledge exists. Thus coverage of essential knowledge tends to displace the inquiry emphasis and force it into an intermediate or long-term rather than immediate role. The teacher who becomes imbued with the mode of inquiry emphasis soon realizes that students are habituated to acquiring a miscellaneous array of facts, have no sense of the basic concepts and principles of the discipline, and have not developed any understanding of or ability in applying the mode of inquiry that characterizes the discipline. The teacher attempt at emphasis on the basis concepts, structure, and mode of inquiry can then move in either of two directions. The first simply adds concepts, principles, and statements about modes of inquiry to the array of facts to be learned. Students learn something about inquiry but have little experience engaging in it. The second moves to a concern for the cognitive development of the students and uses the disciplinary mode of inquiry for this purpose.

With regard to the student orientation, the distinction between the student as a mind and as a person seemed strained to many students and faculty members. Their view was that the teacher who becomes interested in individual development has moved from a purely intellectual treatment of content to awareness of students and interactions with them. Thereby affect is involved and, having introduced it into the teaching role, the teacher can hardly escape realization that affect conditions cognitive development. If cognition and affect are regarded as not completely separable, then the real issue in the student orientation is in the extent to which cognitive concerns dominate affective concerns or vice versa. If affective concerns dominate, education tends to become therapeutic, with emphasis being placed upon self-realization and improvement in interpersonal relations. This argues for separating the student orientation into two types: one emphasizing the cognitive and the other emphasizing the affective development of the individual. This separation poses the alternatives more clearly.

The fourth category (the social orientation) did not stand up in our discussions. Indeed, its meaning and utility became less and less clear. Faculty members and students in professional areas (medicine or law, for example) recognized the societal obligation of requiring or encouraging commitment to professional standards and professional ethics. However, the point was made repeatedly that all teachers regard themselves as contributing to the development of individuals and the improvement of society. Thus the social orientation emerges as a common concern overriding the basic orientations, with all teachers, regardless of their orientations, seeing themselves as making a significant social contribution but disagreeing on how this contribution is best made.

As a result of these discussions and reflections, we arrived at the following four teacher types or orientations:

1. Discipline-centered teaching is defined as a conception in which the content and the structure of the discipline are

rigidly determined and are not to be rearranged or modified to meet the requirements, needs, or special conditions of the teacher or learner.

2. In teacher-centered teaching, the teacher is the expert and the main source of knowledge in the subject matter or discipline for the student. The instructor, around whom all class activities revolve, is the focal point of wisdom in the teaching-learning process.

3. In student-centered (cognitive) teaching, intellectual development is held to be the most important element in the teaching-learning process. Both content and teaching should be adjusted to accommodate the cognitive growth of the student on teacher-specified objectives. Affective development is regarded as inseparable from intellectual development but is dealt with indirectly in and through cognitive-oriented materials and learning experiences.

4. In student-centered (affective) teaching, the personal and social development of the student is considered to be the focus of the teaching-learning process. Both the content and the teaching are adjusted to accommodate the total development of the individual. The individual is expected to develop idiosyncratically rather than adapt to content or teacher demands.

Before we delineate this typology in greater detail, several points about it need be made. It differs from the earlier typology in the discard of one type (social) and in the omission of the two subdivisions initially hypothesized. The typology is not empirically based but is rather a personal resolution and composite of thoughtful but highly subjective reactions of many persons. When the originally hypothesized typology was adapted to the suggestions and criticisms of these reactors, some distinctions may have been lost. But these discarded distinctions were those that caused the most severe negative reactions to the entire idea and therefore seemed likely to interfere with the use of the typology for self-analysis and for group discussion. Aside from acceptance of or disagreement with the types, the mode and purpose of presentation of such a typology is an important factor in how it is received.

In the discussions of the initial typology, a number of faculty concerns were voiced:

- The use of such typologies is demeaning to a professional group in that each professional is unique and should be so regarded.
- Any typology that becomes widely used is likely to have values attached by administrators or other persons and thereby result in inequities in its use.
- There will never be unanimity in definition of teaching types and hence the imposition of any typology designations will confuse and mislead rather than help.
- Teaching is such a complex activity that any attempt at analysis and typing will be useless and perhaps destructive.
- Any set of typologies is an abstraction, so that almost all individuals are not only composites but also adapt their views and practices to changing circumstances.

We recognize and agree in part with most of these concerns, and it is precisely because of them that we sought for an acceptable typology rather than for one rigorously defined by quantitative research methods. However, there are contrasting statements or counterarguments that deserve consideration:

- The potential of teaching for good or bad is so great that all teachers ought to engage in self-scrutiny and seek assistance to determine just how their teaching proceeds, what emanates from it in learning, and how it might be improved.
- Typologies need not be "real" to be useful. The imposition of the four major directions (north, east, south, west) is entirely arbitrary, but it provides a set of four directions against which any movement can be plotted without forcing individuals to a choice of one of the four.
- Simply because teaching is such a complex activity, analysis of it is essential to understanding and improvement. The very extensive range of materials, modes of instruction, and the like, almost certainly means that some are better than others for certain purposes and that some combinations make more consistent and forceful learning systems than others.

Certainly neither the original nor the revised typology was regarded as one in which every teacher could be unambiguously assigned. Rather, the intent was to define each orientation by a list of views and practices among which teachers might identify their own views and practices and thus achieve a profile across the orientations. The individual might then reflect upon this profile, evaluate, and possibly undertake to alter it. Each of the orientations is defined so as to be internally consistent, thereby implying an associated philosophy of teaching or education. Most teachers, however, are eclectic—not by formal choice, but simply because they do what comes naturally from either imitating their own highly regarded teachers or rejecting practices of those regarded as ineffective. Fortuitous circumstances and institutional pressures also play a role. Indeed, few teachers are rigid types, and hence we prefer the term *orientation* as suggesting a tendency toward use of certain teaching behaviors rather than a rigid commitment to them.

The discussions of the initial typology were useful in producing a large number of statements indicative of the views and behavior that individuals related to the various orientations. These were added to the already extensive collection acquired from Axelrod's analysis, from other studies, and from teacher rating scales. Drawing upon all of these sources, we undertook to define the four orientations and elaborate them into a form useful to individuals wishing to review and organize their views about teaching. We shall discuss each of the orientations in turn by characterizing them in reference to several concepts or aspects of teaching and learning and then exhibit the composite results so that the differences in the orientations will become apparent.

Discipline-Centered Teaching. Discipline-centered teaching is defined as follows: The *content* and the *structure* of the discipline are the primary concerns and should not be rearranged to meet the requirements, needs, or special conditions of the teacher or learner. The professorial obligation is to assure that the segment of the discipline covered by the course is presented to students in a sound scholarly manner.

The *course content* is determined by selecting those concepts, methods, theories, and materials that best present that segment of the discipline. The content is determined by the opinions of one or more scholars in the discipline. This commitment is reinforced by the use of a text and of supplementary references that incorporate this agreement. The preferred *method* of instruction uses lectures and a standard text, perhaps supplemented by references, to cover systematically the specified content according to a schedule prepared in advance.

The *classroom setting* tends to be formal with emphasis on scholarly authority and objectivity. The *interactions* of students and of students with the professor relate almost entirely to issues arising out of clarification of course content. All students are given the same or very similar *assignments* to be pursued through use of the text and standard reference materials. Students are *evaluated* and *graded* on specific skills and items of knowledge and on traditional or standard ways of presenting them.

The professor's *self-image* in this orientation is that of an authority or specialist in the discipline or in certain subphases or courses. The professor is responsible for presenting a defined segment of that discipline to a group of students, each of whom is assumed to be motivated to acquire understanding of the content covered. All *students* are treated as though they are prospective majors in the discipline or in a related field to which the discipline has direct relevance.

Rather than making *adaptations* to student interests, the course coverage and teaching methodology are standard for all groups regardless of size. Neither *individuality* nor *creativity* is sought because objectivity—the minimizing of personal opinions —is prized and standards of mastery imposed by expert judgment do not accommodate idiosyncrasies.

There are teachers who so view their role, and they may be very effective with students who are vitally interested in the course and the discipline. Teaching in the disciplinary mode, especially at the graduate level, may be both highly regarded and effective. Such teachers may be vital, warm human beings interested in students who share an interest in the discipline and demonstrate potential for success in it. Such professors are frequently found in mathematics and sciences, but not solely there.

Instructor-Centered Teaching. In instructor-centered teaching, the teacher plays the key role in selecting, developing, and presenting ideas to students. Students are expected to adjust to and learn more from the professor than from reading, discussion, or critical thought.

Instructor-centered teachers are both egoists and actors. They may or may not be good teachers in the sense of motivating student learning but they certainly so regard themselves. *Students* are viewed as an admiring audience and a source of acolytes. *Course content* is based upon the professor's preferences and perceptions of the discipline and may include practical applications or interrelations with other disciplines if the professor finds them interesting and complimentary to his or her own personal insights and scholarship. The *instructional procedures* are chosen to highlight the professor's personality and preferences. *Classroom discussions* (used largely to exhibit the professor's humor, critical facilities, and versatility) focus upon and clarify the professor's views. *Assignments* likewise reflect the professor's interests and points of view. The professor (perhaps without consciously so doing) *evaluates* and *grades* students on their ability to imitate, reflect, and elaborate on professorial approaches, perspectives, conceptions, and formulations. The professor's *self-image* is that of scholar, teacher, or "character" of such stature as to have become a recognized authority. The professor may make conscious or unconscious *adaptations* to an audience, but the adaptations are based on affective rather than cognitive concerns. The professor radiates self-confidence and expects applause. He may deserve it.

The instructor-centered teacher may not give much thought to individualization and may even, without fully realizing it, ignore or resent student originality or creativity as competition. The standards of instructor-centered teachers are highly personal. *Subjectivity* or *objectivity* is a role of the moment rather than a consistent stance.

Within this instructor-centered category, there are identifiable subtypes. Some consciously engage in entertainment and titillate rather than educate. Some simply and uninhibitedly express their natural personality. And some professors have had such a range of experiences and so much talent in communicating them that, without conscious intent, they become the course. These latter types are those implied by the advice often given to students by other students, graduates, and professors: "Be sure to take a course from Professor X."

This instructor-centered orientation is found in some of the best and most inspiring teachers in the institution, and also in some very poor ones. The problem of the student in selecting them is that there are far more pretenders than performers.

Student-Centered (Cognitive) Teaching. In student-centered (cognitive) teaching, the intellectual development of the student is regarded as the goal of the teaching-learning process. Both content and teaching techniques are incidental to and are selected to foster the cognitive growth of the student. Emotions (affect) are not ignored but are expected, in most circumstances, to be controlled and directed by intellect.

The cognitive-oriented teacher regards *students* as individuals who must become self-reliant and capable of thinking for themselves. The knowledge they acquire and the ways they use it are not predictable by the teacher. This cognitive emphasis is conjoined with a recognition that affect often directs and controls cognition. Affect, then, is to be recognized and brought under control to achieve fully rational behavior.

Course content is chosen to be interesting to the students and stimulating and productive of intellectual growth. Teaching methods or learning experiences, chosen primarily to encourage or even to force students to think, include student discussions, Socratic dialogues, experiments, lectures, demonstrations, exhibits—any experience that stimulates curiosity and thought. The classroom setting may be exciting and yet relaxed, encouraging student participation and stimulating students to become creative, analytical, and logical in their thinking. Student discussions and interactions are used as means of understanding and applying concepts and principles. However, the teacher, in focusing on cognitive development, is likely to intervene and redirect discussion whenever it seems to stray from the point. *Assignments* are designed to require and develop cognitive abilities and motivate the student toward self-reliance and intellectual maturity. Students are *evaluated* and *graded* on their ability to solve problems that require new resources and strategies. The teacher's *self-image* is that of one who models effective thinking and encourages students to do so. Teachers, accordingly, view their role as that of developing student capability in a mode of inquiry rather than acquiring an organized body of knowledge. The cognitive-oriented teacher undertakes to generalize the mode of inquiry and extend it well beyond the course concept to problems and materials more typical of those that occur in life. In so doing, the cognitive-oriented teacher finds *individualization* and *adaptation* desirable, both as motivation and as providing real problems without readily available answers. The teacher encourages *objectivity,* recognizing always that complete separation of cognition and affect is both impossible and undesirable. *Standards* are high, but more difficult to define than in a discipline-based course because the objectives are broader and more inclusive. Furthermore, the students are encouraged to move toward defining their own standards. The cognitive-oriented teacher is less concerned with coverage of a specified body of content than with fostering student understanding and ability to use what has been learned.

Student-Centered (Affective) Teaching. In student-centered (affective) teaching, the personal, social, and intellectual development of each student is considered to be the primary goal of the teaching-learning process. Affective and social development is also regarded as a prerequisite for significant intellectual development. Both content and teaching activities should be selected and adjusted to accommodate this goal. Education is therapeutic, and therefore intensive interaction of individuals in groups is an essential aspect of it.

In this orientation, *content* is secondary and is selected to help students grow and develop and to confirm them in their status as adults. The preferred *instructional methods* encourage student involvement, with emphasis on discussion sessions led by students or instructors. Informality and student *interaction* characterize the sessions. Since students are encouraged to work toward self-expression, no formal *assignments* are given. Students are *evaluated* or evaluate themselves on the basis of participation, self-expression, affective development, and personal satisfaction. Grades in the traditional sense are seldom used. Student remarks are highly personal, although subject to group discussion and appraisal. In this mode, it is at times uncertain whether students learn to become *objective* about their *subjectivities* or to become *subjective* about *objectivity*. Both have educational value if not carried to extremes. The affective orientation occurs most commonly in the social sciences (sociology or psychology), occasionally in the humanities (literature or philosophy), and seldom, if ever, in mathematics and the natural sciences. This pattern of occurrence reflects differences among the disciplines and among the individuals attracted to them.

Relations Among the Four Orientations. The specific components of the four orientations just presented are exhibited more fully in Table 1. By reading down the table, one can attain a composite description of each orientation. By selecting a component on the left-hand side of the table and following it across, one can see the distinctive views or interpretations of each component in association with each orientation. Individuals can, if so inclined, read each of the four views for each component and check the one or more that most nearly corresponds to their personal views and approaches in a given course or in general. When responses have been made for all thirteen components, a count of the checks in each column will provide a self-profile. It is unlikely that anyone will make all selections in one orientation, but most persons will find that one or two columns exhibit considerably more checks than the others.

The statements in Table 1 could be arranged in various ways to provide a checklist that could be administered to many teachers and students to obtain profiles and norms. We have resisted this, believing that such a development, by becoming more formal, would become more formidable and would interfere with rather than assist the self-analysis that is (so we believe) a prerequisite to understanding and improving one's own approach to teaching.

Student-centered teaching may be focused on cognitive development, on affective development, or on a complex but entirely natural commingling of affect and intellect that charac-

Table 1. Comparisons of Four Teacher Orientations by Definition of Components

Components	Discipline-Centered Teaching	Instructor-Centered Teaching	Student-Centered Teaching (Cognitive Approach)	Student-Centered Teaching (Affective Approach)
Course content	Course is based solely upon the concepts, principles, theories, and methods characteristic of the discipline.	Course content is based on the professor's preferences and individual perceptions of the discipline.	Course content is composed of materials that are both interesting to students and productive of cognitive outcomes.	The content is secondary—used to help students in their maturation and confirm them in their status as adults.
Method of instruction	Method of instruction is by way of lectures and standard text, with emphasis on systematic coverage of the body of knowledge accepted by scholars in the field.	The method of instruction used, generally lecture or teacher-dominated discussion, highlights the personality of the professor.	Student discussions are the primary instructional methods used, with occasional special lectures to focus on important theses and points.	Instructional method emphasizes student involvement and interaction as a means of personal and social development.
Classroom setting	The atmosphere in the classroom is emotion free with emphasis on scholarly objectivity.	The professor dominates and controls the classroom setting.	Classroom setting is somewhat relaxed but intellectually stimulating, allowing students to become more analytical, rational, and logical in their thinking and encouraging student participation.	Classroom atmosphere is highly informal and encourages free student expression of feelings and concerns.
Student-faculty interaction	The professor discourages familiarity and intimacy with students but is not unfriendly.	Discussions with students are focused on clarifying points made by the professor in lectures.	Student-faculty interactions are planned to be intellectually stimulating to students.	Students are encouraged to interact in groups with instructors acting as moderators or resource persons.
Assignments	All students in the course are given precisely the same assignment.	Assignments reflect the professor's interests and points of view of the discipline.	Assignments are geared to cultivate within the student the desire to move toward intellectual maturity.	No formal assignments are given. Students are encouraged to work toward self-expression.

(continued on next page)

Table 1 (*Continued*)

Components	Discipline-Centered Teaching	Instructor-Centered Teaching	Student-Centered Teaching (Cognitive Approach)	Student-Centered Teaching (Affective Approach)
Objectives and evaluation	Students are judged and graded by comparison with standards of mastery for each unit of learning.	The professor judges and grades students on the basis of their ability to imitate professorial approaches, perspectives, conceptions, and formulations.	Students are judged and graded based on their achievement of tasks that require new resources and strategies and on the basis of their ability to problem solve.	Students are evaluated (perhaps entirely by themselves and their peers) based on their participation and self-expression.
Professorial self-image	The professor identifies with the discipline rather than with the teaching role.	The professor has a strong ego and radiates self-confidence.	The professor's emphasis is on developing the student's ability to analyze, reason, use language effectively, and solve problems.	The professor's image is that of a counselor and resource person.
Students	Students are viewed as majors and graduate school candidates.	The professor views students as an audience and a source of acolytes.	Students are regarded as individuals who must become self-reliant in using their knowledge in ways not predictable by the professor.	Students are viewed as individuals who must achieve self insight and accept full responsibility for their own behavior and goals.
Adaptation to or in student groups	Course coverage is standard for all sections.	The professor, like a good actor, may make some adjustments to different audiences.	In a course, emphasis is on the *how* and the *why* of knowledge to be presented and not on the *what*.	Group interaction is used to help motivate student members to learn.
Originality or creativity	Students are encouraged to arrive at the standard way of solving prestructured problems.	Originality in student responses is acceptable so long as it provides a useful foil for the professor.	Student originality in thinking is encouraged.	Each student is expected to achieve self-realization.

Individualization	Assignments are designed to help students master the materials presented and lead students to answers accepted by workers in the field.	Students are expected to adapt to professorial interests rather than develop their own.	Students are encouraged to develop their own analytic abilities.	Course allows individuals to develop and acquire new resources and new ways of organizing ideas.
Source of standards	Standards of mastery are set for each unit of learning by experts in the field.	The professor sets personal standards based upon acceptance of professorial views.	Students are expected to develop high standards which they apply to their own work.	Standards are individually derived and self-imposed.
Objectivity	The professor strives to minimize personal opinions in the classroom.	The professor may seem to be objective, but this objectivity is strongly subjective.	Instructional methods are analytical, objective, and logical.	Understanding and acceptance are more prized than is objectivity.

terizes all human beings. Since we believe that cultivation of the intellect is the primary concern of higher education, we distrust the validity of completely affective-oriented teaching. This is not to say that affective outcomes are inappropriate or that they do not involve learning. Self-insight, self-acceptance, and a start toward self-realization can be deeply educational experiences, but such experiences, even when successful, are not necessarily accompanied by acquisition of organization or skill and ability to use it. The individual experiencing such affective development may be happier and better able to cope with life. However, there seems to be no more reason for granting credits or degrees for this than for giving credits or a degree in nursing or medicine to one who has recovered from infectious hepatitis.

It is our view that purely cognitive-oriented teaching is impossible. Both teachers and students, whether or not they realize it, come to an educational experience with biases and value commitments. For example, most teachers attempt to communicate to students both the values and preconceptions of the discipline and the satisfaction that can attend knowing and using the ideas, concepts, and methods characterizing it. Nevertheless, it is possible to approach teaching—especially in mathematics, logic, and the natural sciences—as though these disciplines were purely intellectual and theoretical enterprises. Some teachers appear not to recognize any other view, whereas others recognize affective potentials but consciously attempt to avoid them in teaching. This conscious avoidance of affect is in itself an affective commitment, although not always so recognized.

The distinction between cognitive orientation and affective orientation is theoretically possible, but the complete separation of cognition and affect in the actual teaching-learning situation is artificial and impossible. The difference between the two orientations is more one of intent and emphasis than of complete dichotomy.

Similar arguments could be made for the interdependence of all of the four orientations. For example, an otherwise discipline-oriented individual may be sensitive to individual differences and adapt assignments to them. In fact, our observations and experiences to date with these four orientations suggest that most teachers fall athwart all four rather than under any one, and that teachers may shift in emphasis from one to another as they deal with different content, course levels, and students. This is facilitated by the fact that the four orientations are related in pairs. The disciplinary orientation and the student-cognitive orientation can be regarded as extremes on an objective disciplinary continuum. At one extreme is a concentration on presenting the discipline as an organized body of knowledge, with some attention to modes of inquiry. At the other extreme, the emphasis is on developing student cognition by assimilation of the modes of inquiry. The instructor and student-affective orientations present a second continuum upon which the human element takes precedence over the discipline. The instructor can be imbued with self-love or concern for his or her students. Some teachers may have an eclectic and composite orientation rather than an extreme position on either of these continuums.

Other teachers may combine instructor orientation with either a discipline (knowledge) or a student-cognitive orientation. Some (as already suggested) combine the student-cognitive and student-affective orientations. The one combination that seems unlikely, from our observations of teachers and of their responses to our structure, is that of discipline (knowledge) and student-affective. But even this composite orientation may characterize some teachers in psychology or sociology.

We point out these possible composite patterns to emphasize, once again, that we do not view the original four orientations as discrete types. The four orientations are the result of observations and logical analyses of tendencies rather than of statistical analyses seeking independent types. Our whole intent was to develop a pattern of orientations useful in self-analysis. Our personal prejudices favor the student-cognitive orientation and question (at least at the undergraduate level) the extreme positions on the student-affective, instructor, or discipline content orientations. But effective and stimulating teaching based upon any of these orientations or composites is surely possible for some teachers in selected courses and disciplines and faced with appropriate types of students. We do believe that teaching and learning will be improved if teachers become conscious of their stances and consider the relevance of their stances to the objectives, courses, and students that they teach. Teaching practices and underlying values are thereby brought to their attention, and the tendency to imitate others unthinkingly or fall into rote patterns can be corrected.

The Teacher, the Course, and the Program

The four teacher typologies and the specifics under each of these make it possible for an individual to clarify personal views of the nature of the teaching-learning process and the relevance to it of the various concepts and procedures suggested. The teacher may also review past teacher practices and successes or failures with courses and students in relationship to this typology to determine what modifications might be made. Those inclined to think in terms of philosophical and psychological views and assumptions will at once recognize that, in this process of reviewing personal views and activities and the four teacher typologies, an individual is brought to think about a personal philosophy of education and its relationship to an institutional view of education (if one exists) and to the nature of the learning process and the goals of learning. As the statement of the typologies makes evident, no one of these can be categorically stated to be the best, and individuals may see themselves operating in different typologies in relationship to the students and the educational goals. The teacher in this process of self-examination is also brought to review the activities of teaching, the activities of the students, and the types of activity provided in the classroom, laboratory, and assignments to students. The question can be raised as to what types of learning experiences are best provided off campus through practical work, community service, cross-cultural experiences, internships, preceptorships, and study abroad, or simply recognized as having already taken place through unplanned but nevertheless significant educational experiences. The on-campus learning experience can be student oriented, in which case it focuses on learning contracts, independent study, individualized experiences, or self-paced or personalized self-instruction. Teacher-oriented learning experiences, including lecture-demonstration, recitation, discussion, tutorials, seminars, and case methods, can be reexamined in terms of the specific objectives, the justification for the methodology, and some consideration of the impact on the learning of students, in respect to both character and quality.

In this review of educational experiences and outcomes, the teacher may undertake to look at the range of technological aids, including audio-tutorial instruction, computer-assisted or managed instruction, and multimedia instruction and television as a means of programming and coordinating a wide range of materials not readily available in the classroom or on the usual, brief off-campus trips. As one becomes clearer about the anticipated outcomes and considers the immediate relationship between the experiences provided and the outcomes desired, it becomes possible to introduce greater variety into the learning procedures and make them more pointed and realistic with regard to the desired outcomes. All too frequently, some new approach to teaching or learning has been viewed as so novel and stimulating in itself that it has been introduced enthusiastically without adequate analysis as to its relevance or effectiveness. Telephone interviews, field trips, the pyramid plan (involving student-teacher teams), role playing, brain storming, buzz groups, and community study have all been introduced at various times in some institutions by individuals who succeeded in attaining widespread recognition. A teacher really is planning a learning process for individuals and must steer a rather difficult path in this development with full awareness of the following considerations:

1. Overuse of any particular process or technique is likely to focus too much attention on the process and fail to maintain adequate attention to the anticipated outcomes of the process. This includes the possibility that the process is, in itself, so satisfying that individuals fail to recognize that it is a means to an end rather than an end in itself.
2. Any innovation process carried to an extreme so that the de-

mands upon students are continually changing makes it difficult for either students or instructor to perceive clearly the
anticipated results of a course and the particular activities
students are to engage in on a continuing cumulative basis to
achieve these outcomes.

3. Any course that imposes unusual demands upon the time of
the students may detract time from other courses or other
pursuits in which individuals are engaged. The course must
be planned with due regard to the complexities and time requirements of the totality of the tasks imposed upon the students.

As a teacher moves from the delivery of designated segments of a discipline to a professional role in developing courses
designed to interest and motivate students, providing experiences productive of progress with regard to objectives, and
developing attitudes, skills, and abilities that transcend specific
content, that teacher becomes aware that a course has to be regarded in relation to its contribution to the student's total educational development rather than solely in terms of coverage of
a carefully defined segment of a discipline. From this point of
view, teachers are not addressing the problem of teaching adequately until they become aware of the differences and com-
monalities in backgrounds among students as persons and as
participants in other courses. It is not to be expected that a
teacher would make attempts to adapt materials and assignments to each individual, but the majority of the students who
appear in a class are there for some reason other than the simple
convenience of the hour or credit. If we accept, as I believe we
must, that learning by students is the measure of teaching, then
acceptance of a professional role for teachers requires that they
use information about individuals in relation to information
about the process of learning to develop experiences related to
student motivations and goals and designed to facilitate progress
in regard to program objectives.

Suggestions for Further Reading

Anderson, J. "The Teacher as Model." *The American Scholar,*
1961, *30,* 393-398.

Anderson, O. R. *The Quantitative Analysis of Structure in Teaching.* New York: Teachers College Press, 1971.

Baird, L. L. "Teaching Styles." *Journal of Educational Psychology,* 1973, *64* (1), 15-21.

Briggs, L. J. *Handbook of Procedures for the Design of Instruction.* Pittsburgh: American Institutes for Research, 1970.

Davis, J. R. *Teaching Strategies for the College Classroom.* Boulder, Colo.: Westview Press, 1976.

Eble, K. E. *The Craft of Teaching: A Guide to Mastering the Professor's Art.* San Francisco: Jossey-Bass, 1976.

6

Motivations and Models of Faculty Planning

⤫ I recall, as a visitor in a department of education meeting some years ago, hearing with amusement a quick resolution of a curricular issue. One professor remarked that several teachers planning to attend summer school had asked about a course on planning and directing extracurricular activities. There was general assent that such a course was needed; action was authorized to obtain immediate approval of the addition of a three-credit course in student extracurricular activities. The professor proposing the idea volunteered to teach the course. This quick response to an apparent need seems commendable, but I wondered then (and still do) whether the course was really needed, whether the available materials provided sufficient content to justify the course, and whether the professor was really qualified to teach the course.

In another college, a four-year medical technology program was devised and a coordinator hired within the span of two months, because four very able graduates of a nearby high school planned to enter medical technology. Unfortunately (for the college), none of the four enrolled at the college and no other students appeared. The director was paid for one year, and the program was listed for several years before being discarded.

These two examples of curricular actions are extreme, though not unique. They illustrate that undue haste in course and program development can result in proliferation, weak offerings, unduly heavy teaching assignments, and unjustifiable expenditures.

Incentives for Program Changes

If left entirely to the faculty, the fundamental changes in existing courses and programs would be limited, but new courses and new programs would be added as further knowledge justifies further subdivisions of a discipline or the recognition of a new one. New staff members naturally seek to add one or more courses in their specialty. In professional or vocational programs, some courses, recognized as dated and unneeded, may be dropped and replaced by new titles and numbers. In the basic disciplines of the arts, sciences, social sciences, and humanities, there is a tendency to maintain currently unused courses on the plea that someone may want to offer them again. Departments understandably take some pride in the number of courses and fail to recognize that listing currently unavailable courses savors of dishonesty in advertising. Some departments see no need for recurrent course revision. In one highly regarded liberal arts college, the old-timers of the biology staff reported no need for change other than the addition or deletion of a concept or phrase in the course description and occasional change in the textbook used. Course titles, numbers, and descriptions had been largely unchanged for thirty years. In another college, a professor of history used in a course a specially arranged reprint of a text that she had studied as a student in the early years of the century. These examples are extreme and atypical, but they do reveal one extreme of curriculum change—the lack of it.

Expansion and improvement of the faculty in a department will usually result in an expansion of course offerings either at the advanced undergraduate or at the graduate level. This frequently noted trend has led some administrators and writers on higher education to conclude that strengthening a faculty weakens liberal and general education by promoting specialism.

Since any major change in a program or course is a demanding task, most such changes are in response to some crisis. Pressures for change may be generated internally by students (or by lack of them), faculty, or administrative officers, or by financial problems. In the 1960s, student pressures, aided by sympathetic faculty members, effectively destroyed required general education or distribution requirements in many colleges. New departmental chairpersons, deans, or presidents frequently urge a thoroughgoing review of the curriculum. Typically, new administrators have no commitments to the existing curriculum and are the recipients of accumulated criticisms of it. They see a major curriculum revision as a way to revitalize the faculty, attract gifts and grants from alumni, foundations, and government, and gain for themselves some national acclaim as able and innovative administrators.

The comments about internal pressures for change have already noted external factors that may stimulate or reinforce the internal pressures. Falling enrollments immediately generate some concern about curriculum and instruction. Attempts to achieve an appropriate representation of minorities and disadvantaged students may result in addition of developmental (remedial) courses of secondary or lower level for which, after long debate, some degree credit will be granted. Concerns for student retention (reduction of dropouts and transfers) may lead to review of requirements, grades, courses, and teaching as causal factors. Counselors and advisers may have an impact at this point. Efforts to attract community college transfers tend to result in granting of full credit for freshman and sophomore study and abandonment of specific requirements or course sequence requirements that might endanger the effort to attract transfer students. Thereby an entire program design may be threatened. It is difficult to hold to standards and requirements for four-year students once they are waived for transfer admissions.

Certification and accreditation procedures impose some requirements on programs. Typically, these are accepted readily by some faculty members and reluctantly by others. Governmental aid often affects the curriculum by specifying the amount and type of credits required for student support. Attempts to attract adults into a lifelong education program usually involve some augmentation of offerings and a revision of content and standards in others. Career concerns are forcing liberal arts colleges (most of which have long since offered some vocational and preprofessional programs) to expand career-relevant courses and curriculums and to revise some traditional offerings to attract nonmajors.

The values involved in curriculum review and change are, as in all other matters in a democratic society, many and contradictory. Personal recognition, recognized stature as an elite or innovative institution, and concern for growth or survival are all present (and sometimes definitive) in curriculum changes. Relevance to the times and student interests and the attractiveness, appeal, and quality of a program are much more fundamental and obviously not unrelated.

Factors Impeding Curricular Change

The department, even in the small liberal arts college, is synonymous with a discipline or possibly with two or three very closely related disciplines. It provides a list of courses by title and number and offers a limited amount of information devoted primarily to the segment of the discipline covered by the course. In many disciplines, there may be no clearly sequential or cumulative elements in these courses. Thus courses may be added or, less commonly, deleted with little difficulty. The selection of a new text or texts may extensively modify the course, but with course specifications being as brief and uncertain as many are, the original course title may be maintained. Thus the first and most obvious reason for changing courses— that is, to update them—frequently calls for no restatement of the course description and only an addition or deletion of a few words. A complete program revision will require a department to change courses relating to that particular program, but seldom does a departmental faculty find a demonstrable need for completely reconstructing a departmental curriculum.

Interdepartmental programs or supradisciplinary concepts, such as liberal or general education, are secondary interests to department-based faculties. Hence they are unlikely to consider departmental contributions to liberal or general education unless an administrator, a special grant, or widely and favorably publicized changes in a number of nearby institutions provide motivation. Lack of faculty interest or motivation is the *first* factor that impedes curricular change.

A *second* factor is the lack of specific dissatisfactions on the part of students and faculty members. Generally, a course plays a less important role in the student's experience than it does in the faculty member's. The student is usually taking several different courses and no one is likely to loom above the others unless it is viewed as particularly bad or irrelevant or particularly good. The diversity of backgrounds of students almost assuredly means, then, that in a particular course there will be a wide range of comments, both favorable and unfavorable, about the course. Even when a course is poorly rated by a large percentage of the students, it is quite likely that different students are reacting to different aspects of the course.

A *third* factor impeding curricular and program change is lack of leadership. This has been hinted at in the previous comments. Departments take special pride in their course and program offerings, but there is little interaction or exchange among departments on curricular and program problems of broader scope. Indeed, unless an administrator urges the faculty to review the whole curriculum, it is unlikely that such a review will occur. Standing committees concerned with curriculum generally find themselves sufficiently busy dealing with minor curriculum changes, proposals for new courses, and occasionally with new programs. Such committees do not have the time to make a thoroughgoing review of a total curriculum with an eye to current thinking and increased impact on the students.

When the curricular offerings of a department rise to as much as four or five times the number of credit hours required for a major, it becomes inevitable (unless there exist several essentially independent degree programs in the department) that the separate courses are seen as unique offerings. There is, then, very little interest in defining a coherent major other than through a set of specifications to be followed by students in the enrollment process. The complexity of the collective curriculum is such that no one is aware of the significant course interrelationships that might define a coherent program. There are disparate concerns among individual students and departments. Departments are concerned that there be offered, however few the students involved, a significant array of courses that can be characterized as providing a major. Students come and go through these various curricular ramifications with no one fully aware of just how many routes exist or how many courses of what kind combine to make a degree program. There is a tendency to assume that courses are interchangeable and that an appropriate credit accumulation is equivalent to a degree.

The restructuring of a course or program is a complex, time-consuming job. One needs to review all of the recent scholarly work and consider new topics to be added and old ones to be discarded. The instructor may require some release from regular teaching duties. This means that the cost for curricular revision rises markedly. Hence a *fourth* factor impeding curriculum review is the cost in released time for faculty members directly involved and possibly of honoraria for outside consultants. Those faculty members selected to work directly on a review process must keep in touch with other faculty members not directly involved, especially if several courses are interrelated or sequential. It is not surprising that most curricular change is piecemeal, leading perhaps to the improvement of single courses but seldom, if at all, to the complete review and improvement of a total program.

It is unfortunate that more persistent attention has not

been given to program change. There needs to be a continuing review of programs. Too much time has been spent talking about improving teaching and about new materials and methods as though each teacher were autonomous in course and program definitions. If a program plan and curriculum materials are sufficiently good, some students can become their own teachers. Selection of materials and experiences to encourage students to develop broad objectives and significant learning skills aids the teacher in recognizing that the end result of teaching is learning. The role of the teacher is that of facilitating the students' grasp and understanding of the curricular materials presented.

A *fifth* major factor that impedes program change is the lack of any accepted pattern for making program changes. Much has been said about statements of objectives—that is, statements of what students are to acquire as a result of an experience in a course—as a starting point. But these objectives are difficult to agree upon and they provide much less in the way of direction on program issues than some people seem to believe. It is easier in most cases to move to a set of criteria for curricular review that imply objectives but are also sufficiently closely related to the offering of a course that they also imply immediately some thoughts for improving teaching. For example, in previous chapters, the means of structuring and the concepts for so doing have been introduced.

A *sixth* factor complicating course and program review lies in the contrasting views or assumptions of the nature and objectives of education (see Chapter One). Questionable or dubious and conflicting assumptions, no matter how enthusiastically accepted, lead to unrealistic and therefore temporary and uneasy solutions to the structure-content issue. These assumptions include such views as the following:

* Human nature is essentially good and every individual seeks both self-improvement and increased and satisfying interactions with others.
* All individuals are equal and can attain a reasonable mastery of any field of study.
* If content is carefully selected and well presented, it will arouse the interest of every student.

- Personal experiences generate creativity because of their novelty.
- Unrestrained self-expression is good for the individual and for society.
- Requirements and grades interfere with free choice and personal development.
- Students learn more from interactions with other students and faculty members than from structured course activities.

The ardor with which some persons express these views and present them as bases for curriculum planning is exceeded by both the ambiguity of their meaning and the uncertainty of their validity. If statements of the preceding type are intended to be generalizations true of all individuals, they are obviously untenable and false. If they are intended to be generalizations applicable to a majority of individuals, they offer little assistance because of the ambiguity of identification.

Personally, I believe that requirements and formal evaluation are essential to maintain a student focus on the content and the abilities in using it. Structure is the means of accomplishing this, but this structure must be understood, accepted, used, and, in part, constructed by the individual.

Program-Planning Models

Too much planning proceeds with little consideration of how a new course or program relates to other courses and programs. To correct this, there are three models that deserve attention. The first of these, an input-output model of higher education, is shown in Figure 1.

Displayed on the left of this figure are inputs characterized as students, dollars, social needs and demands, and accumulated learning. These inputs into the programs then are engaged in interaction processes with faculty, facilities, materials and equipment, with the environment, and with a curriculum designed to bring the other components together in meaningful ways. From these interaction processes emerge a number of outputs. Three are suggested here: educated persons or, more pragmatically, degrees; new knowledge and insights useful in

Figure 1. An Input-Output Model of Higher Education

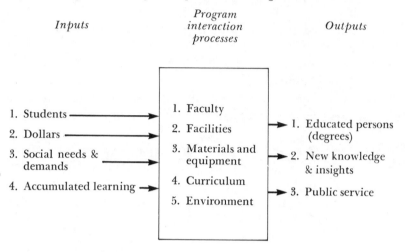

improving the quality of living; and public service, a means whereby educated persons can bring the new knowledge and insights into meaningful contacts with people and society.

There are a number of points in the model that deserve some discussion. People are listed as inputs. People are also included as major elements in interaction processes, and people are indicated as outputs. The model could be revised to reflect a view that faculty members are also inputs into an institution and that faculty members are hired with specific attention to the kinds of facilities, materials, environment, curriculum, and objectives that the institution represents. Indeed, in some ways, the ideas of faculty as inputs could be considered a corrective to the view espoused by many faculty members that the faculty is the university. This model suggests that social needs and demands, to a considerable extent, dictate the nature of the university and determine the dollars for its operation. The accumulated learning as an input changes constantly because of the output of new knowledge and insights. Likewise, social needs and demands are presumably changed by the educated persons produced by the institution and by the new knowledge and insights generated by the public service function, which assists in applying the new knowledge and insights to society. This model, although suggesting that the faculty members are part of the institutional structure into which inputs are fed, recognizes that facilities, materials and equipment, curriculum, and environment are not determined solely on the basis of faculty preferences, but depend, in considerable part, upon the needs of society, the dollars made available, and the expectations of students coming to the institution. In particular, the curriculum, to a great extent, depends upon the quality and characteristics of the educated persons and degrees that the institution presumes to produce.

Just as outputs influence inputs, the interaction processes also overlap with inputs and outputs. Faculty members, in a very real sense, are also students, and the increased knowledge that faculty gain by their experiences in teaching and research result in their inclusion among the outputs of educated persons. The interactions among people, facilities, materials, equipment, environment, and curriculum in themselves can generate new knowledge and insights as to how education can be improved and particularly how public service (a form of education) can be more efficiently and quickly made available to society.

Among the many significant points suggested by this model, one of primary concern in the immediate context is that the curriculum is only one of several factors involved in the program interaction processes of education. The curriculum cannot be solely a matter of faculty whim or preference in that it is one of the intervening variables between certain inputs financed by society and certain outputs desired by society. Thus the planning of a course or of a program is a social and professional responsibility.

Figure 2 moves closer to the curricular problems involved in developing a course or program. The figure is a triangular pyramid, the base of which is a triangle with vertices labeled *instruction, procedures,* and *content.* A point inside the base triangle is labeled *evaluation* and is connected with objectives, instruction, procedures, and content. The significance of this is made evident by an elaboration. The instructor, in teaching a course, must make some decisions about content as drawn from the disciplines and procedures whereby that content is to be

Figure 2. Role of Objectives in Program Development and Evaluation

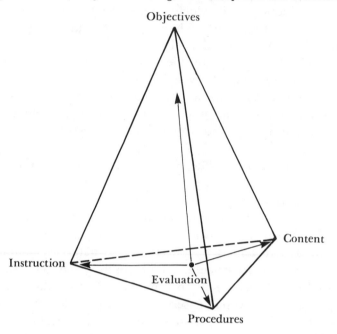

presented, dealt with, and understood by students. Judgments have to be made about the probable effectiveness of various choices and interactions. If the instructor prefers to make these choices on the basis of traditional procedures and coverage of a designated sector of disciplinary content, some evaluation has still been applied, although without conscious intent. If the instructor recognizes objectives transcending course content and procedures, the accomplishment of which will be expedited by proper choice, then evaluation becomes the making of judgments about those combinations likely to be most effective in attaining the objectives. Ultimately, evaluation becomes a review of the actual outcomes and a reflection upon the processes, content, and instructional patterns used to determine whether alteration is needed.

Figure 2 can be used either for thinking about a single course or as a model for thinking about a total program. In a major, instead of a single triangular base, one could have a number of such triangles at various levels, becoming smaller and thus, in some conception, more concentrated as the ultimate objectives are approached. One might also imagine a three-dimensional surface in which various courses are arranged with respect to each other in some meaningful way, but all pointing centrally toward certain ultimate outcomes. Alternatively, instead of representing all objectives by a single point, there might be a number of discrete objectives. This conception is possible, but it is a serious distraction from the primary concern that a course, and especially a program, have a cumulative, integrative, unifying impact on individuals. Acceptance of the idea that each course has its own objectives, and no responsibility for integrating these with program objectives to achieve an educated individual, is a major factor in the fragmentation of courses and programs. There should be, in every course, a set of objectives transcending particular content, procedures, and materials. The professor who views his or her course as an opportunity to bring students into interaction with certain great works or ideas may not wish to accept responsibility for forming the tastes or the analytical powers of students. Nevertheless, that professor would be unhappy if all students taking the course became indifferent or antagonistic to its content and subject matter. The methods and materials used also affect outcomes. Even at the level of mastery of course content, different approaches can lead to different results. The auctioneer who makes no sales will not long remain an auctioneer, no matter how highly he personally appraises his style.

Figure 3 portrays the steps and sequence involved in the development and evaluation of a course or program. The first step is the establishment of need and purpose by assessing societal, economic, and individual and institutional needs. The last category has a number of ramifications. Individuals within an institution have certain aspirations and goals called needs. These needs lead to development of new programs. An institution at a certain stage of development may need an additional program or two to provide the interactions among several programs necessary to produce desired results. And there are also indi-

Figure 3. A Flow Model of Steps in Course and in Program Development and Evaluation

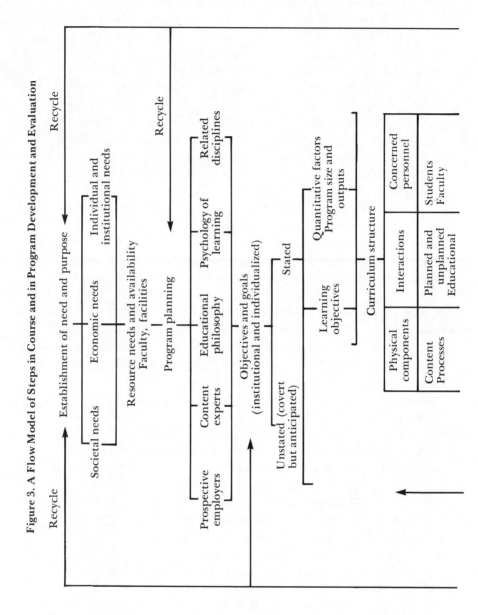

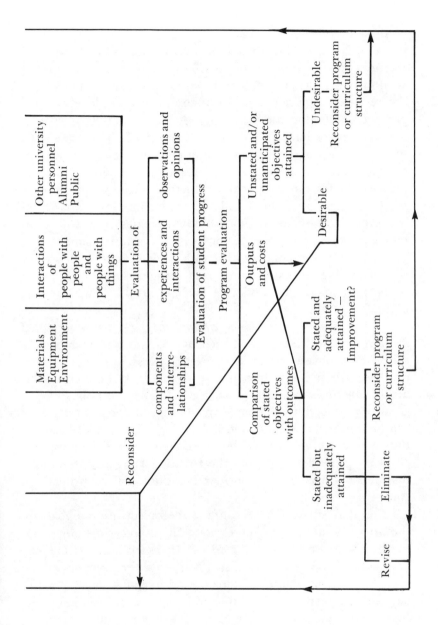

Materials
Equipment
Environment

Interactions
of
people with
people
and
people with
things

Other university
personnel
Alumni
Public

Evaluation of

components
and intere-
lationships

experiences and
interactions

observations and
opinions

Evaluation of student progress

Program evaluation

Comparison
of stated
objectives
with outcomes

Outputs
and costs

Unstated and/or
unanticipated
objectives
attained

Desirable

Undesirable

Reconsider program
or curriculum
structure

Reconsider

Stated but
inadequately
attained

Stated and
adequately
attained —
Improvement?

Reconsider program
or curriculum
structure

Eliminate

Revise

viduals (students) who are seeking education to pursue a career and contribute to social and economic development. If a review of these categories of needs leads to the conclusion that a new program is required or an old one needs extensive revision, then the next stage is that of considering the resource requirements. Without resources, there is no point in further programming. If the resource requirements can be met, program planning must proceed to develop the program in sufficient detail to make resource need estimates and justify support of the program. At this stage in program planning, a number of views and sources of information may be sought. Prospective employers of program graduates can suggest desired abilities and designate some of the specific problems faced. Generally, this source has been less productive than anticipated, but it creates good will. Content experts may include persons who are offering similar programs around the country or who are adept at reviewing their own disciplines and suggesting from those disciplines what concepts, principles, and modes of analysis are likely to be most useful.

The terms *educational philosophy* and *psychology of learning* are not likely to be used by most faculty members in thinking through a new program. Nevertheless, elements of both of these are present. Is a new program in technology to be highly practical or is it to be theoretical? The questions of what is known about how people learn certain skills and of how they can be motivated and assisted in learning must be addressed, although the answers are far less clear than desired. The more a given program deviates from the traditional practice, the more significant it becomes to consider how this departure will affect student learning.

Out of these several sources, the objectives and goals of the program should become clearer. These objectives and goals can be divided into two groups. First, there are the stated objectives and goals presented as justifications for the program and as providing guidance both to students and to course development. Second, the unstated objectives and goals, as defined here, are covert but anticipated. These unstated goals are sometimes reasonably obvious and even commendable but they may also be indicative of motivations and aspirations somewhat at odds with the stated reasons for program development. An institution that opportunistically seeks a graduate degree in a field of no great interest in the institution simply because there is a strong probability that it will be approved does so, in part, because of motivations that are not publicly stated. An institution that seeks a new program largely to bolster student enrollment is unlikely to say so, but an awareness of this motivation would not be altogether irrelevant to a final decision. Both stated and unstated objectives and goals are involved in more detailed statements of the learning objectives and in the listing of the quantitative factors, such as expected program size and outputs, which, in turn, are the immediate factors in developing the curriculum structure.

In determining the curriculum structure, there are three categories of concern. One includes the physical components of content, processes, materials, equipment, and environment. A second involves the personnel concerned in the program: students, faculty, other university personnel, alumni, and the general public. A third category comprises a series of planned and unplanned interactions of people with people and people with things. The inclusion of unplanned interactions does not necessarily mean that there is no hope or intent that certain desired interactions will take place. In fact, there may be, by provision of equipment, environment, and materials, an attempt to encourage unplanned interaction. A convenient departmental library with ready access to books and materials may generate a large number of unplanned interactions among department majors and faculty members. The selection of the physical components, the personnel, and the interactions desired must be done on the basis of some assumptions. Hence some evaluation is required, although this can be highly informal. This evaluation involves looking at the various components and the interrelationships of these components to discern whether they are having the effects anticipated. It entails observing the experiences and the interactions to see whether people and things are actually interacting in modes anticipated and in ways beneficial to the development of the program goals. It also includes seeking observations and opinions from the people involved on how the program is operating. Evidence from these three sources can be brought together with other information to evaluate student progress in the program and to relate aspects of student progress to strengths or weaknesses in the program.

Student progress is the key factor leading to the next stage—program evaluation. There are three aspects of program evaluation. One is the comparison of the stated objectives with outcomes. There are two results here. Some of the stated objectives may not be adequately attained. It may be necessary to revise these objectives in the light of experience, or even to eliminate them as impossible or irrelevant. In either case, there needs to be referral back to either the statement of objectives and goals or the consideration of the basic needs and purposes of the program. This is particularly true when certain stated objectives that are of primary importance appear to have been attained in little or no measure as a result of the program. If the stated but inadequately attained objectives still appear sound, another possibility is to revert to the program-planning stage, or to the development of curricular structure, and attempt to make appropriate revisions to attain these objectives in greater measure. If, in the comparison of stated objectives with outcomes, it is found that some are adequately attained, it might seem that the sequence of steps in program development has been closed for those objectives. The question still remains of whether improvement is desirable or possible.

The second aspect of program evaluation is the examination of outputs and costs. The outputs with regard to stated objectives have already been commented upon, but the matter of costs needs to be added. If stated but inadequately attained objectives are still considered valid and the program or curriculum structure is to be changed in an attempt to attain them, it is entirely likely that additional resources may have to be added and costs increased. If stated objectives have been adequately attained, the question of further improvement may be raised, but, especially if program costs are high, there may be consideration of whether some reduction in costs could be achieved while still maintaining adequate program quality. The third aspect of program evaluation involves the need to be alert to the possible attainment of unstated and/or unanticipated objectives. These objectives will be found only if one looks at the program outputs in a sensitive, creative manner. There is some tendency for the evaluator to seek solely for outcomes specific to stated objectives. Actually, there may be outcomes that were not foreseen. These may be either desirable or undesirable. If they are desirable, it will be to the point to consider the costs involved and to reconsider earlier stages of the program development to make such objectives more specific and then to pursue the stages through the development of the curriculum to consider whether, with these objectives now added, changes in the program might be desirable. Unstated and undesirable outcomes equally call for reconsideration and change at the curriculum structure stage, or possible recycling through some of the earlier stages.

The considerations of unity, sequence, and integration particularly are of concern when this flow model is being used with the entire program as against the single course. Program objectives will make explicit that the program is oriented to any one of several positions on the various continuums developed earlier and structured in various ways according to the concepts presented in Chapter Two. Thus the addition of the six continuums and the various structural concepts permits one to include in the evaluation of the components the interactions and personnel criteria for judgment with regard to the effectiveness of these commitments. This is further reinforced in evaluation of students' progress where the specific nature of the progress sought indicates the extent to which concepts of structure and of the basic continuums have been successfully incorporated. Finally, the program evaluation with the multiple results suggested here provides a basis for review of objectives, outcomes, and desired emphases and characteristics in the educational processes.

The Planning Process

The planning of a new undergraduate degree program, whether within a department or conjointly by several departments, should include representation from several departments.

Usually, there are several members of a university or college faculty who possess a reasonably sound basis in a discipline and also have some overview of the implications of that discipline for various career opportunities. These "outsiders" will not usually be involved in offering the program, but their interest in the university and in students will expand the range of considerations of the planning group.

This proposal for faculty involvement beyond a department simply recognizes that the typical departmental faculty member reacts in terms of views and opinions of immediate colleagues and a general commitment to support expansion and rigor in the teaching of the discipline. In this emphasis, little attention may be given to possible interrelationships among other programs and disciplines or to the career prospects of the program. Once a program is fully developed and presented for review by a college and university curriculum committee, scholarly courtesy seems to demand minimal criticism. Curriculum approval procedures are seldom either penetrating or helpful. Reactions at a formative stage of program development are much more effective.

In the initial stages of program planning, it is desirable to identify the concerns, problems, and subject matter to which the program is addressed. This focuses attention on the social and personal significance of the program and defers the tendency to move immediately to specifying courses, topics, and credits. In an attempt to define the program, it is useful to consider this question: What can an individual who completes this program do that is distinctive from the competencies provided by other programs? The answer should not be by specification of content but by an indication of fields of activity or types of problems with which the individual should be able to deal. This approach moves toward identifying specific knowledge, values, insights, and competencies essential to successful performance. These procedures both defer the too ready definition of a program in terms of courses and provide a background rationale against which courses and instruction can later be reflected in the process of development and evaluation.

In planning a new program, it is desirable to decide upon

the student admission requirements. This factor may be the most potent determiner of output quality. It is likely that some conflict will be found between faculty preferences for selective admissions, institutional concerns about student enrollment and costs, and social pressures for equal opportunity. If these differences are not resolved prior to program planning, operational problems resulting from them are likely to arise. In particular, the question of whether a program should be undergraduate or graduate may become an issue.

The availability of one or more faculty members qualified to teach in the program is highly relevant. They should have not only the disciplinary basis but also a background in the problems and opportunities for which this program prepares. If such individuals are not available within the department or unit planning the program, are they available elsewhere in the university? If not, then the faculty development requirements or faculty selection and allocation procedures required to meet these demands must be resolved.

The early stages of planning should define the procedures to be used in formulating and evaluating the program. If such questions as those previously raised are carefully addressed in the planning process, it will become apparent that there are many alternatives at various stages and that the final program or course is a selection or a compromise among all of these alternatives. Despite this, once a program has been set down on paper and approved, there is a tendency to view it as a fixed entity and to regard evaluation as an imposition on the time and energy of individuals who have already made expert judgments about the program. If the plans for evaluation are developed as part of the process, many issues will arise that can be suggested as questions to be looked at in connection with the evaluation process. If no thought is given to evaluation until after the program is complete, it will be difficult just to get agreement on what the issues are with regard to the program and perhaps even more so to define the relevant data in the process of evaluation.

Several of the points discussed earlier noted that the program objectives designate the expected student achievements. Hence course or program planning should involve more than a

statement of content. As previously mentioned, there are faculty members who dislike to talk about objectives other than in
content terms. Even those who recognize the value of so doing
are troubled by the semantic problems that arise in defining
outcomes other than explicit knowledge. The continuums that
were developed in Chapter Four provide another way of approaching this problem. The first continuum involved the
teacher-discipline dichotomy or emphasis. If the entire emphasis
is placed upon the discipline or disciplines to be covered, then
the planning of a program is simply a matter of agreeing upon
the particular courses and the disciplinary content to be covered
by them. Taken to the extreme, there would be strict adherence
to coverage of the specified content on a rigid compartmentalized basis with little or no attention to differences in students,
flexibility within the program, or interrelationships among
courses simultaneously or in sequence. If in the initial planning,
however, it is agreed that the success of this program or course
depends in large part on the kind and quality of teaching provided, then some specific criteria such as the following may
emerge: The teacher should be one who is interested in students, who interacts with faculty in related departments, who
has an interest in practical applications, who is flexible and
adaptable, who is competent to teach all of the required preceding courses and is knowledgeable about all succeeding courses,
whether in the discipline or in related disciplines.

If there is agreement that the course or program should
give attention to students as well as to content, then such criteria as the following may be specified:

- Select sound materials that the students can read or learn to
  read.
- Select materials in relationship to student interests and the
  prospects of utilization.
- Arrange for some variation in student assignments to take
  care of individual interests and abilities.
- Provide materials that contain at the beginning some review
  of essentials and, from time to time, provide some glimpse of
  coming attractions.

If it is agreed initially that the program should be balanced between the practical and theoretical, then the following principles may be stated:

- Adopt a consistent position as to how much theory is to be presented and required.
- Emphasize assumptions and conditions essential to applying theory to practice.
- Use practical, realistic examples rather than oversimplified or idealized ones.

If, again, it is agreed that the program should retain some flexibility rather than be rigidly planned a priori, the following principles emerge:

- A significant portion of any program will be maintained as electives to adapt to individual interests.
- Each course will retain some flexibility to adapt the content to the background and interests of students, including spending more or less time on some topics as difficulty and interests dictate.
- Individuals with unusual backgrounds will be permitted to complete parts of the program by competency demonstration or by alternatives to the regular courses.

If it is agreed in the beginning that the program should not only have unity and coherence when viewed on paper by qualified individuals but should also give the students some sense of unity and coherence as the program is pursued, then much attention must be given to the interrelationship of courses and to the continuity, sequence, and integration over time in the courses. Courses taught independently by faculty members who know little about what is being done in other courses inevitably become compartmentalized, and students find their total experience fragmented. The concern here is not simply that students be told in detail each day why it is important that these particular things be learned. Rather, it is to take advantage of student motivation by helping the students integrate the learning in each course and experience with that in other courses. A major difficulty is that the faculty members teaching segments of a program are not themselves aware of how courses relate. It is neither possible nor reasonable to expect every professor in a disciplinary department or in an interdisciplinary professional program to teach all parts of the departmental or program offerings. This is not of great concern in the discipline because each discipline has many special emphases that can be dealt with in isolation and with little recognition of any common disciplinary structure and methodology. But in a coordinated program, the instructor who has no sense of the sequence and ultimate integration of the facets of a program is likely to emphasize unduly his or her own course and to cram it with unnecessary and irrelevant materials while failing to develop in the students the capacity to deal independently with the materials and ideas that this particular course embraces. It is these concerns that make it so important that faculty members from other areas be involved in the planning, teaching, and evaluation of any new programs or of any course that serves as a key building block in a number of programs. The planning of a program should also include steps for orientation of faculty members in other departments that require the course as part of the major or program of students in their area. Generally, this orientation of the faculty should include discussions of the following questions:

1. What is this course expected to do for the students that take it?
2. What are the students required to do in the course?
3. How should advanced courses be dealt with more effectively utilizing the insights and competencies developed through this course?

Because of these problems, the planning of a course or program is not complete until something has been said in rather specific terms about how that course or program is to be staffed and how it is to be reviewed, evaluated, and kept up to date. For every professor who develops an outstanding course and maintains his or her enthusiasm over years in giving it, there are several others who, in assuming responsibility for a particular course, drift into slovenly patterns of teaching because they use the same approach each year—perhaps even to using the same materials and questions. Professors who are not thinking as they profess are not likely to stimulate their students to think. A significant educational experience does not result simply because a student has a number of outstanding teachers, each doing his or her own thing in his or her own way. A few very able students may be stimulated and profit from this experience. Most students require some kind of continuing, cumulating, integrative experience that is structured, in part, but not structured to the point where the student simply assimilates. The major purpose of placing structure in a program or course is to encourage students to see the importance and necessity of structure so that they gradually develop and impose their own.

Suggestions for Further Reading

Ahearn, F. L., Jr., Bolan, R. S., and Burke, E. M. "A Social Action Approach for Planning Education." *Journal of Education for Social Work,* 1975, *11* (3), 5-10.

Anderson, O. R. "The Effects of Varying Structure in Science Content on the Acquisition of Science Knowledge." *Journal of Research in Science Teaching,* 1968, *5,* 361-364.

Carpenter, P. *History Teaching: The Era Approach.* Cambridge, England: Cambridge University Press, 1964.

Chickering, A. W., and others. *Developing the College Curriculum: A Handbook for Faculty and Administrators.* Washington, D.C.: Council for the Advancement of Small Colleges, 1977.

Cole, C. C., Jr., and Lewis, L. G. *Flexibility in the Undergraduate Curriculum.* New Dimensions in Higher Education, no. 10. Washington, D.C.: U.S. Government Printing Office, 1966.

Lydo, W. J. "A Suggested Conceptual System for Decision Making in Curriculum Development." *Educational Record,* 1960, *41,* 74-83.

Tamminen, P. G. *A Guide to Resources for Undergraduate Academic Reform.* Washington, D.C.: American Council on Education, 1970.

7

Individualizing Courses and Programs

Individualized programs are to be contrasted with the standard programs approved by the faculty and listed in official publications. Most standard programs include some options that provide limited individualization. The student can choose a course in either economics or sociology. A slightly more flexible form of individualization specifies the credit-hour total required from a group of courses or disciplines. A general education distribution requirement is an example. In some cases, individualization is possible by requesting the substitution of one course for another. In recent years, some individualization has been possible by demonstrating that the equivalent of a course was attained in some other manner. These forms of individualization are limited in extent. They permit the student to choose a course or two on the basis of interests or convenience. One might better characterize these alternatives as permitting limited flexibility rather than as individualization.

There is also a degree of individualization within courses if individual variations in content and experience are possible. The course outline or structure is kept sufficiently flexible so that students have options or preferences in what they do and how they do it. Some of this flexibility may result simply from the need to balance the activities of the students against available resources. These adaptations are certainly worthwhile but they provide quite limited individualization.

Programs and courses planned by the faculty often lack unity and coherence, especially from the viewpoint of the student, because they arise out of departmental disciplinary structures and are focused on content coverage. Moreover, whatever coherence exists is a faculty conception frequently based more on abstractions or theories than on practical orientation or student motivation. The availability of a few options to students does not remedy this basic weakness, nor does it permit the student to regard the program as a personal development and commitment. In contrast, the individualized approach allows students interested in concepts, issues, or problems transcending the usual course and disciplinary lines to build their own programs. This is undoubtedly the best structure if one wants to offer students the widest latitude of choice. However, there are some difficulties and resulting strong convictions pro and con in respect to individualization. Those who are against individualization see students as generally lacking maturity and a sense of purpose required to build a program. Even when students have a career goal in mind, they usually lack the expertise to relate this to courses and programs structured by disciplinary content. Students also lack the knowledge to understand the relationship of particular courses to their own interests and career aspirations. They are quite likely to demand immediate experience rather than recognize the need for a theoretical and conceptual background. The limited information provided about courses presents a difficulty for students and advisers. Although the lack of information is a deficiency in faculty specification or description, many faculty members doubt that elaboration of course descriptions is desirable or that it would be useful to students or advisers in building an individualized program.

The major objection that many faculty members have to program individualization is that students will select groups of courses of little substance and with no significant interrelationship or coherence. A program made up of courses from several departments is difficult to appraise for significance and quality. Many faculty members assert that it is a faculty prerogative to define courses and programs. They argue that academic freedom in research and scholarship is based on recognition of expertise and that only experts in a particular field are able to define a sound program. Although large segments of the faculty resist individualization, my own experience is that most faculty members recognize the value of special arrangements for individuals of unusual backgrounds and abilities. A departmental base could still provide flexibility, but traditional strictures make it unlikely. An understandable fear is that uncontrolled individualization might jeopardize faculty interests, expertise, and control, with resulting chaos. It is not surprising that programs of individualization are tightly limited and controlled.

The arguments for individualization emphasize the involvement of the individual in program planning, with the expectation that the planning itself will be a strong motivational and educational experience, and that the personal commitment made by planning the program will result in high motivation. It is noteworthy that the flexibility of the individualized program in allowing the student to adapt to particular interests, present competencies, and ultimate aspirations is especially appropriate for a mature person who has, as a result of various educational and work experiences, come to a clear focus and strong commitment to a particular career. Obviously, the complete individualization of program planning does not work well for vocations or professions in which there are explicit program requirements for degrees or certification. However, there are many fields in which the specificity of programs is almost entirely based upon faculty judgments and departmental interests rather than on logic, evidence, or professional school admission requirements. The individual who finds part of a prescribed program irrelevant, who believes that actual experience is the equivalent of certain courses, or who prefers to explore idiosyncratic career possibilities often finds that the available choices among the highly structured programs are inadequate.

Although some beginning college students have well-based program choices to which they adhere, others find their initial choices unsatisfactory. Still others have no basis and no enthusiasm for selection among the majors and programs available. This state of mind has often been interpreted by counselors and faculty members as an indication that the first year or two in college ought to be highly prescriptive, emphasizing general education, and thereby laying a foundation for later selection of a degree program. The difficulty is that general education requirements are not greeted with great enthusiasm, and that program pattern postpones rather than initiates the process of career planning. Loaded with general education courses in the first two years, individuals may bypass basic courses in the sciences and mathematics, thereby delimiting later choices. My belief, based upon my early experiences in directing a counseling center, is that students without program commitments should be urged to develop an exploratory program designed to provide first-hand experiences that aid in reaching a program commitment. This is easier to do when unique or fully individualized programs are possible, although I find that students, through such exploration, may claim as their own an already existing program.

Weighing the pros and cons of the individualized program, I feel that such an opportunity is highly desirable. However, I would not expect a large proportion of entering students to elect the individualized program. It is difficult to publicize and describe such programs to students, and students find it difficult to describe them to friends, relatives, and prospective employers. Advisers, pressed for time in advising numerous students and having inadequate knowledge and experience in planning individualized programs, tend to fit students into traditional molds. My observations are that individualized programs are limited to a few students who recognize the possibility and demand it. Even these students are often frustrated and discouraged by the difficulties in acquiring approval of such a program. We should and we can do better.

Individualized Courses

Traditionally, courses meet at fixed times and places. The assignments are standard for all students. Faculty loads and priorities are such that there is little or no direct and immediate follow-up of the day-by-day performance of individual students. The professor "covers" the materials in lectures and may involve a few students in reacting to his or her questions or raising their own. If attendance is not taken, students who have access to the notes of a friend will find other more pleasant and perhaps more profitable ways to utilize their time. This structure preserves the stereotype of scheduled classes as the means of attaining an education. For those oriented to accountability, the presence of professor and students in the classroom for a certain number of hours a week is at least an indication of time spent, whether or not it is productive. In large classes, and particularly in institutions using ten-week quarters or even shorter periods of study, the available time may not permit much more than this deadening production-line pattern. Time is required to become acquainted with students, to learn their special interests and experiences, and to identify possible working groups or combinations of students to engage in cooperative endeavor. Individualization calls for such elements as differential assignments in readings or problems and development of reports and projects sufficiently early in a term that they can be shared with other students. This requires a flexible list of topics and tasks, and some discussion and guidance in selecting among them. If the objective is that individuals learn how to collaborate and cooperate with each other in the study of significant issues, then it is important to identify small subgroups of no more than half a dozen students.

Generally, the individual and group efforts in such a course will proceed at a much slower pace than the usual pattern of professorial-based coverage, so that the content coverage will generally need to be modified. Greater emphasis must be put on what students are able to do than on how much they have learned of some defined body of content. This imposes extensive clerical work on the instructor, both in keeping track of the individual assignments and efforts and in individualizing the evaluation of accomplishment. If, in addition, it is accepted that part of the motivation for individualization is an obligation to report the results to one's peers, then further dilution of the content coverage is required—at least insofar as the instructor-centered presentations in the classroom are concerned. One of the more uncomfortable aspects of this individualization from the viewpoint of the instructor is that the comforting assumption that everyone is at the same stage in doing the same thing must be abandoned. However, an experienced instructor recognizes that some students accomplish very little, even under constant and direct pressure—and still pass. No wonder we talk about what our "A" students do when we describe our courses!

An advanced undergraduate course or a graduate course may take on a seminar character if students focus upon a broad topic and individualize their reading or research and reporting to the group. When this is done, the class structure can move close to a group (or even an individual) independent study model. The independent study model exists in various forms and with accompanying variation in the amount of individualization. One pattern required at one time or another in a few undergraduate programs requires a student to select one course and, using the outline and materials used in classes, study it independently and take the common examination. In effect, this limited approach to independent study says to the student: "You have to demonstrate that you can pass this course without having the advantage of class attendance." In a few cases, a major has been asked to take (by independent study) one of the advanced courses offered in his or her department. Thereby this individual is presumably demonstrating the ability to read a textbook and prepare for an examination without class attendance and with limited contact with the instructor. In some small colleges, certain advanced courses that cannot be given in class simply because of the lack of students are used effectively as independent study. This may be no more than reading a text, but if, by this means, a student learns to read textual materials understandingly and apply them, that pattern of independent study will have thoroughly justified itself.

Some problems involved in independent study are alleviated by study of an existing structured and credited course. The professor need not worry about credits because these have been established. The student knows at once that certain topics and pages are to be covered and that a report is to be prepared or an examination taken. This provides a sound and useful, although still relatively structured, approach to independent study. Even in this pattern, if the work is done well, some students will spend many more hours on the material than would be the case in class. The pace of a class is effectively set by the outline and the instructor. The independent study pace on the same materials is set by the conscientious student who seeks to understand the material and may impose a higher standard than held to in a class. The professor may have to weigh the question of whether coverage of two thirds of the material with an unusually high level of understanding is equal or perhaps superior to coverage of all the material with a barely adequate grasp. Individualization forces us to reexamine standards, coverage, and evaluation procedures.

Another level of independent study is experienced when a professor hands his or her own graduate school notes or materials to the student as an independent study project. The difference is that there is no formal course in existence, no set pattern for just what is to be covered, and the material may be less well organized and rather more difficult to digest than a textbook. This can be very effective study, although it is to be noted that it is highly dominated by the instructor (or the instructor's graduate school professors).

Another level of independent study is one in which the student and the instructor discuss various possibilities and reach an agreement, perhaps even formalized into a contract, as to what the student is to do. Some professors will not permit the individual to engage in independent study of a topic unless they themselves have already delved deeply into this topic at some time in the past. And some professors insist that even this commitment requires an extensive amount of rereading and updating of their knowledge. Such independent study is rigidly controlled and highly demanding on the time of the instructor.

A more flexible approach is exemplified when a student develops a topic, presents it to the professor, and gets acceptance with minimal discussion for an exploratory study. This works especially well when independent study can be pursued over two or more consecutive terms. Credit for exploratory phases seems entirely appropriate, but some professors are reluctant to approve it.

Perhaps the ultimate in independent study is the circumstance in which an individual appears in a professor's office and exhibits an accomplishment. Until recently, few institutions would consider granting credit under these circumstances. There is still widespread reluctance to grant credit for educational outcomes of life experiences. An individual cannot, in most graduate schools, present a piece of research already accomplished and have it accepted as the doctoral dissertation. Independent study for credit traditionally requires advance approval of a project and a culminating evaluation and grade after the completion of the project to justify credit.

In the process of developing an independent study as a significant part of an undergraduate program for most or all students, there are numerous difficulties. Perhaps the first, as most faculty members would probably claim, is that few students are capable of independent study. This may well be true, but it misses the point. My own conviction is that most undergraduates are capable of achieving some independence, but that it must be a gradual development from the highly structured classroom situation to the point where an individual demonstrates capability to plan a significant learning activity and carry it through largely on his or her own effort. I do not believe that anyone should receive a baccalaureate degree unless such capability is demonstrated. A second major problem is that many professors find it difficult to permit students to engage in essentially autonomous independent study. There is a concern as to what the student will do, how much will be accomplished, and whether the professor is competent to make a judgment unless he or she has already delved deeply into the topic studied. A third factor, closely related to the last, is that as students move to select their own topics, the nature of the topic and the treatment of it may not fit into the disciplinary compartments upon which course credit is based. Further, the project may not be within the competence of the professor who was designated as responsible for it, which immediately suggests a multiplication of burdens on the faculty and on the student. This practice tends to raise the time commitments for undergraduate study to the level of doctoral program dissertation direction. Obviously, that is not feasible. A fourth problem with independent study concerns the degree of freedom available for students in selecting and pursuing topics. In part, these problems have been touched upon in our prior discussion about levels of independent study. I believe that limited independent efforts should be encouraged early in a program, and that students should move to the highest level possible within the time constraints.

The fifth problem with independent study arises out of time constraints. These time constraints are of two types. Independent study, because it is an individual effort, tends to require a superior performance level, and therefore more time than the typical course. But the student, in use of time, is usually enrolled in a number of structured courses that make day-to-day demands. The individual completing the daily demands for these courses may wish to defer the even more demanding independent study effort until another day. In independent study, as with contract learning and other individualized programs, students tend to fall behind. The professor only has to take note of personal difficulties in balancing daily demands and longer-term professional and scholarly effort to understand the student's dilemma. Another aspect of the time constraints is that putting independent study in the calendar structure used for classes asks the student, in effect, to do something that faculty members themselves would generally say is impossible—that is, to plan research on a calendar basis corresponding with the teaching schedule and bring papers or studies to a close on that same calendar. Giving deferred grades on independent study and carrying it into another term only makes for more difficulty later on, as carry-over work makes demands on time needed for new work. This issue is also related to the tendency to expect a great deal more out of independent study than a student would do for the same number of credits in a structured classroom. A possible solution would be to have a student sign up for a certain amount of independent study for the entire academic year, with the expectation that reasonable progress at the end of one term would justify reporting of a grade at that time, but that the project involved need not be completed until spring.

A sixth problem with independent study is the amount of credit to be granted. This has already been discussed to some extent. There is always some concern about the relationship between the credit granted a student and the amount of work done, and perhaps some tendency to relate this to the instructor's coverage of materials in a traditional classroom situation. The differences in levels of performance and the amount of originality or creativity involved in independent study are recognized as time consuming, but the tendency of the professor to expect closure on a topic studied causes some independent study projects to end up as master's theses. In many respects, it might be better if variable credits were assigned to independent study and the total amount of credit finally allocated determined on the basis of amount and quality of work done.

A seventh problem in encouraging independent study is the existence of such course proliferation that student interest in independent study can be redirected to taking an additional course or two. Students may also be told that the topic that they propose is covered in one of the courses.

The two most serious difficulties in developing independent study programs are the equating of independent study with honors work, and hence limiting it to a few students, and the unreasonable expectations for accomplishment by the independent study student. Independent study has had relatively hard sledding in modern undergraduate education.

Individualized Programs

Program individualization can take place at many different levels. When a program offers some electives or alternatives among several courses, the choice of these courses constitutes a degree of individualization. When required courses are waived so that an individual can substitute something else, a degree of individualization has taken place. When students are provided opportunity to obtain credit for courses by taking examinations or by evaluation of some product of current or past extra course efforts, some individualization has occurred. Individualization simply means that some adjustments are made in developing an individual's program on the basis of his or her likes, experiences, aspirations, and talents. There are relatively few programs in most institutions that are fully prescribed for all students, and hence a degree of individualization occurs in most programs. However, much of this individualization is at a very limited level.

When individualization moves to the level of waiving requirements or making substitutions, there is a strong probability that bureaucracy will take over. In a typical circumstance that I have seen, the individual student repeatedly fills out a request form that must be countersigned by the adviser, sent to the head of the department concerned, and submitted to the dean or to a committee for approval or disapproval. This is discouraging to both students and advisers.

The next level of an individualized program is one in which an individual student, with the support of his or her adviser and perhaps the endorsement of a review committee or a dean, develops a program subject usually to certain rules or constraints. These constraints may pertain to general education or distribution requirements, limitation on the number of hours in a single department, or completion of specific requirements in foreign language, physical education, or composition. There may also be a requirement that a certain number of credits be at the advanced undergraduate level to prevent an individualized program based entirely upon freshman and sophomore courses. Seldom, if ever, does a student have the opportunity to develop a completely personal program untrammeled by rules, advisers' comments, or the necessity that the proposal be approved by several individuals, offices, or committees. A number of institutions indicate that double or triple majors are possible for students, but this option is severely delimited by the departmental attitude that majoring in a department involves obligations well beyond the taking of specific courses. Therefore, a department might disapprove a major for an individual who was, at the same time, undertaking to complete majors in one or more other departments. I recall a brilliant young freshman who entered Michigan State with a request that he be permitted to take only work in music, chemistry, and mathematics. He had already done outstanding work in all three disciplines, but the departments and deans concerned could not accept such an unusual combination. As a matter of fact, this person had some interests that bridged the disciplines, but since no department or professor represented that bridging, the combination was deemed impossible. In this case, incidentally, the student seeking an unusual program was more concerned with self-development and integration of ideas across disciplines than with any prospects of graduate work or career development. However, it seems likely that no college will effectively develop individualized programs unless there is enabling legislation or a firm policy stating that individuals have the right to develop their own programs. It will also become necessary to state some rules or policies with regard to the nature of these programs and grant advisers some autonomy in interpreting them. Whether that imposed set of limitations or structure expedites individualization or destroys it depends a great deal on the nature of the rules and those who enforce them.

Any attempt to permit the individualization of programs within an institution will be fraught with a number of problems. Since at least the latter part of the nineteenth century, undergraduate programs have been construed as a combination of breadth and depth, with depth largely being defined in terms of disciplinary or departmentally based majors. Any departure from the departmentally based major is regarded with suspicion and distrust. It is feared that such a development carried too far would be completely disruptive to the traditional departmental disciplinary organization. Further, most faculty members doubt that significant depth experiences that cut across majors are possible at the undergraduate level. A second problem is that when an acceptable pattern is developed, there is a tendency to formalize this in a highly structured manner. My own first experience with this came in the late 1930s when, after spending many hours obtaining approval from various administrators of a combination business-agriculture program for a student from Detroit, I found the complete program printed in the next year's catalogue as a new joint major between the two colleges. The introduction of such new programs is, in one sense, a victory for individualization. However, the formalization of the program not only prevents anyone else from having the discovery experience but also tends to reduce the freedom of others who find a rigid program specified. A similar movement to rigidity has appeared in individualized programs structured around themes or problems, such as urban studies, black studies, women's studies, environmental studies, or future studies. A number of colleges that I reviewed at an early stage of such programs offered the possibility of individualized programs but moved shortly to detailed programs, partly for publicity purposes. There are obvious values in the public listing of these programs. Time is saved on the part of advisers, deans, committees, and others in reviewing and approving individual programs. The presence of a formal approved program in the catalogues may attract students. The formal statement of the program eases the problem of the hesitant or uncertain adviser who doubts that any program that he and a student might develop will be accepted by his colleagues. Adherence to rules and to their literal interpretation can be time saving, can provide security, and can be defended as preserving standards; but the existence of such rules and strict adherence to them are sound evidence of a bureaucratic operation that discourages individualization.

The problem of planning degree programs for nontraditional students provides ample evidence on both sides of the rule and rigor issue. By attempting to avoid traditional structure and adapt to the individual's background, purposes, and time limitations, some programs have become so flexible that they are lacking in rigor and meaning. Formal evaluation is omitted other than that of euphoric and self-congratulatory comments about how education has been adapted to the needs and interests of the nontraditional student. In some cases, cooperative education that originally attempted to merge some job experience with education has been pushed to the opposite extreme. An attempt has been made to merge some education with a full-time job experience. It *may* be effective. However, in these non-traditional programs, there is typically a difficulty in maintaining continuity and sequence. The concerns for relevance and integration are not necessarily satisfied simply because nontraditional students have had, and are having, numerous experiences aside from formal education. In some cases, the attempt to maintain the minimal elements of a formal structure have eliminated much of the flexibility for nontraditional students. Some nontraditional master's and doctoral programs have been so stereotyped that every individual follows the same pattern. I have found that even after individualized programs are authorized, the evaluation of them may be on traditional grounds. I recently visited the liberal arts college of a major state university to review an individualized degree program in liberal education, only to find that the faculty review had terminated the program because the programs of graduates revealed that traditional general education distribution requirements had not been met. Apparently exercise of the freedom originally granted was deemed undesirable!

In any sense, any individualization of education can be regarded as the development of a nontraditional program. Any program faces the problem of balancing content and structure. The departure from a common structure in an educational program does not mean the elimination of structure; rather, it means the devising of structures on the basis of individual interests and competencies and the reasonable demands of rigor and quality that justify the award of a degree. Thus one is faced with discussing educational experiences for the nontraditional student in reference to the nature or type of experience, the quality of experience, the level of experience, and its reality. There is also a problem of planning of experience, for one cannot simply assume that experience will be educational. There is also a need to evaluate the experience. This requires appraisal of the values intrinsic to the experience, the values that emerge from the experience, and consideration of possible improvements. In nontraditional education, rather more than in traditional education, such evaluation is essential. Traditional education starts the student into a series of courses, each being relatively independent of those that precede it and those that follow. Evaluation at any point has limited significance because one cannot change what is past and the evidence has very little impact on what happens in the future. In individualized education, on the contrary, the individual has some part in the planning of the experience, and the consideration of such matters as nature, quality, level, and reality adds significance to that experience and enhances the opportunity that the individual has to draw something significant from it. Since the program is individualized, subsequent experiences can be based upon those to date.

Advising and counseling become tremendously important in the process of individualization. But advisers as faculty members are hesitant about how far they dare go in approving nontraditional patterns. In many cases, they have limited understanding of the career prospects of various combinations of study and may not be disposed to spend the time acquiring it. Relatively little is done in the training of advisers and essentially nothing in rewarding them. To encourage individualized programs in a college, it may be necessary to develop a small core of academic counselors who have a sound academic background and do some teaching, but who also have spent, and continue to spend, sufficient time as counselors that they are able to deal with some of the personal as well as the academic and career problems of students. These problem areas are closely related for most college students.

Most attempts to relate education and career development involve self-appraisal by the student and the resolution of a number of problems. To make this effective, the autonomy of departments in spelling out programs and requirements must be abridged by granting authority to qualified advisers or counselors to approve programs. There is reasonable concern that there may be some excesses in approving undesirable programs, but recurrent review procedures can identify and strengthen or eliminate them. Thus the granting of the authority to advisers or counselors would require continuing appraisal of program effectiveness. This would include considering what happens to the students, appraising the programs developed by the students, and reviewing with advisers or counselors their procedures in working with students in developing and approving a program.

For effective individualization, advisers in program planning should start from the individual's interests and aspirations, taking into consideration the experiences provided by various courses. But there is one major difficulty in so doing. The information available on most courses and educational opportunities in an institution is insufficient for effectively planning an individualized program. This is discussed in the following chapter.

Suggestions for Further Reading

Claxton, C. S., and Ralston, Y. *Learning Styles: Their Impact on Teaching and Administration.* AAHE-ERIC/Higher Education Research Report No. 10. Washington, D.C.: American Association for Higher Education, 1978.

Dressel, P. L., and Thompson, M. M. *Independent Study: New Interpretations of Concepts, Practices, and Problems.* San Francisco: Jossey-Bass, 1973.

Givens, P. R. *Student-Designed Curricula.* Research Currents, ED 061 917. Washington, D.C.: American Association for Higher Education, 1972.

Mayville, W. V. *Interdisciplinarity: The Mutable Paradigm.* AAHE-ERIC/Higher Education Research Report No. 9. Washington, D.C.: American Association for Higher Education, 1978.

National Society for the Study of Education. *The Integration of Educational Experiences.* 57th Yearbook, Pt. 3. Chicago: University of Chicago Press, 1958.

Shoenfeld, J. D. *Student-Initiated Changes in the Academic Curriculum.* ED 065 105. Washington, D.C.: ERIC Clearinghouse on Higher Education, George Washington University, 1972.

8

Improving Course and Program Descriptions

The previous chapter has indicated that one of the hazards in the way of individualization in program planning is the lack of information available to students and advisers to tailor a program to individual student specifications. If the planning of a student program starts by reviewing existing programs, as described in the catalogue and in other departmental or college literature, it is likely that some programs will be found that are related to the individual's interests, but so highly structured that variation would be beset with endless red tape. Furthermore, the student who succeeds in attaining some minor modification of an existing program is unlikely to deal with that program in the same depth as a self-constructed one. The student is still following a program with little understanding of what it involves other than a series of courses and accumulation of credit. But the student and adviser who would go beyond existing programs find that course descriptions are unclear, misleading, and sometimes even false.

I am not speaking here of intended deception, but rather of the variation between what formal course descriptions state and what instructors actually do. For example, I recall an honors student advisee of some years ago who enrolled in an honors section of a chemistry course that, according to the catalogue description, specified six hours in the laboratory. After the first meeting, a much troubled student arrived at my desk saying that the professor in the course had asserted that students taking it should clear a minimum of twelve to fifteen hours for laboratory work in order to meet course requirements. Obviously, such unauthorized departures from formal statements constitute motivational and workload hazards within a term as well as in program planning on a longer basis. There are other problems with course offerings that imperil the planning of a program. The nature of a particular course often depends heavily upon the professor assigned to teaching it. With Professor X, the course may be a waste of time to an individual; with Professor Y, it may be just what is needed to round out a program. When ambiguities exist as to term or time of day courses will be offered, program planning becomes difficult. The individual attempting to arrange a special program must adapt to whatever program factors are dominant in college and departmental scheduling. However, these scheduling matters are of less concern than the lack of detailed information needed by the student and adviser. Program and course specifications are, to a large extent, based upon faculty convenience and departmental concerns rather than on adaptation to individual planning.

Students and advisers are not the only persons who need more information than is generally available. Any administrator or committee that undertakes to review departmental offerings soon finds that many questions arise with regard to course content, sequence, credit, overlapping, and duplication that no one at hand is able to answer. At times, there is no explanation as to why certain requirements or courses exist. In visits with accrediting association teams, I have frequently found that no files exist on courses, so that it is impossible to learn what was done in a course offered two or three years ago. The textbook used, examinations, course outlines, or syllabus and other such matters apparently are not regarded as of any consequence once a course has been given. Even the instructor who taught the course a year or two ago may not be able to recall what he or she did at that time. This does not necessarily mean that instruction is bad or that the curriculum is unplanned, but it does suggest that the department or institution places undue reliance on the individual teacher. Successive teachers may have difficulty reconstructing a course. Inquiries from other institutions regarding transfer credit for a course may be inadequately answered or ignored. Students who, because of illness or other factors, withdrew from the course shortly before examinations may, upon return a year or two later, find that no one can determine what this individual must do to complete course requirements. This lack of continuity in course offerings presents a serious handicap in planning programs.

The preceding remarks are not meant to suggest that every course description must specify in detail how that course is to be handled or what is to be covered day by day. Some courses must be highly structured, and the description should indicate this. For independent study, the topic may not be determined until after the individual has signed up for the course. There may also be seminars or discussion groups with an array of optional topics and procedures. If the course description makes specific that a course is of that flexible type, the situation is adequately explained. Even so, it would be appropriate for a department to keep a file on such courses so that, for various reasons already suggested, it would be possible to determine what happened in a particular course or with a particular individual. A statement of program and a description of courses are contained in a document available to the general public. It may be used by individuals attempting to compare a number of institutions; it may be used by prospective students seeking particular types of programs. In these cases, a curriculum and program statement must be regarded as the equivalent of an advertisement. This has two implications. First, there should be truth in advertising; and second, the statement of the

existence of a program or of certain course offerings establishes
the basis for a contractual relationship in which a person seeking admission to the institution expects the opportunity to
acquire the benefits implied by the advertising. Some state and
federal legislative prescriptions now exist with regard to such
matters. These prescriptions have been written primarily to con-
tend with institutions and individuals engaging in unethical
practices, but a sound ethical institution should not have to be
prompted by legal requirements. Its service responsibility and
its general concern for seeking and advancing knowledge and
truth should be an adequate rationale for insisting that professors, departments, and colleges be accurate and completely
honest in describing the various patterns of learning experiences
available. Since the ultimate concern in education must be for
the individual, the intent should be to supply as much information as is possible within reasonable limits to assist the individual in planning an educational program.

Information Needed on a Program

In many respects, the information needed on a program
by students and advisers corresponds to the information needed
when a program is proposed or reviewed. The basic purposes
should be part of the formal statement of the program, and the
extent of flexibility and the possible variations of the program
should be made explicit. Purposes and objectives, even of a liberal education program, should include some consideration of
the career and vocational possibilities. The statement of the objectives for the program should indicate the accomplishments
that students must demonstrate to satisfy the program requirements. That statement of accomplishments should point out the
significance of liberal education outcomes as well as any specific
vocational or career competencies. The statement of objectives
should be sufficiently detailed that the various program requirements can be related to and justified by their contribution to
the learning objectives.

The admission requirements of a program should be made
explicit and justified for programs requiring advanced standing.

Any specific college-level prerequisites should also be stated and justified. Both students and instructors should be aware of them and anticipate that the course level will be consistent with the prerequisites. If enrollment limitations are imposed upon the program, the reason for this should be indicated, as should the criteria and procedures utilized in selecting among applicants to fill the quota.

The career implications of a program should be stated on the basis of the intent and purpose. Further, after a program has been offered for several years, a few sentences or a table indicating the nature of the positions acquired by the graduates should be provided.

Program Recommendations and Requirements. Most program specifications are excessively demanding in regard to required courses. This is, in part, a response to the insistence from various disciplines that existing courses be included in program requirements rather than devising new ones. New courses could cover essential material more efficiently than when existing courses having some relevance are included, but the omission of traditional topics and a reorganization of others is not readily acceptable either because of conviction or the extra work required. Some courses are required by accreditation practices, certification policies, or state laws. Usually, these courses can be waived for individuals on the basis of certification of equivalents. There are other courses required only by action of the local faculty. Awareness of this latter group could inject an element of flexibility into many unnecessarily rigid programs. In addition to the required courses, there should be an indication of options or selectives among a group of courses. Here it is desirable that there be some indication of the implications of the choices. If there are sufficient options to produce a program variant when combined with appropriate electives, this is the place for such a statement. The details required may be excessive for inclusion in the catalogue, but there should be descriptive statements available to advisers and students. The statement of the electives and options for a program should include an indication of appropriate courses from other departments or colleges than the one in which the program is based. It may also be possible to work out a number of combination programs in which the essence of two or even three somewhat related programs is drawn together for a particular individual. It would be desirable to indicate some principles or bases for planning and approval of these combinations, but all such programs need not be spelled out in detail.

It is appropriate to specify required experiences other than formal courses; and the requirements should be made sufficiently specific that the student entering the program is aware of the existence of the requirement, its precise nature, and the time and cost requirements. Such experiences may include study abroad, one or more periods of internship, work-study programs, some form of writing or oral presentation requirements, or possibly some form of participation, such as tutoring of lower-division students to demonstrate mastery of material and the ability to explain it.

General Education Suggestions. Whether or not a program should make specific suggestions or impose requirements on the choices that students may have in the general education area is debatable. There are many who would argue that general education or breadth should be considered as entirely separate from the specialization or depth. My own view is that a rationale for choice, a personal commitment, and a sense of relevance are highly desirable in planning the breadth experience of students. I have seen all too much of student irritation and time wasted by taking so-called general education courses having limited relevance to general education and no relevance to anything else. In my view, the task of liberal education is to develop persons who seek interrelationships among experiences and knowledge. Consequently, anything that can be done to help individuals see the pervasiveness of certain concepts and values and the possible ways of interrelating materials from various disciplines in the context of problems is highly desirable. Thus I see no harm and some value in a program statement that includes suggestions for general education—for example, that certain courses be avoided or others taken, or even that certain options have specific requirements. There will be certain sensitivities here that need be regarded. Advisers well might caution students to avoid particular courses that are poorly taught, unreasonably demanding, or simply irrelevant. I regard the implied criticism of colleagues as justifiable in fulfilling an obligation to students. Any published statement about the avoidance of certain courses would have to take a different tack. For example, a broad-gauge general education course in biology might be out of bounds for a program drawing heavily on other courses in biology. In contrast, a general education course in biology that provides a sense of the structure of the discipline of biological science, its basic concepts and principles, might be strongly urged. The rationale for including any course in a program must be sound and communicable to students and advisers. If this is so, it becomes easier to determine whether that rationale applies to a particular student.

Information Needed on Courses

Courses are the building blocks for a program, whether that program is predetermined by faculty formulation and administrative action or developed by the individual. In building a house or wall, the individual must be concerned not only with the structure as a whole but with the content and quality of the individual bricks or blocks used in that structure. In contrast, my own experience in observing the building of programs is that existing courses are sometimes thrown together without much more information than the title of the course and the number of credits involved. Alternatively, a new course is designated by title and credit, and a faculty member is given the responsibility of creating a course that fits its niche in the total structure. The net result is that individuals teaching one course in a program know little about what is done in other courses. There may be no consistency or connectivity in what is done from one offering of a course to another. A further problem in this crude structuring is that the concepts of continuity, sequence, coherence, and integration as one progresses through a curriculum are apparent to neither instructor nor student. The result is that progress in a so-called program is largely the completion of a set of requirements rather than the acquisition of increasing insight into basic concepts and principles and the ability to use and apply them. My general observation is that programs are more clearly and tightly defined than the units that make up the programs. This becomes a special problem when one contemplates the possibility that individuals might make up their own programs if they could find the specifications as to content, size, or composition of the available units required to build those programs. A pile of bricks is not a wall, nor is an unorganized collection of courses a program.

Catalogue Information. Catalogue information on courses is generally held to a bare minimum. It should include a course title, a number, and an indication of the department or discipline but not necessarily the professor responsible for the course. Despite the fact that dual and triple listing of courses in several different departments is somewhat wasteful of space, there is no other effective way for faculty members and students in one of the departments involved to become aware of such joint offerings. A complete listing under one department with cross references from others, if it is acceptable to all units and does not give an erroneous impression of department responsibilities, is probably the best way to exhibit such courses. In my experience, the indication of joint offerings by cross references to a single department poses a problem. Both students and faculty members are prone to favor enrollment in courses listed in their specific departments or programs and to take no responsibility for or interest in other departments.

The listing of a course should also indicate the types of sessions involved and the hours required for each. It may be important in some cases for students to know how the credits for the course are broken down and related to session types. In any case, this information is vital to analyses of program costs. The types of sessions listed should use an agreed-upon terminology in an institution rather than the vocabulary peculiar to each unit. *Lecture, discussion, seminar,* and other such terms should be defined in some uniform manner, as indicated in Table 2.

The prerequisites for a course should be clearly specified and a distinction made between recommended and required prerequisites. It is unfair to students to specify requirements and

Table 2. Types of Learning Experiences

Method	Description	Instructional Materials and Processes
Lecture	The faculty member takes the dominant role. The primary emphasis is on transmitting a body of knowledge or information, explaining ideas or principles, and giving specific assignments.	Syllabus, text, or reading list, evaluation of individual learning.
Lecture/ discussion	Includes student participation by means appropriate to the subject matter—discussion, performance, reporting, peer exchange, etc.	Syllabus, text, or reading list, evaluation of individual learning.
Laboratory	Primary emphasis on learning by doing with the burden of course activity placed on the student, under faculty direction and supervision, for the purpose of giving first-hand experience, translating theory into practice, and developing, testing, and applying principles.	Syllabus or manual, evaluation of individual learning.
Field study	Arranged by a faculty member for a student or group of students to carry out a project outside the classroom by observation, participation in a work experience, or field research.	Careful advance planning involving faculty, students, and field supervisor for activity and for evaluation of learning.
Independent	Usually initiated by the student and proposed to and approved by a faculty member. Includes thesis and dissertation work, research apprenticeship, tutorials. Implies one-to-one work with an instructor.	Careful advance planning between faculty and student, with goals, parameters of project, and evaluation method prearranged.
Seminar	Designed to provide a small group of students with independent and interdependent learning under leadership of a faculty member, with maximum opportunity for individual research and peer exchange. Topics can be interdisciplinary or highly specialized.	Broad outline of possible topics and procedures, including basis for evaluation.
Practicum	Professional practice under careful supervision of faculty member and experienced professionals.	Broad outline of possible topics and procedures, including basis for evaluation.
Internship	Professional activity under general supervision, with a high degree of responsibility	Specific job description and provision for

Table 2 *(Continued)*

Method	Description	Instructional Materials and Processes
	placed on the student. Involves placement as a professional in a job situation.	evaluation by supervisor.
Workshop	An organized learning experience with the same purposes and methods as the laboratory, usually offered in a concentrated period shorter than a term.	Broad outline of possible activities and procedures, including basis for evaluation.

Note: This table was modified from a more elaborate outline prepared by Margaret Lorimer, Office of Institutional Research, Michigan State University.

then waive them for any individual so requesting. However, to omit any requirements or recommendations may be equally unfair to students of marginal capability who may enroll in such courses and experience serious difficulty because of lack of background. The waiver or specification of prerequisites for a course should be something more than an instructor's option. If students with weak backgrounds are promiscuously admitted to a course, it becomes something different than originally was intended, wastes the time of some students, and may fail to fill its role in a program. If, to the contrary, unrealistically high prerequisites are established, students may be discouraged from entering a course, or large numbers may fail. Since, in some sense, every course becomes a part of one or more programs, these matters are departmental and institutional decisions rather than instructor preferences.

There are several special factors that ought to be included in the catalogue description of a course. In some institutions or departments, recitation and laboratory sections of a course may be listed as separate courses. Occasionally, this may mean that the segments of the course can be taken separately, but this separate listing may be more a matter of convenience in crediting faculty load or in separating the two components so that if only one is failed the student need not repeat the entire course. But if, as is common, simultaneous enrollment is required in the two courses, each course description should include that infor-

⸻ mation. It is also desirable to list them together and to indicate by consecutive numbers (111, 112) or by a letter attachment (111a, 111b) the relationship of the courses. A second aspect of a course that could well be noted is a listing of any courses for which this course is a prerequisite, required or recommended. This information can be helpful in student program building in that a major reason for taking a particular course could well be that it is a prerequisite for a later course of importance to the student. Presumably, the prerequisite could be picked up in viewing the later course, but the information is a vital part of appraising the significance of a course and should be indicated. Another course characteristic that should be included in the catalogue is the equivalence of a course to other courses. This may relate to courses within the same department or to courses in other departments. Within a single department, there may be several courses covering essentially the same material, but doing so in slightly different ways to accommodate the backgrounds and interests of students or the needs of particular programs. It is important that such courses be identified so that individuals do not waste time or select an easy program by duplication of coverage. It is usually more difficult to identify equivalent courses across departments than within one. Departments have been known to offer, by accident or design, courses equivalent to those in another department. The purpose may be to provide a distinctive course (statistics, for example) in an easier or more relevant manner for a particular group of students. If a number of such equivalent courses exist, they should be identified and each should note its relationship to the others with an indication of restrictions on duplicate credits.

Each catalogue course listing should provide a description of content. In some cases, this may be adequately covered by specification of such factors as chronological period covered, names of individuals, and designation of ideas, major concepts, or principles treated or used. Frequently, however, the nature of the course content is much more complicated than a very brief description would imply. The course title generally will indicate a discipline, but the discipline may be used to deal with certain social issues or problems (subject matter) or it may be focused upon the clarification and elaboration of the significance of certain disciplinary concepts and principles in a new area or at a more advanced level. Indication that a history course covers a particular period in a region or country, without further detail, tells almost nothing about the focus or purpose of the course and the nature of the experience. In particular, course descriptions are frequently written with a focus on the discipline and under the assumption that the course will be of interest only to professors in the department and to majors. Students and advisers in other departments and colleges learn very little from the brief descriptions provided with some courses. They may not even be able to identify the course as one worthy of consideration.

Enrollment limitations on courses should be indicated in the catalogue description if they are regularly held to. These limitations may pertain to class size, level, or types of students admitted to the course, and the necessity of special approval by the department or an individual may also be included. When enrollment limitations are specified, the reasons should be indicated. The limitation may have to do with the availability of equipment and facilities, the nature of the interactions required among students and between students and teacher, or the need for close supervision, as in an internship experience in the health field. I recall a limitation on a course in veterinary medicine imposed by the number of horse carcasses that could be refrigerated. In any case, the enrollment limitation and criteria for admission should be specified and documented.

The catalogue is not usually the vehicle whereby individuals learn when and where courses are being offered. The catalogue should indicate how frequently the course is offered: every term, alternate years, and so on. Increasingly too, with many institutions offering programs on a flexible basis for nontraditional students, it is important, even in the catalogue, to show if the course is offered in the evening or on an off-campus basis. The schedule book for a given term will make this explicit, but an individual doing some advance planning with regard to a program may wish to know whether or not and under what circumstances a particular course might be available.

Although not included in the catalogue, any statement about when a course is offered should take into consideration whose convenience is considered in scheduling.

Supplemental Information. Certain supplemental information is useful to advisers and advisees and perhaps to others, but it involves a detail and type of information rather more variable than that indicated for the catalogue. The student who is developing a carefully designed idiosyncratic program will want to know more about who is teaching the course, what kinds of learning experiences are provided, what specific things the student has to do, how much study time is required, and the like. In a large multiple-section course, the number of separate sections and instructors may make it impossible to provide in detail all of the information that students would like to have. Yet, at the same time, it should be pointed out that multiple-section courses offer a unique possibility by assignment of teachers to generate distinctive sectional experiences that may be more attractive to or educationally beneficial for some students than others. The more information that can be placed in the hands of students and advisers, the better the planning that can emerge. However, there are some problems of scheduling that make specific commitments sometimes difficult to maintain. On an occasional basis, failing to fulfill a printed obligation may be justifiable, but wholesale violation of a priori published commitments may mean either that a department is trying to provide too much in detail about a course or that the department itself is not well managed.

It is desirable that students be able to find out what instructor or instructors are assigned to a course or particular section thereof. The point is not so much that students should be enabled to avoid bad instructors, although a case can be made for that. The answer to that as a general problem is to eliminate the bad instructors. The problem still remains that students differ in their preferences and some will be more challenged by a particular type of teaching and personality. It goes without saying that the time and place of meeting should be indicated when the person enrolls, but I have known of a number of institutions in which the assignment of rooms in relation to the size or activity of a class was so badly done that last-minute confusing changes were commonplace. There have also been circumstances in which the assignment of classroom space seemed contrived to perpetrate the maximum inconvenience and discomfort for everyone concerned.

The types of learning experiences provided or required should be described to the student. This would include information on the quality and character of teacher performance when available, although the kind of information provided through summaries of the student rating scales has not been impressive. But beyond this, as already suggested in connection with the discussion of program specification, individuals should know in advance the expectations with regard to field trips, laboratory work, lectures, use of videotaped presentations, and the like. In addition, it is important that the specific requirements be stated. This includes the number of papers, number of examinations and types of examinations, reading reports, laboratory reports, field study reports, and the like. From this, the student and the adviser can determine whether this course offers particular opportunity to an individual who needs more experience in writing, who wishes to prepare for a career in writing, or who simply enjoys courses that include certain patterns of activity.

The amount of time and effort required of the student is a reasonable area for information before enrolling in a course. Fulfillment of course requirements varies greatly from student to student and the time required to fulfill them varies, but it is also true that professors, in specifying what students are expected or required to do, differ greatly in their estimates of the total time required and how much students can do in a specified amount of time. The professor who enjoys giving a tough course and requires an unusual amount of work should let students know before they enroll in his or her course.

The matter of grading and performance standards is also of importance. By analysis of past grading of professors, it is possible to determine high and low graders. It is even occasionally possible to find one who has given all As or another who has never given an A. More important, perhaps, in the present day is the issue of whether an instructor grades students by comparison among those within a class, by some personal standards, or by means of a mastery grading pattern, specifying in advance a minimum satisfactory performance level on all examinations. This information has implications not only as to how hard a student may have to work but also with regard to the extent to which a course is structured. Almost out of necessity, the teacher who insists on something approaching mastery of material has to select that material in advance and emphasize it. He or she is unlikely, therefore, either to encourage or permit individuals to deviate from that specified pattern. The supplemental information about a course should also include the text or texts and major references and other learning resources used or available, especially if these must be purchased by the student. And this leads to the last supplemental item—the additional cost involved for materials, clothing, travel, and equipment.

Other Issues

There are a number of special issues that arise with regard to course and curriculum descriptions. One of these is the problem with transfer students. In earlier years, many of the smaller liberal arts colleges did not make any special plea for transfer students but rather emphasized holding their own underclassmen through the junior and senior years to the attainment of a degree. There are significant advantages when a curriculum and programs drawing upon it can be planned on a four-year basis. The demise of the early completely required program specified for all students greatly simplified such problems as continuity, sequence, and integration and eliminated any need to worry about prerequisites and individualization. The introduction of the breadth-depth conception and the gradual inflation in the range of courses offered, along with the use of options and electives, made it increasingly difficult to establish any common base for students entering upper-division offerings. Even so, departments offering majors found little difficulty in arraying courses with a major in a sequence and requiring students to follow that pattern. As it has become more and more necessary that colleges adjust to accept transfer students from other institutions—and especially the community colleges—we may be approaching a situation in which competition for students will so undermine any conception of depth and sequence that colleges and universities will move very close to what seems to be the pattern of some nontraditional institutions that apparently presume to offer a course in anything, anytime, anywhere, to anybody, and ultimately to grant a degree of some kind. Another factor undermining the quality and rigor of educational programs arises with the disadvantaged students. What should be called remedial work has come to be called developmental. In order to maintain controls over such offerings and collect money for them, many of these have been moved into the credit structure. Thus it becomes impossible in reviewing catalogues in many institutions to know whether particular courses, whatever their numbers may be, are offered at the level of the junior-senior year, at the freshman-sophomore year, or even as the equivalent of secondary or elementary school courses. There are those who have argued that the curriculum is a minor aspect of education—that ultimately the quality depends upon the faculty. Yet some faculty members may allow the curriculum to deteriorate when the circumstances threaten their own security and the future of the institution. It may be that our present concerns should be focused, to a considerable extent, on redefining the curriculum and restoring quality and rigor to programs, further insisting that professors assigned to courses offer these courses as specified rather than to satisfy their own convenience or that of their students.

A second major issue with regard to the curriculum is the offering of special sections. One of the difficulties with many core course programs or required general education options has been the tendency of faculty members to offer special sections built upon their own particular interests. The practice can be defended on the grounds that it provides variety and meets the needs of particular students. Special sections of courses may be offered for any one of several reasons, including: (1) a limited size to permit more personal contact and interaction with students and their efforts; (2) limited to prospective majors in order that the course can be offered at a more advanced level; (3) limited to individuals with outstanding talent or high grades so that they can have a different experience or perhaps simply more work demanded of them; and (4) limited to students with physical, educational, or mental handicaps in order to meet their particular limitations and assist them to deal more effectively with routine offerings. The problem with proliferation of special sections is that, although it permits flexibility and adjustment to individual interests and needs, the approach too readily becomes a vehicle for indulgence of special interests by faculty members, for lowering or eliminating standards for certain students, for increasing costs (without necessarily increasing quality by limitation on class size), and for further proliferating the curriculum to the point where no one really knows what is going on either in a multiple-section course or in specific programs.

A third special issue deals with supplementary independent study opportunities. This is an appropriate addendum to a course and one that, if available, should be stated. It goes beyond the extension of some degree of individualization within a course to holding out the possibility that students within the course may sign up for additional credits and do a special project for that purpose. The difficulties with it are many. They are reminiscent of the expectation in many institutions that a graduate student enrolling in an undergraduate course will do extra work. The problem is that arranging that extra work is an additional chore for the instructor, who eases out of the task by stating the expectation that the graduate student will do a more thorough job and go deeper into a number of topics without providing formal evidence thereof. Students vary greatly in the amount of time expended in a course and in what they accomplish. The basis for deciding whether a given individual has done everything required for an A and done sufficient beyond that to justify two or three credits more is not easily made specific. Thus the extension of the opportunity of additional credits for independent study in the context of a given course may turn out to be nothing more than granting more credit to those students who do more work. That is an educational principle of merit worthy of attention, but it is an entirely different principle than that under which we now operate. At present, all students get the same credit and the grade indicates differences in the accomplishment.

A fourth special issue with regard to programs and courses is that of attendance. Many professors avoid the issue of whether attendance is required by simply reserving and occasionally utilizing their prerogative of giving unannounced examinations. If permission to make up an examination is restricted to medical excuses, this knowledge should be provided in advance, but any professor who thinks that this specification will solve the problem is naive, both in lack of awareness of professional willingness to oblige a client and the possibility of forgery by the student. Taking attendance and reducing grades for absences seems to me to be completely unjustified and encourages a different type of dishonesty, particularly in large classes where attendance checks are by filled and unfilled seats. The best assurance of attendance is a set of demands imposed upon students by day-to-day work and examinations, making it difficult for them to meet course requirements without reasonably regular attendance. In the case of internships, work-study programs, and the like, attendance takes on another character and can reasonably be specified as an end in itself. Since the learning experience is dependent on the student's presence, a lack of attendance is ample indication that no learning took place.

One other issue deserves brief attention. I have found that, in many departments, courses exist by title and number without any change over many years. One may reasonably ask whether there should not be some indication of how recently a course has been reviewed. There is a consumer responsibility here quite analogous to the selling of canned or packaged goods, many of which include a label indicating that they should be used prior to such and such a date. Courses and programs are also packaged goods and they can deteriorate. There should be some recurring review that ensures that the contents of the package are still digestible and nutritious.

Implications

The views expressed in this chapter are consistent with the general trends toward consumer protection and toward providing such information that the consumer may make some judgments of whether a given commodity meets his or her needs. To apply this in an educational institution requires a degree of care in program and course development and a degree of specificity, alien to higher education, in defining the nature and effect of programs and courses. In the past, higher education courses and programs have been based largely on an authoritarian approach, with the authority residing in faculty members highly specialized in disciplines that have little immediate and direct relevance to life or work. There is currently a move in the country, even in liberal arts colleges, toward giving concerted attention to career development as well as liberal education. I believe that the requirements specified in this chapter constitute a major move in that direction. As professors and their departments have to make evident why courses and programs exist, what students do who enroll in these courses and programs, and what consequences they may expect by that enrollment, the necessity of relating the curriculum to the later life of the individual becomes apparent. And as advisers and students work together in the delineation of student programs, it is inevitable that both will look toward the long-term significance of a program rather than to the immediate course-credit accumulation. Even students who might, in existing circumstances, seek the easy way out in regard to courses may be led to look at their immediate educational experience in a somewhat different way when they relate that to their future prospects.

Suggestions for Further Reading

Cohen, A. *Objectives for College Courses.* Beverly Hills, Calif.: Glencoe Press, 1970.

Council on Education in Geological Sciences. *Audio-Tutorial Instruction: A Strategy for Teaching Introductory College*

Geology. Washington, D.C.: Council on Education in Geological Sciences, 1970.

Dressel, P. L. *College and University Curriculum.* (2nd Ed.) Berkeley, Calif.: McCutchan, 1971.

Levine, A. *Handbook on Undergraduate Curriculum.* San Francisco: Jossey-Bass, 1978.

Stark, J. S., and Marchese, T. J. "Auditing College Publications for Prospective Students." *Journal of Higher Education,* 1978, *49* (1), 82-92.

9

Role of Evaluation

In the context of this volume, this chapter might more appropriately be entitled "Evaluation of Curriculums, Courses, and Programs." I have instead used the one word *evaluation* because evaluation is such a complex and comprehensive task that, done well in any of its aspects, it inevitably has beneficial consequences well beyond the immediate focus. My view is that the evaluation of teaching, of courses, of programs, and even of the performance of individual students form an interrelated complex such that evaluation in any one of its aspects interacts with and, in part, determines the nature of the results found in any other aspect. Evaluation at any level and in any form in an educational institution should be an incentive to learning. That incentive may be directed to the student or to the teacher. I start from the premise that no task is as effectively done as it might be, and that no educational program and no teaching can be as effective as they would be if conscious attention were given to review, criticism, and improvement. And I would apply this equally to teachers and students. Students who are asked to participate in the evaluation of a program, as well as of its individual courses or teachers, by that very act of evaluation gain insight into the significance and sequence of a program that they would not otherwise achieve. At the same time, the insights contributed by the students help the teacher to learn something more about the art and science of program and course development. Unless continuing constructive evaluation is evident in some form, both teaching and learning degenerate to rote patterns that hardly justify the designation of education. Immediately intertwined with the concept of evaluation as an incentive for learning is the development of capacity for self-evaluation—again on the part of both the teacher and the student. My major objection to much of teacher evaluation done through use of checklists filled out by students is that these checklists reflect a very inadequate conception of learning and teaching, and there is seldom any constructive use of the results. That is probably fortunate. Basically, the central objective of higher education is to develop the capacity of individuals to make a judgment. This includes self-evaluation, as well as the evaluation of others. Evaluation of teaching should promote improved self-evaluation on the part of the teacher. A procedure used with students to permit evaluation of a course or teacher should first be introduced to evaluate both the educational processes and the teacher's use of them.

If evaluation is regarded as an incentive to learning and a means of developing the capacity for self-evaluation in both the student and teacher, then it becomes evident that it should lead to improvement of teaching and also of courses and programs. Teaching, after all, is directed toward student learning, and the course and the program are structures within which teaching and learning take place.

Evaluation also provides the means for certification of progress. This refers not only to grades given to the student or comprehensive examinations at some stage of progress but also to evidence provided within the institution itself and to accrediting agencies that the institution and its programs are under regular review and that every effort is being made to improve the program. Evaluation is not just something done to students or faculty for the sake of reward or retribution; it is something that must be done with and for them, for the very process itself is educational and beneficial. Furthermore, the patterns of evaluation used should provide attractive and useful models for both teachers and students so that evaluation becomes part of their life-styles. This does not imply that in the ideal situation when everyone would be self-evaluative there would be no need for external evaluation. There remain problems of bias, subjectivity, self-interest, and accountability. But evaluation that is always and solely done to judge people and their efforts is never very effectively carried out for either reward or punishment. Seldom, if ever, is it effective in bringing about improvement. The evidence in attempting to evaluate major national social programs involving millions of dollars is that external evaluation of a program that is anything less than completely eulogistic usually results in driving out the evaluator rather than changing or curtailing the program.

Evaluation of Student Performance

Perhaps the first purpose served by careful evaluation of student performance is the clarification of objectives. This clarification is not solely on the part of the students. Inability on the part of a teacher to evaluate an objective usually means that the objective itself is unclear and probably ignored. For example, if one considers the differences between knowledge of a definition or a principle and the understanding of that definition or principle, the distinction becomes clear only when one recognizes that rote knowledge of a definition can be achieved without any understanding. A depth of understanding is revealed by the ability to state the principle or definition in other words, by pointing to a specific example, or by applying the definition or principle to a new situation. Neither students nor teachers are likely to understand fully any objective until a number of concrete tasks involving that objective have been carried out.

A second reason for evaluating student performance is to provide feedback for indication of progress or lack of it. Either progress or the lack of it is further elaborated and clarified by diagnostic information explaining a performance. This should lead to insights that may improve future performance. Students often confuse familiarity with an idea or process with mastery. Only when faced with the necessity of executing a particular task do they become aware that there are aspects of it that they do not understand because of lack of practice with the task.

A third reason for evaluating student performance is to provide personal satisfaction and motivation. All too frequently, the conduct of evaluation activity emphasizes inadequacies and weaknesses and arouses antagonism and defensive mechanisms. Only if evaluation provides some sense of personal satisfaction and some expectation and assurance that improvement is possible is an individual likely to be motivated toward improvement. I have always insisted that there be something positive about an evaluation, even if one is driven to the extreme of commenting "nice use of the word *and*" in regard to a theme or response to an essay question.

A fourth reason for evaluation of student performance is to provide in-course feedback to a teacher and in-program feedback to those who are responsible for the program. Unsatisfactory student performance may be a result of a number of things or the interaction of them. It may be poor planning of a program or course, or poor teaching, or poor materials. Conceivably, it might be a totally unsatisfactory environment. Only as there is feedback to program planners and course teachers on group and individual performance, and on the nature and reasons for variations in this performance, is it possible to determine whether a course or program is effective and to what extent teaching or student effort is a major factor.

A fifth reason for evaluating student performance is to make both teacher and student cognitive of the fact that there are multiple objectives and outcomes for a course or program. Not everyone who takes a math course expects to become a mathematician. And there may even be, once in a long time, a would-be artist who takes some mathematics for insight into the characteristics of curves and surfaces in two and three dimensions. There is an intimate interrelationship between the tests that are given in a course and the grades given to students, on the one hand, and the effort expended and results obtained, on the other. The content of a final examination, coupled with the grades given to those examinations by an instructor, constitute probably the best evidence both as to the objectives of the course and the quality of it.

A sixth reason for evaluation of student performance on a regular basis is to emphasize and clarify the difference between outcomes considered as essential for achievement of credit and those regarded as important and desirable but not subject to grading in the usual manner. Whether one likes or dislikes mathematics after taking a course in it should not enter into the grade given to the student, but evidence that almost all students dislike mathematics after having had a course from a particular teacher should be regarded as highly significant with regard to the course, the teacher, or both. Affective outcomes are important in education. The teacher who believes himself or herself to be offering a value-free course, whether in mathematics or in religion, does not understand values and their pervasive involvement in all human experience. Equally, the individual who would throw out evaluation of students on the basis that each student must determine his or her own objectives and his or her own accomplishments with regard to them deceives both the students and society. He deceives the students by permitting them to assume that they have accomplished something that they have not, and he deceives society by permitting individuals to receive unearned credits and degrees. Recognizing the importance of affective outcomes in all facets of education, one must also recognize that there are cognitive outcomes and skills that can be evaluated in a reasonably objective format, and it should be regarded as the responsibility of the teacher to do so.

The orientation in evaluation is a matter of great importance with regard to the quality of the education that takes place. Much of education, especially in the humanities, has been past oriented. The student studies the accumulated heritage and the reactions and appraisals of other individuals of that heritage. I am reminded of a doctoral dissertation with the title "Twentieth-Century Commentaries on Nineteenth-Century Commentaries on Eighteenth-Century Commentaries on _____ ." The blank referred to a document written in the seventeenth century. Education is a process not only of becoming acquainted with great ideas but also of learning how *others* have appraised those ideas. In that emphasis, it is quite likely that students develop no capacity for self-judgment and may even endanger their grades if they attempt to do so. In the cumulative fields, such as the natural sciences and mathematics, there is much more tendency to orient evaluation to the present. Even in these areas, evaluation often focuses on what the student has just covered in a course and primarily on whether he or she knows, recalls facts, or is able to solve problems of the type dealt with in the course. Present-oriented evaluation is still deficient because learning becomes significant only if it is grasped in such manner that it can be used in the future. Students need to be faced on occasion with tasks or problems that have not been dealt with in class. They need to learn that they can organize their thoughts and apply their knowledge in such a way as to deal with these tasks. In short, they need to learn how to use knowledge, and they are not likely to do so unless evaluation is, to some extent, oriented in that direction. And from this there emerges one other thought: Individuals who have tried to solve new problems find that this task may take some time and a significant amount of trial and error. Setting new tasks for individuals and then requiring that they be done within a one- or two-hour period is quite simply unreasonable. Comprehensive evaluation oriented to future use of knowledge is not to be assessed in one- or two-hour examinations, whether these are objective, essay, or oral.

Evaluation of Teacher Performance

In Chapter Five, it was noted that there are distinctive conceptions of teaching, varying from the teacher solely as a deliverer of disciplinary content to the teacher perhaps excessively concerned with the development of individual students as persons. These various roles and combinations of them all have a legitimacy and validity in appropriate circumstances. Our difficulty with defining and evaluating teaching grows out of the vastly different emphases that have been given to the teaching task. The major problem, as I see it, is to make teachers aware of the necessity of some preplanning of a course and of each class in relation to the programs of which that course is a part. There should also be a marked degree of sensitivity to the backgrounds and needs of students taking the course. The extremes of bad teaching are found when the teacher goes to each class with a prior commitment to cover a certain amount of content, whether a set number of pages in the textbook or a prepared lecture. In this emphasis, the teacher is so content bound that there is little sensitivity to whether students are learning anything and no variation to take advantage of motivational opportunities. The other extreme is that of a teacher going into a classroom and, in effect, saying, "What would you like to do today?" This is a pattern so purposeless and unstructured that it simply wastes the time of all concerned. The teacher has a professional responsibility to provide a structure within which significant content materials and learning opportunities are brought to the students in such manner as to enable them not only to learn significant ideas but also to grow in a sense of being able to use these in meaningful ways as they deal with issues and problems arising beyond the course.

This professional responsibility is modified by an institutional and social responsibility which requires that the teacher take into account the relationship of any course to the total experience of students and the competencies that they are to achieve through a college education that provides them with the opportunity to live in a way satisfying to themselves and productive in respect to the society that supports higher education. Hence one of the first aspects of evaluation of teacher performance is to assist teachers to discern—through discussion, observation, and checklists or rating scales—how they view the teaching responsibility and what they do to prepare for the task. At the same time, it is important that teachers come to recognize that whatever a priori judgments and plans they may make with regard to a course, ultimately the effectiveness of these must be viewed in light of the impact on students in regard to the educational objectives of the institution. In a sense, this aspect of teacher evaluation aims at leading the teacher to develop a philosophical point of view about what education is, what the responsibilities of a teacher are, and how a teacher can best achieve results within this framework.

Another aspect of evaluation of teacher performance involves looking at the teacher in the classroom and in interaction with students in the office or after class. It takes no professional evaluator to note and report back to a professor that appearing before a class with hair uncombed, straggly beard, unkempt fingernails, remnants of breakfast egg on tie does not promote student respect, and may lead to an undercurrent of exchange among students detrimental to whatever the teacher does. The mathematics teacher who talks to the blackboard, the pedant who stands erect before a podium and reads his speech or makes his remarks in a monotone from an endless set of cards—these may not be bad teachers in respect to student learning, but they could be better. There are repetitive mannerisms in speech, gestures, and body movements that are equally distracting. All professors ought occasionally to have videotapes made of their classroom performance and review it themselves or, even better, with someone who has sat through several of their classes.

The teaching styles discussed in Chapter Five seldom occur in the categorical form discussed there, but since teaching styles are usually matters of imitation and accident rather than the result of careful consideration in relation to the objectives, teachers should, through the eyes of an observer or by self-examination, come to see their teaching activities as others see them and to examine the question of whether this is what they really intend and whether it is effective. The teacher who is troubled by the inattention of students may find, as I have noted in many classrooms myself, that the inattention is a direct result of the inadequacies of the teacher. Thus students, indirectly and directly, provide feedback on a teacher's performance, and the critical and sympathetic observer, over time, can provide even better insights than do the students.

Another aspect of teacher performance that should be reviewed and evaluated is the fairness and validity of the teacher evaluation of student performance through examinations, essays, recitation in the classroom, or other means. An experienced evaluator can readily review examination questions and student answers and determine whether evaluation is emphasizing memorization or stimulating the individual to think and apply knowledge and develop his or her own values. The mere review with the teacher of how an assignment or examination is prepared and how it is reviewed and rated or graded is likely in itself to bring many teachers to a realization that there are aspects of their performance requiring improvement. What they may not have fully realized is that the kind of evaluation imposed upon their students determines the emphases that students place on their preparation and on the objectives that they attain.

Any appraisal of teacher performance ought also to look at the quality and quantity of instructional materials: textbooks, reference books, handouts, and other materials and associated requirements in the course. A review of the syllabus or course outline in connection with the review of instructional materials immediately gives some insight into the mind of the teacher and the basis for planning. Evidence of an overwhelming amount of material suggests that the teacher is more interested in impressing individuals with his or her own scholarship than with making an appropriate selection of materials that can be reasonably covered and understood by the students. The text used in a course, the outline indicating what is covered in that text, and the examination reflecting what the professor expects the student to know will frequently provide insights into the adequacy of the planning for a course.

Another area in which teacher performance should be evaluated is the teacher's knowledge and the use of applications in related fields. In discussions of the adequacies of liberal education in respect to career development, it is often noted that one of the major problems is that teachers in the liberal education areas hew very closely to the disciplinary lines in coverage of material and display both little knowledge and little willingness to go beyond them to interrelate concepts, ideas, and principles to other disciplines or to problems and issues in the world. As was pointed out in Chapter Four, there are places for purely theoretical discussions, but, especially at the undergraduate level, long discursions into theory without some examples indicating the significance and practicality of that theory fail to arouse student motivation and to assist in the process of understanding and retention.

The approach to evaluation of teacher performance suggested in the preceding paragraphs is rather different from that proposed by many professional evaluators, most of whom seem to focus on the use of student ratings. With greater concern for the improvement of teaching, specific materials may be developed so that teacher behavior, assumed to be more motivational and more readily suited to students' learning styles, can be observed.

Evaluation of Courses and Programs

The need for evaluation of the quality of instructional materials in the appraisal of teacher performance makes evident the difficulties involved in separating teaching from course and program structures. There is a kind of mythology about teaching that seems to assume that a really good teacher rises above content, subject matter, and materials and inspires students by presence and flow of ideas. To a considerable extent, this may be true of advanced graduate-level instruction where the professor represents a segment of a discipline in which he is the local authority, and the course that he teaches is at such an advanced level that no other courses or teachers are dependent upon the content or manner in which that course is taught. For much of undergraduate-level teaching, especially the lower division, the content of a course as prescribed by a catalogue statement and other delineatory materials places the teacher within a structure in which he or she is obligated to perform to keep faith with students taking the course and with colleagues who will relate their instruction to what is assumed to have happened in the course.

In a certain sense, the course or program takes precedence over the instructor. The evaluation of the classical curriculum, for example, was implicit and based largely upon the historical considerations and philosophical presuppositions. The content and substance of the classics regarded as the heritage of the Western world was viewed as incontestably valuable in its own right. Its proponents also were convinced that the classical liberal education had practical utility—at least in the professions. Clearly, the teacher in the classical program was not free to do as he or she pleased with a course because that was a vital link in the whole sequence. However, the classical curriculum failed to adapt and maintain utility and relevance and gradually disappeared. Although historical and philosophical validation was still adequate in the minds of a few classicists, an external and more objective evaluation decided that the classical program was inappropriate in modern society.

Another approach to program evaluation starts with a different rationale. Identification of the assumptions, principles, and policies upon which the curriculum is based and validation or rejection of them may be an initial step. The specification of the content of particular courses and justification of it is of concern. The hours and types of field work, clerkships, and internships, as well as traditional courses, may become standards for program evaluation. This approach is through a specification of the process and the experiences as derived from the original rationale, which, in turn, was presumably based upon its anticipated effectiveness in bringing about the desired outcomes. Verification of that effectiveness is a further step.

Liberal arts programs can be evaluated on a process basis. Are the various types of courses prescribed in the catalogue or departmental statements really available? Do students fulfill the various requirements that have been specified? Is there evidence that the students and faculty understand and accept the rationale for the curriculum? Does an understanding of the fundamental nature of the discipline emerge from the program? Do students obtain insights into other disciplines and into current social issues? What behaviors or tasks provide evidence of success? The culminating project is intended to afford evidence on this point, but does it work? Are students in adequate numbers attracted to the program?

Still another approach to evaluation of a program might consider aspects of quality, the currency of offerings, the appropriateness of content of particular courses, bibliography, and instructional techniques and methodology. Faculty preparation in relation to courses taught is another factor. The existence and appropriateness of courses for nonmajors is, in many departments, an issue of importance. This is true especially in science, mathematics, and statistics, which frequently provide essential backgrounds for students in other fields. The adequacy of classrooms, laboratories, and other facilities is an important consideration. Library holdings and their usage require assessment.

In such evaluation, opinions of various groups may be sought. Students and former students may have views worthy of collection and consideration. Faculty members in other disciplines may have opinions about the adequacy and quality of courses offered. Their views too may be communicated to students in various ways and affect student attitudes and performance in courses. The comments or criticisms of external groups, such as employers or accrediting agencies, are relevant. Recommendations or standards suggested by professional societies or committees should be used in reviewing curricular offerings and requirements. Some may be inappropriate, but this is a decision to be reached by deliberation rather than by omission.

The most difficult task in evaluating a program is in determining its impact upon students. To what extent have individuals become aware of the problems of society and internalized values involved in considering the solution of these problems? Have the students seen their education as providing resources for coping with personal, family, and social problems? Breadth and depth should be interrelated in a manner transcending the usual distinction between majors and general education. The evaluation of a program in reference to outcomes requires that the program developers specify what the student is to obtain from the experience and attempt to find out how much progress has been made. Unless program outcomes are defined in terms transcending individual courses, program evaluation and revision by assessment of student performance are hardly possible. Focus on processes and rationale is likely to be more productive. Program evaluation is sorely needed if unity and sequence are to be restored to the undergraduate curriculum. The lack of effort in this regard is a composite result of the altogether natural professorial preoccupation with courses, the lack of clear objectives transcending courses, and a consequent lack of sequence and cumulative character in disparate courses. The effort, costs, and changes in view required also tend to discourage comprehensive curricular and program evaluation. It is, therefore, not surprising that administrators rather than faculty initiate such activity.

If one takes the view that a program and the specific courses in it exist apart from the individuals assigned to teach the courses or administer the program at any given time, then one step that would materially improve program evaluation would be to insist that each teacher report on experiences in teaching a course and on the seeming relationship of that course to the program. To accomplish this, the teacher, at the close of a given term, would be asked to file immediately a report commenting on the adequacy of the text, the course syllabus, and associated materials and to make suggestions with regard to the improvement of these in the future. This set of comments is appropriate even if the teacher is the person who was primarily responsible for the course syllabus and selection of the text and materials; but there may be others involved in teaching of the course, and the decisions may have been made at some point in the past by others than those currently involved. Frequently, no such report is made, and even the same person teaching the course a year later may not recall and take advantage of specific observations made in the prior year. Commonly, when somebody else takes over a course, there is no material available about prior experience.

Another type of evidence that the teacher should provide is the course coverage in relation to the time and credit given for the course. Course outlines and syllabuses frequently are much too optimistic in coverage, in respect to both time and credits, and they may be based upon a term in which the number of class sessions exceeded what is currently available. Just after reading the final examinations, the teacher should be able to make realistic commentary on this problem.

Another area of comment by the instructor should be the

adequacy of student preparation. The assumptions made in developing a course are not always met when individuals enroll in the course. Hence there may be a problem of adjusting the course to the kinds of students served, or it may be that more careful screening is required to prevent ill-prepared students from entering and to encourage those with superior backgrounds to enroll in something else. Any comment on this point is likely to lead to some discussion of the grade distribution, for this ought to reflect directly on the match between student interests and ability and the character and difficulty of the course.

Still another point on which comment is appropriate is the placement of the course in the program. The individual just finishing teaching the course may have some tentative conclusions about its relocation in respect to other courses in the program. Perhaps it should be delayed until students have had another course that would provide much better background for understanding the concepts and principles in this course. Perhaps the course is unfortunately placed in a group of courses, all of which are overly demanding on students in that particular quarter. From these comments, the individual making the report should be able to record some suggestions for possible changes in the course, whether for gradual change or for a radical overhaul and perhaps complete replacement. The record for such course commentaries over a period of time would provide much more insight than is usually available at a time when program review is undertaken.

One additional point should be taken into account at the time of this review. The individual ought to engage in some self-evaluation with regard to the course and record any problems or deficiencies faced in teaching it. Obviously, no individual wants to record in detail personal inadequacies, but a retrospective statement on unjustified views, attitudes, and prior experiences that handicapped the individual in teaching this course would be useful to others and might serve also as a guide to the department chairman in making later assignments. Students should be asked to engage in a similar kind of evaluation. In my experience, it seems that students enrolled in a program made up of a group of required courses—undoubtedly organized in sequence on the basis of some faculty considerations—may be entirely unaware of these factors. Even with such prior organization, a course taken at a given moment in time may be so taught that it seems not to lead anywhere and to be unrelated to other courses. Obviously, there are aspects of teacher evaluation and program evaluation that are closely related. Too much emphasis has probably been given to the evaluation of teachers rather than to the evaluation of programs. The latter requires evaluation of the teacher in a specified context.

There are some individuals who feel that students are incompetent to evaluate teachers' programs fully. I agree, but would also note that Aristotle in *Politics* says, "The dinner guest not the cook is the best judge of the feast." To this one might add that a cook might, under some misunderstanding, serve a very excellent meal, but one intended for a very different person than the guest. In this case, the judgment of the guest regarding the quality of the meal would have to be interpreted either as based upon error or a misjudgment by the cook. Whether or not one decides to remodel a course on the basis of student comments depends upon a number of factors. If students respond frankly and honestly, their insights must be taken as valid in some sense, and some consideration of their views is appropriate on the next round. Changes in either process or content may increase insight, improve motivation, and achieve better results.

There should also be, from time to time, departmental review of course and teaching assignments. The department chairman and possibly his or her advisory committee should develop some principles with regard to teaching assignments. The mere desire of an individual to teach a course should not become the basis for assigning it to that instructor. The fact that an individual has done very well in teaching a certain course should not mean that he or she is reassigned year after year, very likely with the result that the quality of teaching diminishes. And even with advanced courses, it is seldom appropriate to let a given individual monopolize the course indefinitely, with the result that in a sabbatical year the course cannot be offered or, if the professor leaves, a hiatus occurs. More information is usually needed to perform this teaching assignment function than is available. That is one reason why the suggestion was made earlier that each teacher provide a complete report at the conclusion of instruction in a particular course.

From time to time, there should be a review of course and programs involving the use of individuals outside of the immediately responsible unit. This may be part of a recurrent review or self-study, such as is described in the following chapter. There is a tendency, once courses go into the catalogue, for them to reappear year after year in much the same form; hence there should be, now and then, a reexaminaion of the rationale of a course and its place in the program. In this process, the course purposes and the specific objectives should be reviewed. The course organization and content and its actual operation should also be considered. Again, unless there is some kind of accumulated record on the experiences of individuals teaching the course and of the students taking it, the significant issues will probably not be raised. It is indeed because of this lack of accumulating evidence that the assumption seems generally to be made that the departmental curriculum and courses do not require an in-depth review. As the next chapter indicates, there are many sources of data that should be organized and brought to bear in such a review process.

Summary

In this chapter, the multiple purposes of evaluation have been discussed, ranging from an incentive to learning for the student to the improvement of teaching and of the courses and programs for the sponsoring unit. The evaluation of student performance, of teacher performance, and of courses and programs have been shown to be interrelated activities that have significance at points in time. These evaluations should also be accumulated over time to achieve their most meaningful effect on program improvement. There are other aspects of evaluation that are important in a department or college. Careful program evaluation will inevitably raise questions about the unit's approach to program development and administration. The evaluation of teaching quite naturally raises questions about an individual's background and preparation, and these issues result in at least the recognition that there are other aspects of the faculty members and of a departmental performance that require evaluation. Performance in research, public service, or other functions may have highly significant and either good or bad effects upon instruction and curriculum, depending upon the attitudes of faculty and on administrative policies and practices in recognition and reward.

Suggestions for Further Reading

Anderson, S. B., and Ball, S. *The Profession and Practice of Program Evaluation*. San Francisco: Jossey-Bass, 1978.

Bowen, H. R. *Investment in Learning: The Individual and Social Value of American Higher Education*. San Francisco: Jossey-Bass, 1977.

Bruner, J. S. *Toward a Theory of Instruction*. Cambridge, Mass.: Belknap Press, Harvard University Press, 1966.

Commission on Science Education. *An Evaluation Model and Its Application*. Washington, D.C.: American Association for the Advancement of Science, 1965.

Council of Graduate Schools in the United States. *Assessment of Quality in Graduate Education: Summary of a Multidimensional Approach*. Washington, D.C.: Council of Graduate Schools in the United States, 1976.

Dressel, P. L., and Mayhew, L. B. *General Education: Explorations in Evaluation*. Washington, D.C.: American Council on Education, 1954.

Eble, K. E. *The Recognition and Evaluation of Teaching*. Project to Improve College Teaching and the Committee on Evaluation. Washington, D.C.: American Association of University Professors and Association of American Colleges, 1971.

 10

Purposes and Criteria of Program Reviews

~~~~ In my observation of program review in the many colleges and universities over a number of years, I have found it to be both erratic and perfunctory. Core requirements, interdisciplinary offerings, and other curricular issues transcending the departmental structure come in for sporadic review as administrators and curriculum committees change. But the basic programs provided by the departments and professional schools are subjected only to minor tinkering unless enrollment problems, costs, complaints from students or outside sources, or an accrediting review raise enough issues and generate enough pressure that a program or perhaps the total curriculum offering of a department or college is scrutinized. Occasionally, professional society committees viewing requirements for undergraduate majors or for the graduate school recommend reconsideration of a course or the addition of a few more. Reviews initiated

214 Improving Degree Programs

under these several circumstances may be productive, but it is also possible that departmental resentment engendered by the pressures may simply lead to defense of the status quo or to limited changes made more to meet the criticism than to innovate and strengthen the curriculum.

There are a number of alternative patterns for program review, almost any one of which is likely to be more productive than forced reaction under stress. Some universities have a policy of a recurrent or rolling review of each academic unit at specified intervals of time. Such a schedule ensures that each academic unit comes under detailed scrutiny at reasonable intervals and that, at each of these intervals, the total program and operation of a unit is reviewed by the unit itself, by others within the university, and possibly by an external evaluator. Faculty, instructional quality, enrollments, and costs also should be reviewed. Unless these additional factors are included, curriculum review alone may be done quite superficially. Internal and external criticism of courses and programs may reflect as much on faculty or instruction as on curriculum. For this reason, the total responsibility for the review cannot be left solely to the unit.

Certain aspects of program review involve concepts or concerns that cut across several programs and require the collaboration and integrated effort of two or more departments. The major portion of the instruction provided in many departments is of service nature to other departments and colleges. Maintaining an appropriate balance between the heavily disciplinary orientation of the department and the practical or applied concerns of the departments or schools served is usually a matter of continual concern, rising at times to critical levels because of lack of communication or conflicts in personalities. Review of the programs in a liberal arts college requires comprehensive involvement, for a liberal education transcends majors. There are also some common factors in any concern about undergraduate career preparation in relation to liberal education. There are undoubtedly a number of steps that apply equally well in all disciplines: definition of liberal education outcomes, statement of disciplinary competencies, and career implications of the disciplines, among others. Such considerations as these probably should have a significant place in any departmental curriculum review, but a complete institutional curricular and program review involving these factors is more likely to be followed up by detailed analysis of them at the departmental level. Another possibility in program review is to include it in an annual review and evaluation in relation to budget requests both for the immediate upcoming year and the subsequent four or five years. This combination is appropriate but tends to limit the scope and intensity of the review. The problem is that time and the multiplicity of pressures concerned with salaries, operating budgets, new program requests, and other such factors almost certainly make it impossible to combine budgetary processes with critical and detailed curriculum review. A second weakness of this combined approach is that curriculum matters have traditionally proceeded through an entirely different hierarchy of committees than does the budget. Thus individuals involved in budget formulation may not be as sensitive to or knowledgeable about curriculum matters. The budget review process tends to be focused on the particular unit reviewed at the moment, whereas many curricular problems require attention to issues that transcend departments and other curricular units. Finally, to the extent that curricular considerations do come into the budget review process, it is likely that they will involve primarily such matters as teaching load and costs, such as faculty size, unnecessary course offerings, class size, use of independent study, or other practices that make heavy demands on the faculty.

Purposes of Program Review

Perhaps the major reason why the curriculum and programs in academic units are not regularly reviewed is because of faculty specialization and the limited point of view taken with regard to course offerings and program specifications. Most courses and programs are developed on the basis of faculty expertise in the particular discipline or area. For many programs, there are recommendations or (in the case of professionally accredited programs) specifications which are rigorously followed in setting up and maintaining them. With regard to courses, there exists in most academic units an extensive range of faculty experience in other colleges and universities that is reflected in course organizations, titles, credits, and sequence of a program. The further assumption is made that since the faculty members involved in teaching these courses can, within the very general framework provided by a course title and brief statement of content, adjust courses to changing circumstance, there is little need for time-consuming review. There has not been, in the past, any widespread concern that program statements and course specifications communicate to students, other academic units, or the public the details about how a course operates, what it covers, and what it requires of students. The specification of the contents has usually been sketchy because of the assumption that so long as the specified content is covered, the instructor may pursue teaching responsibilities in whatever manner he or she finds most satisfying and convenient.

In fact, there are a number of different and distinctive criteria and associated purposes in curriculum review. One, and perhaps the foremost in the minds of the faculty, is the quality of the program or course. But quality has often been gauged indirectly by the quality of the text, the bibliography, the stature of the professor, relevant library holdings, or the ability of the students enrolled in the course. These are not irrelevant, but the quality of a course ought to be judged in relationship to such criteria as the currency of the ideas and materials upon which the course is based, the appropriateness of the objectives in respect to student learning, and the experiences of the students in promoting the attainment of the objectives, the completeness and accuracy of program statements and materials, and, above all, the evidence as to the actual accomplishment of students completing the course or program. There are other criteria. One obvious one is the need for the program or course. In one sense, the existence of the program can be reviewed in connection with its continuing consistency with the university mission and the adherence of the academic unit to its assigned role.

Need can also be examined in terms of student demand, enrollment, and degree recipients. The existence of a program (especially a graduate program) is often an indication of faculty or departmental need or reputation or ego satisfaction. The demand for or the existence of a professional school may reflect institutional ego rather than real need. And some programs are little more than a commitment that no university can be a really good institution unless it offers, for example, the classics.

Another criterion in review is that of program or course costs. There is general recognition that some programs, particularly those in the health sciences, are expensive, but there has been a tendency to ignore the fact that the proliferation of courses in an institution or a department tends to lower the average class size and increase the instructional burden on the faculty or necessitate an expansion in the teaching staff. Class size is certainly a factor in costs. It may be a factor in educational quality, although that is uncertain. What is certain is that course proliferation reduces class size and raises costs. The offering of a large number of one- and two-credit courses increases the burden on both students and faculty, complicates the use of space, and generally detracts from program quality by breaking student experience up into an unnecessarily large number of discrete segments. The number of contact hours required in a course in relation to the credit frequently (especially in the case of laboratory and fieldwork programs) involves an unnecessary, even unreasonable, number of contact hours, thereby again adding to costs. Repetition of courses in each term tends to lower the enrollment at each offering, raise costs, and possibly reduce quality simply because a teacher, repetitively teaching the same course, may become bored with it. Duplication and overlap in courses from one department to another or even within a single department may weaken the quality of student programs by permitting a few students to get double credit for the same material, but it also raises overall costs of education by dividing the basic group of students seeking contact with certain materials into smaller and more homogeneous subgroups than may be necessary or justifiable. The major expenditure in instructional units is the salaries of teaching faculty. The number of faculty members depends on how the curriculum is organized and administered. Thus one of the major purposes of recurrent program review is to ensure that colleges and departments recognize that management of the curriculum is essential to effective management of the budget. The management of the curriculum also involves considering regularly the interrelationships and possibly changing relationships with other programs and program units. The essential point is that a departmental course or program is not solely the property of that unit, to be offered in any manner it prefers. Sound management of the instructional budget does not permit complete departmental autonomy on curricular planning and operation. Furthermore, so many of the offerings in program units are, or should be, useful to students and faculty in other units that institutional cognizance of courses and program operations and requirements is essential.

There is one further aspect of program review that is deserving of attention, although it is, in many respects, incidental to the process. Many institutions generate, either by intent or because of their recognized stature, significant amounts of alumni and public reaction to curriculum review and change. Harvard, for example, within my own tour of duty in higher education, has generated two reports on liberal and general education, each of which has very likely had more impact on the public and on other institutions of higher education than on Harvard. Frequently, the publicity handouts on new programs (regardless of institutional source) are naive. Anyone who knows anything about higher education and its history in the United States can only be amused at a publicity statement emanating from a college announcing, with great fanfare, such items as a new statement of distribution requirements, individually designed majors, or the possibility that an individual might qualify for a degree without ever enrolling in a course. I do not object to publicity about program changes, but much of it is premature, and those changes that achieve the most publicity are frequently superficial and lend themselves to misrepresentation. The more profound and continuing program review and revision can be interpreted to alumni who have some association with the institution, but it is not likely to attract much attention in the public press.

Content of Reviews

Program Review. In Chapter Eight, the information needed on courses and programs for various purposes was presented in some detail. Any program review should take into account those factors. But it is also likely that any review of a program will need to follow a more orderly procedure in order to take all aspects into account. Table 3 shows one way to look

Table 3. Program Planning, Operation, and Evaluation

	A *Planning*	*B* *Operation*	*C* *Evaluation*
1. Assigned role	accepted rejected or qualified ignored	Is the program operation, includ- ing the processes used, consistent with plans? If not, why altered?	Evaluation ap- plies to both A and B (1 - 7) and should consider balance of costs and benefits.
2. Institutional goals	consistency with role clarity		
3. Program objectives	consistency with 1 and 2 clear, mutually con- sistent, and com- plete	Are operations effective in pro- ducing desired outcomes?	intended unanticipated a) desirable b) undesir- able
4. Program structure	relation to objectives relation to processes		
5. Processes	relation to 3 and 4		
6. Program unity and sequence	criteria for unity and sequence		
7. Outcome appraisal	intervals methods		

at a program by reviewing the stages involved from planning through evaluation. Column A, Planning, indicates, at the first level, that the assigned mission and role of an institution has been accepted, rejected or qualified, or ignored in the process of setting up the program. The second level in this column deals with the consistency and clarity of institutional goals. Thus Column A and the subsequent levels, three through six, make explicit the need to attend to each of the items on the left. The seventh item, outcome appraisal, requires a statement of the levels at which outcomes are to be appraised and the methods used. Column B, Operation, reflects back to the initial list and to Column A. It calls for a review of the consistency of the operation and processes with the intent. Column B also directs attention to the program effectiveness thereby pointing to Column C and the need for evaluation. Concern for the effectiveness of the operations moves the analytical sequence to Figure 3 in Chapter Six, which depicts the various steps and checkpoints in the development of a new course or program. Column C, evaluation, applies to each point of the initial list, to their interrelationships, and to the planning and operational phases. The concerns in evaluation are with quality and with the balance between costs and benefits. All program outcomes should be identified and a distinction made between those intended and those unanticipated. The latter may be either desirable or undesirable.

Table 4 (actually an outline developed in the context of

Table 4. Program Definition or Characterization

1. Degree description, specification, and disciplines or fields of specialization.
   1.1 Degree
       Examples: Ph.D. in history, urban history, chemistry
                  Ed.D. in curriculum, science education
   1.2 Program purposes, objectives, and career prospects
2. Relation to other degrees.
   2.1 Why is this degree designation (Ph.D., Ed.D., D.A., and so on) proposed?
   2.2 Upon what degree attainment is this program based? Baccalaureate, Master's, Educational Specialist?
       What majors or specialties in these lower-level degrees are acceptable?
   2.3 To what advanced degree program might this degree lead?
3. What specific criteria or examinations and standards are imposed at various levels?
   3.1 Admission and acceptance of transfer credits
   3.2 Qualifying examinations
   3.3 Comprehensive examinations
   3.4 Residence requirement
   3.5 Dissertation, thesis, research project, or other product appropriate to the degree
   3.6 Final oral presentation or defense of dissertation
4. Specific scholarly or research skills.
   4.1 Foreign languages

Table 4 *(Continued)*

  4.2 Statistics or mathematics
  4.3 Computer programming
5. Curriculum.
  5.1 Courses that may be required to make up deficiencies
  5.2 Display of all courses available in this program
  5.3 Core requirements and credits required of all students in the program
  5.4 Alternative specialties
  5.5 Cognates or minors in other fields or disciplines
  5.6 Electives
  5.7 Research seminars
  5.8 Field experiences, internships, practicums
6. Dissertation, thesis, or other culminating product.
  6.1 Point in program at which student is encouraged to develop proposal
  6.2 Procedure for defining and approving proposal
  6.3 Composition of group and procedures in giving final approval
  6.4 Publication requirements
7. Exhibit of several complete programs typical of what might be expected for persons completing the program.

---

reviewing graduate programs) exemplifies another way to consider the definition of a program and the characterization of its teachers and operations. Reflection on this outline will indicate that, as its title suggests, it is primarily devised to attain a complete definition of the program or characterization of the program in terms of all of its features. With this detailed characterization in hand, one can make comparisons with other programs in the same institution or in other institutions in the same region. It is possible to look at the actual products of the program —that is, the students, their dissertations, jobs, and other outcomes—to determine whether the program is effectively achieving the purposes for which it was introduced. It is also possible to consider in detail the steps and processes involved in the program to determine whether what is said and intended about the program's operation really is carried out in practice.

Course Review. In some respects, course review is more difficult than program review. It is generally accepted that a degree program exists for some purposes and that there must be a rationale relating the various aspects of the program to criteria for appraising whether the program is effective. In a certain sense, program review is of less immediate concern to individual faculty members and less threatening to them because they are much more concerned with their own immediate teaching chores and courses than with the composite program made up of courses taught by many different individuals. There is also a tendency to see the course as a significant end in itself. It covers a segment of a discipline or some significant subject matter that is worthy of study in its own right, apart from whatever contribution it may make to a degree program. When individual courses are subjected to a detailed review, both the judgments of those who developed and approved the course in the first place and the judgments and practices of those who presently offer the course are put under review.

Table 5, an outline for course analysis, indicates the range

Table 5. Outline for Course Analysis

1. Identifying and descriptive information.
   1.1 Catalogue course description, including:
       1.11 Departmental or generic title and number
       1.12 Descriptive title
       1.13 Prerequisites
       1.14 Terms offered
       1.15 Credits so presented as to identify hours and type of instruction provided (lecture, discussion, laboratory, independent study)
       1.16 Statement of objectives, content coverage, and students to whom directed
   1.2 Outline or syllabus, including:
       1.21 Detailed statement of objectives
       1.22 Test and other materials to be used
       1.23 Day-by-day or week-by-week indication of topics covered, types and amounts of work expected of students, standards to be met, and methods of evaluation to be used
       1.24 Bibliography
2. Analytical information.
   2.1 Instructional model: credits, hours and types of instruction

Type of session	Preferred class size	Staff required[a]	No. of hours per week	No. of credits
Lecture				
Recitation or discussion				
Laboratory				
Fieldwork				
Independent study				

Table 5 *(Continued)*

2.2 Special or additional resources and personnel required

    2.21 Special facilities (classrooms, auditoriums, laboratories, and so on)[b]

    2.22 Library and other learning resources required (books, films, slides, prints, and so on). List with indication of whether the items are here available, can be ordered, or must be made.[b]

    2.23 Special staff competencies required

        2.231 Number of persons now on staff qualified to teach course

        2.232 New staff requirements and individual competencies needed (project for at least two years)

2.3 Relation to other courses

    2.31 Offered by the department

        2.311 Course or courses replaced by this course

        2.312 Prerequisite courses

        2.313 Courses for which this course is a prerequisite

        2.314 Courses covering some of the same content

            2.3141 Safeguards against acquiring of duplicate credits by students

    2.32 Offered by other departments

        2.321 Courses in which enrollment may be reduced by the selection of this course

        2.322 Prerequisite courses

        2.323 Courses for which this course is a prerequisite

        2.324 Courses covering some of the same content

            2.3241 Extent and nature of relationships

            2.3242 Distinctive factors justifying existence of this course

            2.3243 Safeguards against acquiring of duplicate credits by students

    2.33 Offered by other colleges or universities

        2.331 In the immediate community

        2.332 In the state

2.4 Size and source of enrollment

    2.41 Departmental majors (indicate whether required or elective, number involved)

        2.411 Submajor within department

    2.42 Majors in other departments, curricula, or colleges (indicate for each whether required or elective, number of students involved)

    2.43 Anticipated enrollment in first and second year of offering, in summer, fall, winter, and spring quarters[b]

2.5 Details of instructional planning

	Experiences especially related to objective	Means of evaluation of student achievement
Objectives		
1.		
2.		

(continued on next page)

Table 5 *(Continued)*

	Experiences especially related to objective	Means of evaluation of student achievement
3.		
4.		
5.		
6.		
7.		

2.6 Estimated new funds required by addition of this course:[b]
    Salaries
    Supplies and services
    Equipment
    Remodeling
3. Historical information (for courses under review).
    3.1 Enrollment during the previous two years

	19 ___	19 ___
Summer		
Fall		
Winter		
Spring		

    3.2 Sources of enrollment previous year

	Fr.	Soph.	Jr.	Sr.	M.A.	Ph.D.
Majors (departmental)						
Students from Department or College A						
Students from Department or College B						
and so on						

    3.3 Section size for the past year

	Smallest section	Mean	Largest section
Lecture			
Recitation or discussion			
Laboratory			

    3.4 Number (head count) of senior staff involved in past year _____
        Full-time equivalent _____
        Number (head count) of junior staff involved in past year _____
        Full-time equivalent _____
    3.5 Instructional salary cost per student credit hour

[a]Indicate separately the number of senior staff (instructor or above) and junior staff (graduate assistants, assistant instructors) required.

[b]New courses especially.

Source: Paul L. Dressel, F. Craig Johnson, and Philip M. Marcus, *The Confidence Crisis: An Analysis of University Departments* (San Francisco: Jossey-Bass, 1970), pp. 179-182.

of information involved in the review of a course and provides substantive information about course content and mode of operation as well as detailed statistics on the number and types of students involved. Thus this information is both current and historical. Some parts of it can be provided by the immediate department in which the course is based, especially if the recommendation made in Chapter Nine regarding an instructor's report at the close of a course is followed. But some parts of this information must come from registrar's records or from a computerized information data bank maintained on the curriculum and regularly updated. Analyses of the relationship between courses in one department and related ones in other departments can be provided only if the type of detailed information on a course suggested in Chapter Eight is regularly collected, updated, and computerized for ready access. If the curriculum is to be managed effectively, such data must be available; and they must be collected with a view to using the data and review process to make some decisions. Decision making is really the subject of the next chapter, but, in order to provide a basis for summarizing the content of the review process, it is appropriate to emphasize here that there is no point in accumulating large amounts of data on the curriculum and engaging in recurrent reviews unless there is a definite intent that this investment will lead to decisions about the curriculum and the departments and individuals involved in offering it.

Criteria for Decisions. Perhaps the three major concerns in the review of courses and programs, viewed from the dimension of quality, costs, and other factors discussed earlier, are those of (1) quality and currency, (2) need and enrollment, and (3) number of specialties represented. Depending on the way in which these factors are related, a decision might be made to expand the program, adding some new specialties or new dimensions not now covered, and perhaps expanding the enrollment. Another possibility might be to eliminate the program because of low enrollment and no authoritative demonstration of need. A third possible decision is the combination of several subspecialties into a single program, or the combination of two or three closely related programs based in different units in the institution. Such combinations eliminate some specialization, but, by placing more emphasis on broad conceptualization and on the development of skills and knowledge of principles and concepts, they open a wider range of career prospects to the graduate. A fourth possible decision is to revise the program in major respects, a decision that might involve some aspects of all of the previous three: expansion, partial elimination, or combination. In weighing these prospective decisions, it is important to have them in mind from the beginning and to consider the nature of the evidence and procedures required to justify a decision. Viewed in reference to the ultimate concern for reaching a decision, the review process can be described in somewhat more orderly and detailed fashion.

The Review Process

A natural question is: What is the first step in starting the review process? The opening paragraphs in this chapter raised the issue of alternative schedules for review. Some such schedule agreed upon in advance is an essential step in beginning the review process in any unit. If there is no policy on this matter and no scheduled time for review, the mere suggestion that a particular unit undergo a review of any aspects of its operation generates concern, alarm, and rebuttal. And if there is no accumulated background of data on a program, such as has been discussed in this and preceding chapters, the tendency on the part of those threatened by a review is to assert that there is nothing wrong with the program. They are satisfied with it, and they know it is operating well. If there is still an insistent demand that the review go on, there will then be a significant period of discussion and argument as to the essential data required. Each decision on this matter will become a point of great significance with this particular unit because of the fear that the data have been suggested primarily with the expectation that they will demonstrate that something is wrong in that unit. In such circumstances, it seems obvious that the first step is a clearly defined and recurrent review procedure, backed by a regular cumulative collection of data uniform across the institution and immediately available at the time the review is imminent. The range of data suggested should be adequate to determine almost immediately the existence of serious problems in the program and course offerings of a department. If nothing serious is suggested, then the immediate reaction of heavily pressed administrators and of a department desirous of avoiding the review is quickly to reach an agreement that the review can be waived. This, I think, is not an appropriate practice. Once the matter of waiving reviews becomes a possibility, the expectation on the part of even those units most badly needing such a review may well be that, at their request and evidence of their satisfaction, the review can be waived. If a review is called for at a certain time, the organizational pattern for conducting that review should be brought into operation and a task force or committee (or whatever other designation is used) should be brought into being. It is important that the organization and the personnel not be solely departmental or even solely from the college or school in which that department is based. Central academic administration should be involved, and a number of academic units drawing upon or having some common concerns with the unit under scrutiny should be included. The selection and appointment of outside consultants can be delayed, especially in those cases where there seems to be nothing serious in the way of program or of malfunctioning in the department. Once this group is formed, it can proceed to look at the data, discuss the unit and its programs, and call for any comments from students or faculty across the institution. If everything is commendatory, rather than simply bringing the study to an end and so reporting, the group should turn its attention to how the department operates and what persons deserve commendation and what practices justify dissemination in the institution. The advantages in this procedure are:

1. The policy of curriculum review is maintained intact.
2. There is a definite record that a review was made and recommendations reached.

3. The review process will come to be viewed as one that may yield commendation and possible reward as well as decisions considered negative or undesirable by the unit involved.
4. The recurrent review process may, despite surface indication of harmony and perfection, turn out to raise serious difficulties not yet apparent at the operational level. Some possibilities are a significant minority within a department that proposes to change departmental emphases and programs, a well-entrenched control by a dominant and prestigious minority, and an accumulated but as yet unexpressed dissatisfaction in certain segments of the campus because of a department's unwillingness to accommodate to their requests.
5. Regular conduct of a recurrent review admits the possibility of involving a larger segment of any unit and of related units over time, possibly leading to opening up new lines of thought and a different view of operations than when the views are sporadic and conducted largely by the power group.

Summary

In the preceding remarks, a number of suggestions have been made about tactics and strategy and politics. The importance of continuing recurrent reviews on schedule has been emphasized as a clear indication that all units are being treated in the same manner. The singling out of a unit for review will not, then, become a cause for confrontation. Another factor is that there should be a recognition of a number of alternatives as outcomes of any review. The suspicion that a particular outcome or action is sought in initiating review is one of the more irritating aspects of the unscheduled review process. The involvement not only of individuals within the department but also of those from other units and from central administration makes evident that no unit operates solely for its own benefit. The involvement of students in the review process is an effective way of demonstrating to them that the faculty is indeed concerned about their welfare and their views. It is also a good public relations tactic. I have doubts about the effectiveness of undergraduates as committee members in a review process, but I believe that extensive interviewing of students and open hearings at which they are free to express themselves are desirable. Although few alumni are sufficiently aware of current operations on a campus to offer any advice in detail, informing them about reviews and providing some opportunity for their comments on significant issues can be a welcome alternative to the more common and more obvious way of assisting the institution by a cash contribution.

Finally, the continuing or recurrent review is an excellent political ploy in that the institution that engages regularly in this process is able to provide information about itself in an honest and forthright manner and is able to demonstrate, in its own management practices, responsibility and accountability. And perhaps most significantly, many curricular decisions that previously have been irrational compromises generated out of long-continuing discussion and argument involving conflicting values and attitudes would be brought into a rational context based upon actual evidence and extensive discussion and reached in the best interests of students and the university as a whole, rather than in terms of the narrow vested interests of particular units.

Suggestions for Further Reading

Axelrod, J., and others. *Search for Relevance: The Campus in Crisis.* San Francisco: Jossey-Bass, 1969.

Babb, L. A., and others. *Education at Amherst Reconsidered.* Amherst: Amherst College Press, 1978.

Cross, K. P. *Accent on Learning: Improving Instruction and Reshaping the Curriculum.* San Francisco: Jossey-Bass, 1976.

Givens, P. R. *Student-Designed Curricula.* Research Currents, ED 061 917. Washington, D.C.: American Association for Higher Education, 1972.

Kaysen, C. (Ed.). *Content and Context: Essays on College Education.* New York: McGraw-Hill, 1973.

Miller, R. I. *The Assessment of College Performance: A Handbook of Techniques and Measures for Institutional Self-Evaluation.* San Francisco: Jossey-Bass, 1979.

 **11**

Collecting Data and Making Decisions

In the preceding chapter, the importance of relating data collection to the various possible decisions to be made was emphasized. This does not imply that every bit of data gathered is to be related to some immediate decision, even though taking no action is also a decision and should be so recognized. Data collected without any intent that it be related to decisions can become an end in itself for a few persons and a source of continuing frustration and irritation for others.

Decisions on Programs

As already noted, the decisions with regard to a program can be any one of the following:

1. Update, extensively revise, or redefine in scope or specific intent. Generally, one would expect that such actions would be taken by those directly involved in the program. This would imply that the decision should be made at that same

level, but the fact is that there are cases in which the necessity of program revision becomes evident only when individuals and agencies outside the sponsoring unit are consulted.

2. Eliminate, severely contract, or reduce the numbers involved in a program. The units immediately involved will seldom initiate a recommendation for elimination of the program, but they may concur in a limitation on the program, especially if this is related to quality.

3. Combine with one or more other programs locally or regionally. In large universities with a number of colleges, it is not unusual to find two or more units operating in much the same area and providing quite similar programs. So long as the several duplicating or overlapping units are well beyond some minimal critical size, their continuing existence may not be a matter of concern, but in times of resource deficiency and/or diminishing enrollment, the combination of two or more closely related programs within the institution may bring about some significant economies by reducing the number of courses and increasing class size. The combination may also result in a stronger and better-based program than any of those replaced. When several similar programs exist, there is a strong possibility that each may be overly specific in nature, in regard both to the careers contemplated and the courses required. Replacing several similar programs by a single one may permit options to be extended to students and bring all of the students in contact with examples from several related fields, thereby increasing the quality of the educational experience and providing greater flexibility in the job market.

A further possibility in combination of programs is to conjoin programs of several institutions in a region. This possibility needs careful investigation because it is sometimes only a face-saving device on the part of those who are attempting to achieve economy by program elimination and combination. The combination of two or more programs based in different institutions and the provision of a joint degree may greatly complicate the life of the student involved because of disjunction in program and in residence and the uncertainty as to who makes the final decision about completion of program requirements. However, the resources of two or three distinct institutions may be nicely combined into a unique educational experience if good will and close interaction exist among all parties concerned. This is different from a combination of several programs for expediency's sake.

In making any one of these decisions, it is necessary to review in detail costs, resources, courses offered, materials, methods, and staff involved, the availability of internships or practicums, and the employment prospects for the graduate. Where there is any possibility that several programs may be combined or the program eliminated or contracted in size, it is desirable that the review initially take into account all of the possible programs that might be involved. A piecemeal approach will almost certainly result in complications in getting cooperation and acquiring comparable data and in dealing with possible faculty backlash and the politics involved. Obviously, the nature of the possible decision has some implications for the level at which a study is launched as well as the level at which the decision may be made. Most decisions dealing with departmental offerings emerge as recommendations from the unit and are processed through one or more committee and administrative levels before a formal decision is made. Yet, in normal circumstances, the department makes the decision because the review at other levels is perfunctory. Anyone who has reviewed programs in depth over time will find that the units involved frequently make significant changes that have never been recognized or acted on at other levels. Program statements do not always determine or validly reflect practice. However, the way in which a particular aspect of a program is viewed depends upon the perceptions and the values of those involved. Departments typically have somewhat different concerns and a rather different viewpoint, influenced heavily by the disciplinary orientation, than do higher levels. Especially in those units where segments of the curriculum are extensively used by other than departmental majors, the colleges—and ultimately the university

—have legitimate concerns. These concerns are much better taken into account when there is a regular recurrent or rolling review of curriculum stimulated from central administration than when such matters are left entirely to the academic units offering courses and programs. When the prospects involve possible elimination of a program or combination with one or more other programs within a state or region, it is appropriate that the system coordinating body initiate the review process and take responsibility for the collection and analysis of data. Indeed, unless the study and review are initiated at that level, the prospects for program elimination or combination are very dim.

Decisions on Courses

The possible decisions regarding a course overlap, to some extent, with the decisions regarding a program, but they also offer some additional possibilities. A course may be eliminated or replaced by something more appropriate. For example, some years ago many engineering schools required a credit course in use of the slide rule. I know of none that does so now, but there has been, in many cases, replacement by a course in the use of computers. Latin was, for many years, required in colleges of medicine and pharmacy. It is still occasionally listed as an elective, but I know of no case where it is required. In some instances, the program discussions have made a case for biomedical statistics as a form of communication more important in the modern day than Latin. Thus programs change over time. Some courses are eliminated or replaced because they are simply nonfunctional. Other courses are terminated because, when a course is no longer required for specific groups, lack of interest may soon eliminate the offering. In some cases, an attempt by a new faculty member to introduce or upgrade a course has resulted in a course of such great difficulty that student failure and negative student reaction have caused it to be discontinued or replaced. It is unfortunate when decisions come about in this traumatic way, for it shows a faculty and administrative lack of sensitivity to a developing crisis and failure to move in time to prevent it. This experience reflects also the unfortunate circumstances that often arise when, after agreeing upon a new course, the program planning committee assigns responsibility to a department or individual without continuing to monitor the development.

As noted in some of the earlier discussions about course offerings, some courses are required in a program; some options exist among a group of courses; and some purely elective choice is possible in many cases. Thus the decisions with regard to a course permit movement from one to another of these possibilities as well as elimination. Latin, once required, became elective, and in many cases was thereafter eliminated. A course open as an elective or possibly as part of an option may become so important, or sufficient pressure may be exerted by concerned faculty members, that the course is promoted to one of the requirements. Such additions made without thorough review of the total program soon lead to unrealistic loads of twenty or more credits per term. In addition to these possibilities, the position of a course in a sequence of courses may be changed. Experience may show that students are inadequately prepared for the course and could perform at a far more satisfactory and higher level if it were postponed until one or more other courses were completed. Another possibility is that a prerequisite will be specified for the course. It is also possible that a particular course which, for one reason or another, might have been taken out of sequence by a number of students, will become recognized as an essential prerequisite for other courses and so designated. Review of a course may indicate that it is desirable to change some aspects of the delivery system: the number of credits, the standards and means of assigning grades, a better qualified teacher, a change in methods, technology, or equivalent. It may be determined that in the nature of a particular course, it should be offered in an independent study pattern or as a clinical experience rather than a traditional course. The cumulative effect of such isolated modifications can destroy program integrity.

One of the most difficult decisions regarding a course— and usually a continually recurring one, because of changes in content and contrasting views of individuals concerned with various parts of a program—is in the desired degree of under-standing of the material covered. Discussions of this are often oversimplified by pointing out that individuals in technical pro-grams learn how to do certain things in a routine way without understanding the theory or research underlying the technique. Presumably, at professional levels, individuals relate theory and practice. In fact, this is not true. The students in medical school learn something about radiology and they learn something about biostatistics. In the first case, they apparently at least learn how to use the results of radiological studies. In the sec-ond case, biostatistics, many students fail to rise even to the level of understanding the concepts, and only a relatively few learn how to use them. Beyond the first level of learning, that of rote knowledge and use, an individual using any technique might, in some circumstances, be expected to know its rationale and be able to prove, derive, or demonstrate the validity of it. This is the second level of learning. At a third level, a person might understand a particular technique or method in such depth and know the various assumptions involved so well that, recognizing a somewhat different situation, he or she would be able to specify the assumptions in this new situation and derive or adapt a formula or procedure for it. In planning and offering courses, there are continuing tensions among faculty and stu-dents as to which of these three levels is involved in the course objectives. Generally, faculty members teaching in the arts and sciences like to think that their students can function at the third level. However, because of the amount of coverage in most courses and the range of background and ability among stu-dents, the usual result is that many students function at only the first or second level. Unfortunately, there is never any cer-tainty that all those below the first level receive failures. Mas-tery, whatever its level, is difficult to define and enforce.

Alternative Triggering Systems

The usual approach to program review is not systematic and tends to be initiated by complaints from sources external to the instrumentalities involved in setting up and managing the curriculum. Students complain but, to a large extent, they complain among themselves. Their complaints are not brought together where their significance can be assessed. And those students who do try to record a legitimate complaint through administrative channels are sometimes ignored or perhaps courteously heard and then forgotten. Faculty members in units other than the responsible one are chary about complaining about their fellow academics, and they seldom do so in any concerted fashion. The concerted reaction is evident occasionally in a college of business or engineering that decides that the mathematics or statistics taught by the department thus designated is inadequate or inappropriate to the needs of the professional program. This extreme action usually comes about only after a lengthy period of heated discussion that brought no change. This type of decision has implications for both costs and quality. At times, the complaints of certain employers or a survey report carried out by the institution will raise doubts about a program or even a specific course. Accreditation reports may focus on weak links in the curriculum. Usually these complaints are taken seriously only when they come from some influential source or when the cumulative impact of complaints generates campuswide or even public concern, compelling some adjustment.

It is unfortunate that we have not developed some early warning system or quality control procedure that makes it possible to keep track of what is happening in courses and programs. I believe that there are indicators of this type, but they are seldom accumulated consistently and reviewed to examine their possible significance. Drops and adds are normal after registration because of the confusions, course discontinuances, and other matters. But a department chairman could readily review the drops in all courses in the department and take note of any course or section in which the number of drops is noticeably greater than in the past. A review of grade distributions from one term to another will often indicate developing problems in that a very high rate of failures or low grades suggests either inadequately prepared students or poor or inappropriate teachers. If student ratings are made on courses and reported to department chairmen or a dean, marked shifts in these from one term to another may be indicative of trouble. Marked changes in enrollment, either increases or decreases, suggest a range of possibilities. The dean who first hears a faculty member suggest that a required course be dropped from the required list will do well to investigate the significance of that comment. It is undoubtedly much easier to operate this type of early warning system in smaller institutions than it is in large ones. My own observation is that the signs are usually there, but they are invisible to many different people who never coordinate their observations to derive a significant level of concern. Thus the periodic review may be much more of a necessity in large institutions than in smaller ones, where much of what is found in the more extensive recurrent review becomes more quickly evident if people are sensitive to the signals.

Data Required for Decisions

In both this and the preceding chapter, the importance of accumulating basic data over time and in a manner that facilitates detection of trends has been repeatedly emphasized. These data serve several purposes. First, they become the basis for the initial stages of the planning and completion of the recurrent review. Second, they sensitize departmental chairmen, faculty members, and others to the fact that various curricular decisions have consequences and that these consequences should be examined at the moment when a decision is contemplated rather than waiting for them to be revealed by the data system. A third purpose is that if one or more individuals regularly review the data in the context of prior data of the same sort, the data system can serve as an early warning system, bringing out certain matters that need action before the next review or that suggest particular foci for that review. Some care should be taken that the data system itself does not get overloaded with details to the point where time for application of it is no longer available. There is a difference between keeping basic information in the system and processing that information into reports examined in detail. A few examples will make the point. Suppose that the college of business is considering the elimination of all

or part of a mathematics requirement. In this situation, administrators and faculty members are not always completely frank
about the rationale for the proposition. One may wish, then, to
determine immediately whether there is evidence of inappropriate teaching assignments to the mathematics course for business students, whether the grade distribution has been unrealistic, or whether students and business faculty have come to the
conclusion that the course is simply irrelevant to the needs of
business students. At some point in the emerging discussion, the
mathematics staff may assert that the quality of students admitted to the business program has been continually decreasing
and that this, rather than the inappropriateness or inadequacy
of the course, is the source of the difficulty. Clearly, the additional data that might resolve these complaints or accusations
would not be needed on a regular basis, but they should be
made available when the issues arise.

In recent years, there have been numerous examples in
universities of graduate committees that encourage students to
take all of their work within the immediate department in order
to maintain credit hour productivity. In a particular instance,
one needs evidence as to whether this practice exists or whether
it is simply a rumor—perhaps an expansion of some comment
made by a dean or a faculty member. If there is evidence that
this is actually happening, then issues of quality, overspecialization, and other basic educational concerns need consideration. As alternative decisions are envisaged, additional data can
be collected for a different diagnosis.

As another example, an instructor or group of instructors
may decide that certain courses are to be offered on a mastery
basis and that all students will have to complete all requirements to an A level. It is relatively easy to determine whether
indeed all students do complete all requirements or whether
many of the students simply fall by the wayside, as is typical in
such programs, and do not complete the requirements. It is also
possible to determine whether the mastery level itself has to be
set so low that, in the process of defining mastery at a level
attainable by all students, the average performance of the group
as a whole is significantly lowered because the best students are
no longer challenged to meet the mastery level.

These examples suggest that, for a wide range of curriculum or program decisions, there are sets of relevant data that can be a priori defined and made available as a background and partial basis for the ultimate decision. The immediate reaction of many faculty members and administrators is to wince at the prospects of maintaining and processing these data. Yet one must weigh against this the actuality that many of the issues regarding programs and courses are heatedly discussed at many different levels over long periods of time and with undocumented assertions from various sources that either a new world or the end of the world will result if certain changes are made.

Assumptions and Values

One of the major difficulties in reaching a decision in the academic world is that faculty members, by virtue of experience, have convictions about what ought to be done and how it should be done, but, in many cases, these convictions are based largely on experience and an orientation growing out of their disciplinary emphases rather than on a recognition of the underlying assumptions and values. Thus program issues are often resolved by compromise, but the basic differences that generated the need for compromise are not clarified. The argument as to whether ten credits or fifteen credits should be required in science can be readily compromised at twelve credits, with associated compromises in other requirements. This is why so many actions are taken without consideration of the possible impact and of the unanticipated and undesirable results as well as the desirable ones. Many institutions that undertook to organize small residential colleges in universities did not foresee some of the consequences of this approach, and understandably so. But in many cases, they moved rapidly to set up such colleges by name, thus embedding them securely in the structure of the institution so that, at a later point, any attempt to modify or eliminate the unit became a source of major difficulty. Further reflection on possible unanticipated or undesirable results might have at least sensitized individuals to the possibility that these units would be a source of difficulty. They should have been set

up on an experimental basis and carefully evaluated for determination of their long-term viability.

There is a variety of values involved in program decisions.
Quality is the perennial concern, yet it is never defined and
never well understood. It is always a source of disagreement
among the various groups and individuals. Quality becomes
equated to adherence to an approved process. *Relevance* is an
oft-repeated concern and value, but what is relevant to one person may not be so to another. Some decisions are motivated by
the most *pragmatic considerations,* for example:

- Lowered admission requirements in order to maintain enrollment and continued employment of the faculty.
- Decreased credit hour requirement for graduation from 130
  to 120 because the additional faculty load and costs are no
  longer tolerable, and also because some students, having
  noted the additional 10-hour requirement, are attending another institution where the degree requirement is specifically
  120.
- Decreased credit hour loads for various courses from five to
  three to enable students to have a wider range of choice. An
  unanticipated and possibly undesirable result is that the number of courses taken by students and taught by faculty increases under the reduced credit hour per course pattern.
  Both students and faculty find themselves with a heavier load
  than before simply because of the need to adapt to a larger
  number of courses in teaching and learning.
- Increased credit hours for courses so that students will generally take only three or four courses and no faculty member
  will have to teach more than two different courses, with the
  probably unrecognized result that a student wishing to emphasize such fields as foreign language, mathematics, and science is faced with some serious difficulties in getting started
  and maintaining all three in a sequential pattern.

Judgments and opinions of individuals on program, as on
other matters, are based upon a limited series of considerations.
Perhaps the most obvious is that of *self-interest.* One can hardly

expect a faculty member to vote for a requirement that will eliminate his or her position, but it is unfortunate that the self-interest of faculty members and departments is a prominent though covert factor in many program decisions. *Comparison with other institutions* is a common basis for a decision, whether one talks of the salary of faculty members, load of faculty members, requirements for students, or size of the library. Occasionally, there are *theoretical* or *empirical models* that have come to have wide acceptance, and these become a factor in making particular decisions. Table 6 shows one such model. This model was based upon examination of a wide range of college requirements. It can be seen as something of a normative model that could be adapted to an institution and then made a formal requirement for every major, or accepted as a model under which an individual student could develop a personal program. *Absolute standards* are very difficult to achieve in educational matters; yet faculty members and administrators share in common a feeling that there should be some definite standards and some absolutes to be enforced. Undoubtedly, it is because of this that such matters as credit hours for a degree, specific number of credits in a particular field, and the requirement of specific courses for majors are sometimes regarded as inviolable by faculty members. There are, as a personal survey in one university indicated, many students who failed to receive a degree despite a surplus of credits and acceptable grades. They lacked one or two specific course requirements.

In recent years, there has been much discussion of *cost benefit* or *cost effectiveness analysis* as the basis for decisions. These discussions do not help much in decisions about higher education programs because we are unclear about benefits and differ markedly about those on which we are reasonably clear. We are equally uncertain about effectiveness. Furthermore, there has been a tendency (aided and abetted by concern about fairness and equal opportunity) to feel that effectiveness and benefits ought to be judged by those who demand them, regardless of costs. Thus *consensus* (or sometimes just a bare majority) becomes the basis for decisions on most internal issues in colleges and universities. Some few colleges, related to the Friends,

Table 6. A Curriculum Model

Curriculum Component	Percent of Degree Requirements (Based on 120 Semester Credits)	Arts and Science Majors	Technical and Professional
A. Universitywide core	25	Basic courses in Composition, Social Science, Science, Humanities	
B. General requirement in Arts and Science	30	Foreign Languages, Mathematics, additional breadth	Concentration in the disciplines upon which field is based
C. Collegewide or divisionwide specialization core	10	Divisional requirements to buttress majors	Common requirement for all specialties included in a college
D. Major or concentration common requirement	15	Departmental core required of all majors in a department	Common requirement within each of the several specialties included in a college
E. Major or concentration electives	10	Electives within major field	Electives within specialty
F. Free electives	10	Preferably not to be taken in department of major	Preferably not to be taken in professional or technical college

Note: The percentages presented in this model are arbitrary, but analysis of a number of undergraduate curriculums indicates that they are reasonable. Physical education and other nonacademic requirements are ignored in this model.

Source: Paul L. Dressel, *The Undergraduate Curriculum in Higher Education* (Washington, D.C.: Center for Applied Research in Education, 1968), p. 81.

attempt, apparently successfully, to achieve a consensus. On many of the issues involved in decision making about programs, consensus is essentially a compromise achieved out of general weariness. Thus it becomes difficult to set general principles, policies, and a rationale for planning and operating courses and programs. Decisions tend to be specific and inflexible. Even sample or model programs come to be regarded as *the* program, both by students and by faculty, and any variation therefrom requires a form in sextuplicate, signed and countersigned by various persons and agencies.

Economics and Politics of Decision Making

There are perils in the way of eliminating courses and degree programs that cause even the most decisive administrator to hesitate before moving into that arena or even suggesting that the faculty do so. The reasons are reasonably clear but deserve review.

1. Faculty members directly involved in threatened programs tend to view program elimination or reduction as reflecting discredit or dissatisfaction with their own efforts. This may or may not be so.
2. Faculty members directly involved in these programs are concerned about their futures and the possible need to change institutions, change assignments, or even, in the present scene, move out of the academic world.
3. Students in a program face a loss of identity and institutional attachment and are easily aroused to join with faculty in opposition.
4. Faculty members in other programs (especially those falling in numbers or of low quality) are likely to rise to the support of any threatened program.
5. Students in the first or second year of college who are contemplating that program as a possibility, and others who have never heard of the program before (especially those of an activist orientation), may join in the confrontation over program review or elimination.
6. Since faculty members are understandably reluctant about program termination and reductions, any such decisions are unlikely unless there is strong administrative direction. From the viewpoint of many faculty members, this is an unreasonable administrative intervention into faculty matters, and their general attitude is that any administration-sponsored program review should be halted as an invasion of academic

freedom and faculty autonomy. Even state coordinating and governing boards have found program elimination a difficult task fraught with political implications.

7. Quite likely, there will also be some public reaction to any stringent move on programs. Alumni who majored in the threatened field tend to view elimination as an attack on the integrity of their own degree and a weakening of their attachment to the institution. Executives or employment personnel in business and industry or other fields possibly related to a program tend to view with alarm the elimination of the program and indict the institution as irresponsible and insensitive to public need.

8. Especially in public institutions, members of the legislature may rally to the cause of those fighting program elimination or retraction by proposing that the elimination of the program will be taken by the legislature as a basis for withdrawing all funds associated with it at the next budget session. Thus one of the primary economic considerations involved in program review, that of acquiring resources for reallocation to support underfinanced or new programs, is greatly weakened. So far as I have ascertained in a limited review with state officials, there are few cases in which the elimination of a program has resulted in such retribution by the legislature. Nevertheless, the threat generates a further review of the situation and usually indicates that, in the immediate future, no great saving, if any at all, will result from program elimination. This only reflects the fact that program costs, in many cases, are primarily determined by faculty salaries. Hence if faculty members are retained, there is no visible gain. The fact that there is usually little immediate gain of resources further supports the hesitation of administrators to take action. If resources can be gained only five or ten years down the road after some faculty members leave, why complicate one's life at the moment and possibly for the ensuing five or ten years?

Many of the preceding issues or problems involve personnel decisions complicated by tenure and job security agreements and policies. There is considerable difficulty in relating personnel actions and program actions. Actions on promotions and tenure are on a different calendar and are often dealt with through other channels than actions on curriculum. Hence it has not been unusual to find that while a task force was studying the possibility of eliminating certain programs, steps were being taken to give tenure to the faculty involved, thereby almost negating any possible action.

The phasing out of programs is another troublesome aspect of program elimination. New admissions can be curtailed, but if a program must be continued for two or three years to take care of those individuals already in the mill, it can be expected that contention will continue. Faculty members may be out combing secondary schools and community colleges seeking individuals who will demand access to the program. A phasing out decision is never final. New faces in administrative posts and faculty committees generate hopes that the whole matter can be reconsidered.

My own conviction, after viewing the difficulties faced in program elimination, is that it is better for all concerned if arrangements are made, wherever possible, for students in the program to be transferred to other nearby institutions and that no more than one year should be allowed to phase out those students entering the last year of the program. This action can generate somewhat more immediate trauma, but, by moving immediately to take care of the problems generated for students and faculty, the situation is brought to closure and permits committees and administrators to turn their attention to other problems and programs. So long as one program remains in contention, few individuals are desirous of tackling a second or third.

Finally, there is a failure generally in program review to relate the need for new programs, expansion of programs, and major revision of programs to actions involving the elimination of programs. Even at the state level, coordinating boards or governing boards and their staffs have tended to separate the two tasks, sometimes by assignment to different persons. Under these circumstances, there is no immediate incentive for faculty support of any plan for termination. A broader view could be taken of program review, including the need for new programs, expanded programs, and vastly altered ones. If the beginning of new programs were in some way related to termination or reduction in others and the gradual transfer of resources, both the politics and economics of curricular decision making could be changed. Possibly, although less likely, programs could be seen as responses to particular needs at particular times, subject to elimination and change as necessary or appropriate. Here, of course, the administrative and organizational structure of the institution into colleges and departments poses a major problem. How does one eliminate home economics or even change its name in an institution that has had a college of home economics for eight years or more? There is indeed a relationship between structure and content, and there is a tendency for structures developed to facilitate the offering of certain content to dictate at a later date the continuation of that same content rather than adjustment to changing circumstances. Altering the mission of a unit may be as difficult as eliminating it.

Stability, Flexibility, and Change

In a technological society, change is the order of the day, but change is interrelated with growth. Under circumstances of continuing growth, new opportunities and new needs arise, and change is seen as providing both opportunity and recognition. Even so, there are always conservatives who resist change and, at least in words, prefer the "good old days." Under growth, change is reflected by additions throughout the university: additions in departments, courses, programs, equipment. In this process, the demands and opportunities of new programs attract people and resources. Old programs and courses can sometimes be phased out with no alarm because everyone is too busy doing a new thing. The old withers as its strength is sapped by preoccupation with the new. Under growth, with ample funds, even long-existing units—such as colleges of agriculture, home economics, engineering, and business—undergo major change, but they do so in an atmosphere of expectancy and enthusiasm.

Most of these changes have been gradual, and rightly so. A complete new program of general education installed in six months is the rare happening in higher education. No faculty or institution can function well in a state of continuing revolution; but neither can the university accommodate to the stability that some members of the faculty would like to have. The contention of some conservatives is that sound education is the same at all times and places. If this is true, it can only mean that we have not yet found out what a sound education is. The problem always, and especially in the curricular area, is that of balancing the need for continuing change with the need for some stability. In addition to being disruptive, continuing change prevents careful examination of the nature and effect of the contemplated changes as they appear in practice. It provides no assurance that we are bettering education. Enthusiasm is a poor substitute for substance. The best evidence of this is a review of program and curricular changes over the years in American colleges and universities. What this review convincingly demonstrates is that one institution's innovation is the discard of another institution a number of years before. Real innovation and improvement are notably absent. Renovation is frequently only a return to earlier practices under a new designation. Tinkering in terms of course titles, credit hours, and teaching methodology, after the initial furor, gradually retreats to the more traditional pattern that it replaced. It is not surprising, then, that administrators and other educational leaders in higher education, recognizing the costs in energy, time, and dollars required in the process of curricular and program review, frequently conclude that it is a waste of effort. Thus it is that resources are often used in supporting add-on activities that may possibly alleviate some problem. Shortly that add-on may disappear, but more likely it will become part of the traditional structure as the administrator turns to something else. Everything remains much the same, except for the increase in total program costs.

Another factor discouraging forthright attack on program review is found in judging the relative importance of the professor, the student, and the curriculum. I always recall, in this connection, the remarks of a professor at a major university who, after listening to some of my comments on these issues, dismissed them all by saying that I had forgotten that the university existed to provide a working base for the professor. In part, I agree, but the tendency to accord a high degree of autonomy on curricular and course matters to disciplinary units and to individuals within them is unfortunate. There are too few outstanding teachers and program developers to justify the view that the professor and the instructional process are the key factors in learning. A curriculum or program soundly organized with appropriate indications of readings, exercises, and experiences provides a structure within which highly motivated individuals can proceed with their own education. Professors are not necessarily to be found only in classrooms or on the television screen. In the majority of learning situations, the best teachers are found in good books and other materials developed usually by people far more competent in the area than the professor in charge. Thus I assert that the relative importance given in the program decisions should be, first, to the nature and purposes of a total program; second, to the student; and third, to the professor. Placing the student in the middle is not to say that the student is less important than the content. The educational process is actually a process by which an individual masters the accumulated wisdom of a culture to a level where he or she can use or even add to it. In the educational process, the development of means of educating individuals to assimilate and use the accumulated culture is the major task—one in which professors are simply mediating agents. In good professional programs, it is evident that the development of the total program is guided by the product to be produced: physician, dentist, lawyer, or other professional. Our program development and review should accept the obligation to modify content and instructional approach to fit the particular needs of the situation. The outstanding professor in this circumstance is not, with few exceptions, the one who does his or her own thing, but rather the one who does what the program required in an unusually capable mode that recognizes that the students and their progress furnish the real focus for teaching. Acceptance of this view injects elements into program planning, evaluation, and decisions that are usually notable only in their absence.

Maintaining flexibility and the suitable intermediate point between erratic change and rigidity poses a problem touched upon in several of the preceding chapters. Faculty members, if they give attention at all to the need for flexibility in curriculum change, tend to provide it through electives or selectives within groups. The alternative is flexibility that permits the development of student-designed programs with assistance from advisers and others. The problem in providing this latter type of flexibility arises out of the lack of a statement of principles or criteria for deciding whether a program is sound and acceptable. That lack is a reflection on the quality of thinking that undergirds the curricular offerings and programs of most departments and colleges. Actual programs do indeed tend to be disciplinary and oriented to the professors rather than to the students and their prospective careers. This can change only as the criteria and the procedures and bases for decision making on course and curricular matters are clarified and used.

Suggestions for Further Reading

Dressel, P. L., and Mayhew, L. B. *General Education: Explorations in Evaluation.* Washington, D.C.: American Council on Education, 1954.

Giddens, T. R., and Kenny, J. W. "Research Models for the Evaluation of Interim Programs." *Research in Higher Education,* 1975, *3* (4), 393-401.

Lydo, W. J. "A Suggested Conceptual System for Decision Making in Curriculum Development." *Educational Record,* 1960, *41,* 74-83.

Morrisett, I. (Ed.). *Concepts and Structure in the New Social Science Curricula.* West Lafayette, Ind.: Social Science Education Consortium, 1966.

Parlett, M., and Dearden, G. (Eds.). *Introduction to Illuminative Evaluation: Studies in Higher Education.* Berkeley, Calif.: Pacific Soundings Press, 1977.

Pfnister, A. O. *Planning for Higher Education: Background and Application.* Boulder, Colo.: Westview Press, 1976.

12

Advising Students About Programs and Courses

Student advising—especially in its relationship to teaching and program planning—presents a series of problems and concerns that must be addressed if the curriculum and the programs derived from it are to serve their purposes in preparing students for living, learning, and working. The decisions involved in relating programs to individual abilities and aspirations reflect conflicting values. Consequently, coordination of curriculum or program change and advising in improving the education of students will require continuing administrative concern and action.

The typical faculty member quite naturally views a curriculum or a program as a series of courses based largely on selected discipline content, and he or she regards the disciplinary proficiency of the professor as the chief consideration in designing and packaging courses into a degree program. Students

250

are not expected to grasp the significance of courses other than as a body of content, nor are they expected to understand how several courses are sequenced and integrated into a program. Student course and program selections are made with the aid of an adviser, but the choices are limited by specific distribution requirements, by credit hour regulations, and often—especially in applied fields—by designated course requirements. In this conception of student program planning, the adviser's role is strictly limited. The adviser should know the requirements and should enforce them upon students. Beyond this, he or she helps to guide the student through a maze that even the adviser does not fully understand, either in its rationale or its policies and rules. Deviations require approval by some agency or individual other than the adviser, and the wise adviser therefore avoids deviations in the interest of efficiency and avoidance of difficulties. Students are widely regarded as too immature and too uncertain about their goals to have a vital role in planning. The adviser of lower-division students is not expected to know anything about disciplines and their vocational implications (except possibly for his or her own). The adviser is usually expected to be conversant with general education and institutional curriculum requirements within the first two years and to hold the advisees to them. Occasionally, if flexibility permits, an adviser may undertake to assist the student in building a program around specific interests, but then soon finds that sufficient information is lacking. The adviser's task is not unlike that of the instructor who attempts to structure a course around those students who enroll. It is time-consuming and requires continuing adjustment to a changing student population. Even so, there is likely to be sufficient disparity between the instructor's judgment of student needs or wants and the actuality that the effort is not repaid by the results. The institution soon finds that constrained flexibility for student programs is a difficult goal to achieve in a faculty-structured and discipline-based curriculum. Similarly, advising is caught up in a no-win situation in a culture predominantly devoted to content coverage, the departmental-disciplinary orientation, and a reward system that, at least in the universities, has little to do with the quality either of teaching or of advising.

Except for the appreciation of students, there is little recognition and no reward for the adviser who encourages deviation from standard patterns. There may even be reprimand and retribution for unusual or extreme deviations. The reward system remains in the discipline and the department. The faculty assignment to advising is a chore. Poor advising *may* earn a relief from the task. Though disdaining advising as a meritorious task, departments insist upon retaining the function because it provides access to new students and the opportunity to recruit majors. Control of the advising responsibility by departments also wards off a central counseling or advising system that might draw resources from the departments. Despite the difficulties and hazards involved, there are some exceptional advisers whose rapport with students and whose grasp of the intricacies of the curriculum and its career implications result in excellent advising. However, my observations suggest that such faculty members are unlikely to remain long as advisers. They find the task both time-consuming and frustrating. Furthermore, the abilities exhibited by a good adviser are likely to attract attention and assignment to other chores.

I am personally convinced that the lack of good student counseling and advising and the dominance of the pattern of a choice determined by the existing range of majors and professional programs are major factors in the high dropout rates of many institutions. But I am equally convinced that the repeatedly used techniques of orienting advisers through short-term workshops, and arranging visits of businessmen to campuses and of faculty members to business, will not solve the problem unless faculty members also become aware of the career relevance of their disciplines. It is essential that we have alterations in policies and practices in our colleges and universities as they relate to advising, teaching, the curriculum, and program planning. If advising is to become and remain a challenging task, advisers must be granted *some* authority in approving deviations in old programs and planning new ones.

Alterations in Policies and Practices

The needed alterations in policies and practices would eliminate the dominance of departments or other program units over the definition of course and program requirements. The rules, policies, and rigidities that reinforce this domination at present should be replaced by general principles providing flexible structures and guides for students and advisers. The curriculum array and the programs drawing upon it should be developed and regularly reviewed by interdisciplinary or collegewide study groups. More information should be provided on the courses and programs, and students should be given greater flexibility and opportunity for individualized programs. The following policies are intended to be exemplary rather than definitive, and any such statements should in themselves be regarded as subject to interpretation and alteration by advisers under justifiable circumstances.

Policy No. 1. All published degree programs should be developed by interdisciplinary committees or task forces that include representation from the departments or units providing the courses. For example, in a liberal arts college, programs involving disciplines in the social sciences would be developed by task forces made up primarily of representatives from the social science departments but would include at least one carefully selected faculty member from each of the other divisional groupings, such as the sciences, humanities, and arts. Programs would then tend to emerge as arrays of courses across departments. This would eliminate the departmental major as the primary factor in the undergraduate program and require that some other integrating principle or concept be identified. Programs could be developed on the basis of a theme, a career focus, or a combination of courses from several disciplines that are or promise to be of considerable composite significance in the future. The result would be that departments would no longer control programs and could not insert course requirements simply to ensure that particular professors would have courses that they prefer to teach. With this principle operative, the prospects of approval of individually planned programs should be enhanced.

Policy No. 2. Provide for individually planned programs. Emphasize the opportunity for students and advisers to plan such programs and indicate that this is the preferred pattern, as opposed to unthinking acquiescence in some model suggested by a department or curriculum committee. Recognize that some students may prefer a rather traditional disciplinary-based program. Even when selection is from formally approved and published programs, student options should be increased by minimizing specific requirements and by generally regarding program outlines and specifications as suggestions or examples.

Policy No. 3. Require all teachers of a course to become thoroughly grounded in the relevance of the course content to other courses in the field. Teachers would then be authorized to modify the course as necessary to maintain or even increase its practical relevance. Some sacrifice of coverage may be necessary in order to achieve the deeper or broader understandings desired.

Policy No. 4. Provide for each course a detailed course outline or syllabus for review and comment by curriculum committee, other faculty members, advisers, and students. This course syllabus should provide in detail the information indicated in Chapter Eight, so that advisers and students can select among courses to build a program with reasonable insight and with some certainty that the rationale for selecting the program will be fulfilled by the actual experience. The syllabus should indicate options in content coverage, application, or learning experiences that are available to students within the course.

Policy No. 5. Focus all program planning, published or individualized, on objectives, competencies, and outcomes as the basis for specifying content and learning process. This policy need not de-emphasize knowledge. Rather, it is based upon the conviction that acquiring knowledge is fundamental in any program, but that any attempt to define a course or a program by content coverage without regard for utility and application casts doubt on the worth of the content.

Policy No. 6. Require liberal education experiences for all students. The choice of words here is deliberate. The intent is neither to suggest specific distribution requirements covering several disciplines nor to prescribe a core of general courses. Rather, the intent is that liberal education be defined by competencies such as those discussed in Chapter Four. Experiences that involve and foster such competencies should be included in various courses (whether regarded as vocational or liberal) and be made specific in the course description. Either demonstration of competency or reasonable involvement in a sequence of experiences and ultimate demonstration of competency should be apparent in every degree program. There is no single prescription for attaining a liberal education, and there is no course or discipline that cannot contribute in some measure to a liberal education. Neither is there any course or discipline that can assure a liberal education impact for all.

Only if program planning accepts the possibility of motivating students to become deeply involved in and responsible for educating themselves is it possible for students and their advisers to make wise choices and build programs from course units. Unless policies such as these can be introduced, advising will remain, as it is in most institutions, a perfunctory series of contacts with students in which the adviser is obligated to inform the student of rules, regulations, and requirements, approve the current schedule of the student, and, at appropriate intervals when grades are reported, congratulate or offer condolences to students.

Were such policies as these to become operative, students and advisers would have an opportunity to work out unique programs. Adequate information is provided to do this. The task of the adviser becomes significant. I suspect that many individuals currently serving as advisers might not like or function well in this open system. Some could not be trusted to do so in that they would too readily yield to student whims. The question then arises of how to select, educate, and reward advisers. A quick review of past practices indicates that they are not likely to suffice. In many institutions, the advising function has been handled differently for freshmen and sophomores than for juniors and seniors. Assuming that initial indications of a major by an incoming freshman are subject to alteration by dropout, death, or change of mind, and that the first two years are filled with general education and required courses, freshmen and sophomores are advised by most any faculty member available. In some colleges, I have heard the boast that every faculty member is an adviser. This policy is equivalent in significance to that of several major universities that require every professor to teach freshmen. This may be good for the professor, but is it good for the freshmen? It may be instructive to faculty members for each to have some advising experience, but it may be disastrous for the student if the faculty member is uninterested in curriculum matters and knows little about general requirements and nothing about courses other than in his or her own field.

Undoubtedly, at some place and time, advisers have been evaluated and perhaps rewarded. However, I have never found a formal plan for so doing. I have found institutions that paid a small additional stipend to advisers or granted a slight reduction in teaching load when the number of students advised was fairly high. I have also found a few instances in which advisers were given a few dollars for entertaining advisees. I once directed a faculty advising program involving about 100 faculty members, each having from 50 to 100 advisees, and all being granted a 50 percent reduction in teaching load. As might be expected, some of these advisers (as advisers) were impossibly busy and some had very little to do. Despite a continuing training program, the situation did not improve much, and the costs were disproportionately high for the results attained.

Advising simply has not been recognized as a critical task requiring both commitment and skill. An additional stipend for the extra work of advising rather misses the point. In fact, it only underlines advising as an extra task of relatively low status —somewhat like teaching a noncredit evening class for adults. The small allocations for salary or entertainment also raise questions about similar allotments for other faculty functions and services. Overload payments completely miss the fact that time spent in one function is almost invariably withdrawn from another. Since advising is quite low on the list of priorities in the academic world, an extra stipend for advisers is inadequate to compensate for the time required and the loss of prestige that might otherwise have been attained.

The addition of the advising chore to full-time teaching usually means that the teacher has no time for acquiring the necessary background adequate for the advising task itself. The teacher actively interested in the career implications of his or her discipline has the potential for being both good adviser and good teacher, although either could be a full-time job. Paying individuals for full-time advising becomes unduly expensive, and it is a guarantee that the adviser will have neither faculty status nor stature with the academic faculty. This anomalous status is a precursor of difficulty for the students. The hiring of full-time counselors (using the title *counselor* to designate individuals whose degree work is in that field) is also expensive and poses the same problems with regard to interaction of counselors and faculty.

There are definite advantages attached to faculty status, teaching experiences, and involvement in faculty committees. Whereas advisers of the typical faculty disciplinary orientation seldom know much about other disciplines and little or nothing about careers, counselors may know much about the latter and little about the former. Moreover, many counselors regard counseling as a form of psychological or psychoanalytic therapy dealing with personal problems, trauma, marital or sex concerns, and nonacademic difficulties. Among these are special demands for drug counseling, abortion counseling, rehabilitation, financial counseling, and counseling for the handicapped. Such counseling needs are obvious but do not relate immediately to teaching and curriculum matters as perceived by the faculty. For these various reasons, solving the advising problem by hiring a group of full-time counselors who deal primarily with academic and vocational problems is unlikely. However, good advising will certainly identify students requiring counseling. In fact, bridging the gap between today's specialization in counseling and the faculty disciplinary orientation is the major challenge and task of advising. One pattern attempts to solve much of the routine advising through the faculty advising role and by establishing in the dean's office, or closely connected with it, a number of coordinating advisers with some academic background who hold title (and achieve status thereby) as assistant or associate dean. The adviser with faculty status is much better situated to feed student views and problems into discussions and policy formulation regarding teaching and curriculum. The administrative title also grants sufficient autonomy to develop individualized programs that transcend the usual restricted and rigid program. Occasional teaching (especially if it is of superior quality) adds responsibility and stature to such an individual in the eyes of both students and professors. Such individuals, working in association with professional counselors, can usually and easily relate this additional source of information to the interests and abilities of students in planning a career.

This pattern provides a three-echelon approach to advising. At the first level are selected faculty members who are effective in dealing with young people and willing to spend sufficient time to understand the institutional program and acquire some sense of the range of careers related to various programs and majors. At the second level are individuals associated with deans' offices who have sufficient status and authority to make modifications in programs and arrange combined programs across departments and colleges. These individuals have sufficiently close relationship with professional counselors—the third level—to enlist their cooperation when required. Psychiatry may be required as a fourth level in a few cases.

Another possible solution to the advising problem is one that I have heard discussed but never seen in operation. This pattern uses a combination of individuals with academic background and faculty status who have demonstrated particular interest in young people and success in working with them and who are willing to spend some time in preparing for advising work. These individuals are organized into groups of five to ten, with an academically oriented counselor coordinating the activities for each such group and serving as a resource to deal with more complicated personal problems. In a small college or moderate-sized university, such a group of individuals might function at the all-institutional level. In larger universities, in which each college may itself be a unit of some size and embrace a number of relatively unrelated programs, the organizational unit for advisers will be at the college level but will still need to have some all-university coordinator or unit from which advisers and individuals can obtain help in planning programs that draw upon several colleges. The implication involved in any such pattern of organization and staffing is that advising is seen as an important assignment. It would be viewed as a special task force or service demanding abilities and interests transcending those of the department and discipline.

I believe that advising deserves recognition and reward as a quasi-administrative function. It is also essential that a degree of autonomy be assigned to advising if it is to be more than a perfunctory clerical duty.

Career Advising

The relationship of undergraduate education to career development has been and will continue to be present in any discussion about curriculum and advising. Because the department is regarded as the unit for offering both courses and programs, and a liberal education is erroneously thought to be attained by taking courses distributed over several disciplines, attempts to solve the career problem have almost invariably involved add-ons. Special courses on career development, expansion of the placement office, adding a vocational counseling office, and the preparation and dissemination of vocational materials exemplify the add-on approach. These additions increase costs but accomplish relatively little because they do not solve the problem of relating a liberal education to the world of work. Indeed, I believe that it is impossible to do so as long as the disciplines are taught as organized bodies of content having little or no relationship to reality and presented as though all students were headed for graduate study. As earlier suggested, the most potent force for changing this situation would be to have the continuance of courses depend on their appeal to students and advisers as useful units in career-related programs. Because of the career-planning function of advisers, I believe there is merit in continuing teaching assignments for advisers. Courses that provide an orientation to various professional or vocational fields and demonstrate the relationship of liberal education competencies to various career fields are especially appropriate. Such a course could be justified in a number of disciplines. The course would develop the nature of the discipline and pursue the application of the concepts, structure, and modes of inquiry of the discipline as used in several fields. Liberal education is concerned with values, and values are also of primary concern in all vocational and career fields. Indeed, the difference between performing in a humanistic fashion in any job and performing a job in a rote way without regard for individuals is a matter of personal value commitment. Senior integrating seminars bringing together the insights that students have achieved over a span of years in college and relating these to current and continuing problems are also valuable courses that are appropriately taught by advisers. The size of the adviser group could be such that the adviser continues with a group of students throughout the college years. This pattern would provide a continuity and cumulative impact that is lacking in colleges and universities.

Although I have never found any corroboratory evidence, I have long suspected that lack of continuity in advisory contacts is a significant factor in student dropouts, discontinuities in attendance, and apathy about college continuation. College attendance, especially in liberal education programs, provides no clear goal and has no obvious relevance to the future. Advisers and students, recognizing the short duration of their contact, see little advantage in expanding it. Neither has any set of expectations for the other, and hence there exists no basis upon which the continuing adviser contact can become a mutual bond encouraging continuance—especially when the student's current program provides no coherence or career prospects. If advisers were selected because of their interest and competency in assisting students, and if each adviser maintained contact with his or her advisers for the entire undergraduate program, a continuity and cumulative impact would be generated that could have beneficial effects for both students and institutions.

If education could be interpreted to students as a valuable and cumulative experience relative to later living as well as to a career, dropouts and discontinuities in attendance might be reduced. Even if they were not, a strengthened advisory program in which students achieve a vision of the composite nature of the total program and its possibilities would ease the strain of withdrawing and returning to school for both full-time and part-time students. If education is indeed to be a continuing lifelong process, the individuals who engage in it must have some sense of the significance and of the sequence to achieve desired goals. In many ways, good advising may be a more critical and more significant academic function than teaching.

Problems with Career Advising

One of the problems with any new educational model is that there are many people against it. Some faculty members are likely to view a move in the directions just discussed as a softening of the educational process and as requiring additional resources that will deprive the faculty of possible salary increases, new program development, and other benefits. Those who have long decried the organized disciplines as providing any satisfactory means for education and have emphasized education as personal development may view the continued demand for substance and for relevance in terms of career as contradictory to their own concern for education as a process of personal development. Those who have made a strong plea for the role of student personnel programs in higher education are likely to see this model as infringing upon their own prerogatives. In rebuttal to all of these concerns, I would suggest that it is difficult to achieve a well-rounded education from an educational experience compartmentalized by the existence of discrete noncooperating or even competing units. Indeed, the separation of academic and student personnel programs has provoked a dichotomy such that students have had to choose between extensive activity in student programs or primary commitment to the academic aspects of the program. The advising-focused model here suggested would not unite these separate units and the various extant philosophies of education into an integrated whole, but, if career planning is made an integral part of the educational process, there is at least the prospect that a sense of unity could be restored to the undergraduate program. If students could be assisted by advisers to engage in significant learning and development and realize that these processes are intimately interwoven with their hopes and aspirations after college is over, both motivation and performance might increase.

Questions can be raised about the costs and effectiveness of this model relative to its success in achieving the desired results. I doubt that the costs would be excessive if some competing or overlapping student personnel functions were discharged and if class size were maintained at a reasonable level. The real problem in exploring such a model lies in the reluctance of individuals, whether academic faculty, student personnel worker, or some other type of functionary, to change existing patterns. We have become so accustomed to assuming that an educational problem must be solved by inserting another office or function that any fundamental change that questions this conception will be difficult to achieve. Even the foundations seem more likely to support new or add-on services and functions than the reshaping of the fundamental operations and services.

A careful analysis of the processes involved in this advising model will show that the model is based upon or interrelated with the continuums and competencies described in Chapter Four. I believe that the major reason for the failure of our complex, although inadequate, evaluation efforts is that we have expected a range of outcomes from college attendance but have organized the college experience in ways unrelated to the results that we would achieve. Thus the desired results are fragmented and invisible to students and faculty. It is not surprising that most of the desired results are also invisible when an attempt is made to evaluate them. Process and product are interrelated. So are structure and content. The college or university cannot be structured to suit the faculty, student personnel workers, and coaches and, at the same time, achieve as effectively as it should the results desired by students and society.

Suggestions for Further Reading

Eddy, E. W., Jr. *The College Influence on Student Character.* Washington, D.C.: American Council on Education, 1959.

Feldman, K. A., and Newcomb, T. M. *The Impact of College on Students.* San Francisco: Jossey-Bass, 1969.

Perkin, H. J. *Innovation in Higher Education: New Universities in the United Kingdom.* Paris: Organization for Economic Cooperation and Development, 1969.

Perry, W. G., Jr. *Forms of Intellectual and Ethical Development in the College Years: A Scheme.* New York: Holt, Rinehart and Winston, 1968.

 *13*

Administering Program Development and Review

Professional schools have typically defined and administered their own programs. This is justifiable because many professional programs are accredited by associations that set specific standards for courses, credits, and clinical experiences. These programs are also planned and controlled by a faculty with professional and social responsibilities to monitor carefully the preparation of professionals. Higher administrative levels have generally regarded professional schools and colleges as essentially autonomous on curricular and program matters, but this is not always the case. In a university in which basic science departments serve all colleges, including a college of medicine, a disagreement between basic science departments and the medical college as to content and credit for basic science courses may ultimately require intervention by central administration to resolve the matter. In somewhat more flexible undergraduate programs, such as nursing and engineering, which generally provide a liberal or general education breadth experience, the nature and extent of these requirements may become a matter of university policy for all students rather than an autonomous decision by each of the several colleges.

As the professional component of a degree program becomes less massive and less rigid, there is an increased need for a set of guiding policies or principles for the undergraduate program. The departmental focus is on majors and on its graduate programs. There is an understandable lack of interest in or motivation for broader concerns about undergraduate education unless administrators or institutional curriculum committees press for reflection and action on the character and quality of all undergraduate programs. The lack of specific dissatisfaction by students and the focused interests of faculty members, combined with the complexities of the collective undergraduate curriculum, tend to cause curriculum committees to adopt a policy of noninterference in program unit proposals. The larger and transcendent issues regarding undergraduate programs become of concern to most program units only to the extent that college deans or academic vice-presidents, through the prevailing curriculum structure, press for the development of policies, procedures, and program principles to be regularly applied in critiquing new program proposals and reviewing existing programs.

Role of the Chairman in Curriculum Review

I have talked with many university departmental chairmen who disclaimed direct responsibility for the undergraduate program and indicated that an assistant or vice-chairman was responsible for its coordination. The chairman, selected because of his or her scholarly prestige and research more than for administrative ability, desired to continue past activities largely unmodified by current responsibility. In a private university with a large graduate program, deans and other officials may be satisfied with this interpretation of the chairman's role. In a public institution, it is an irresponsible conception. The chairman has the initial responsibility at the departmental level for assuring and demonstrating accountability in the use of public funds. This means that the chairman must accept responsibility for the following matters:

1. A continuing review of course enrollments should be carried on to determine necessary expansion or appropriate contraction and elimination.
2. A recurrent review of the service courses and functions of the department in respect to other departments should be undertaken to determine the satisfactions or dissatisfactions that exist and to demonstrate departmental concerns that the service functions be well fulfilled.
3. A regular review of teaching, grading, and evaluation practices is essential. Some chairmen adopt a policy of reviewing with each staff member the grades in all courses before these are reported. Others deal with this by occasional departmental discussions of the associated problems and by reaching agreements on general policies with regard to testing, grading, and teaching. Student and faculty comments and complaints about instructional practices that reach department chairmen who evidence interest and concern provide another input, although one that must be tentatively and cautiously used.
4. Consultation with other departments of similar nature about departmental policies on grading, evaluation, and teaching is advisable. Departments are and should be reasonably autonomous on these matters. However, marked variation from one department to another, especially for students whose programs involve both departments, can be frustrating and demoralizing to students.
5. The chairman should be concerned with staff assignments. His or her primary concerns should be for effective resource utilization and for maintenance of quality instruction. The time of day at which various courses are scheduled should be examined, for occasionally a professor becomes more concerned with personal convenience than with that of the students. Some advanced courses may tend to become individual holdings, thereby causing a problem if a sabbatical or

departure occurs. The development of younger faculty members may be advanced by wisely allocating experiences in teaching particular courses. In addition, the assignment should take into account the range of experience and knowledge of the teacher relative to those taking the course. A professor who knows nothing about applications of the discipline should not be assigned to applied courses. Teaching assignments constitute one of the major ways to assure good teaching to particular groups of students. It is the chairman's responsibility to see that this is done.

6. The possibility of development of junior faculty through teaching assignments has already been noted. The sensitive chairman knows that some individuals will do an unusually fine job with new courses or existing ones that they have not previously taught simply because of the effort that they put into it. Such experiences may add considerably to an individual's stature in respect to teaching other courses and even enhance their scholarly grasp of the discipline. Other chores in the department, such as advising, development of new courses, and preparation of teaching materials or examinations, all represent activities that can be so assigned as to promote faculty development as well as to provide the best possible experience for students. At the same time, the assignments can be varied to involve additional faculty members and encourage a broader grasp of the departmental functions.

7. The use of student evaluations of courses and teachers varies not only among institutions from unit to unit but also within institutions. These evaluations should be of concern to faculty and to the chairman. The granting of tenure and the promotion and financial reward of faculty members should depend upon the quality of teaching. Student reactions are only one index of information on this, but the chairman should encourage faculty members to discuss their student ratings thoroughly with the chairman, an associate, or some of the students. If the ratings are made available to the chairman and/or dean for use in recognition or reward, a formal statement should be provided to both faculty members and students on how this evidence is used.

8. No matter how the decisions regarding selection and recommendation for reward of faculty members are reached, the chairman has the responsibility to see that this is effectively done. I have noted a tendency in the current scene for departments and chairmen to avoid difficult decisions—especially those involving women and minorities. This avoidance is understandable in view of the complicated appeal mechanisms and the possibility of court involvement. Yet avoidance of this responsibility can only result, in the long run, in a weakening of the quality and autonomy of a unit. The major problem, in most cases, when these delicate situations arise is that the department chairman has not collected adequate evidence to justify the recommendation that should be made. When adequate supporting evidence is lacking, a negative recommendation is almost certain to be successfully contested.

9. Whatever may be the policies, rules, and procedures for developing majors and undergraduate programs, they will be effective only if they are interpreted and enforced. Errors and oversights are one common source of unintended violation. They weaken the program for a particular student and set precedents that present difficulties with other students and advisers. When it becomes known by advisers and students that no one reviews programs to determine whether requirements have been met, a variety of planned evasions of requirements may appear. The registrar's office or the dean's office may be responsible for checking program requirements, but a department chairman should not assume that these responsibilities are always carried out. Furthermore, the chairman of the department ought to have some concern about the total pattern of education of students who take a significant segment of their work in that department. If review of the actual records of a number of students raises no problems, one has only to note that the review was conducted and no errors found. If no review is conducted, error or deliberate evasion may go unchecked—at least until someone beyond the department takes note of the matter and calls the department and chairman to task.

Role of the College Dean

In the absence of college or institutionwide policies with regard to courses and programs, departments and other program units vary markedly in their practices. Those with an elitist conception of education may impose standards and requirements that eliminate all but the most able students. Others, in an attempt to attract students, may adopt such flexible standards and policies that both the department and the institution suffer in reputation. The dean's lot in attempting to deal with this wide variation in the absence of any policies is difficult. Recourse to standing committees is unlikely to be helpful because committees, in the absence of well-documented policies, lean toward departmental autonomy. Hence the dean who takes seriously his or her responsibilities for course and program review will seek development and acceptance of college and institutionwide policies upon which to base the program review. Budgetary allocations can also take into account the efficiency and the effectiveness of departmental operations. In particular, a department that ignores policies on unnecessary course repetition and small classes can be forced into line by a decreased budget.

It is important that the chairman seek the reactions of other departments toward departmental offerings, quality of instruction, and appropriateness of courses. Some chairmen will do this; others will ignore it, taking the stance that each department is fully responsible for its course offerings and programs and that only the departmental staff is competent to make decisions about them. Discussions among the deans can bring to light such attitudes. Appropriate measures, especially in the delineation of duties and choice of departmental chairmen in the future, can eliminate such irresponsibility. The dean's office is likely, in one way or another, to be the recipient of complaints from students, parents, and individuals external to the institution. The dean who ignores or immediately refers such complaints to the department or individual directly concerned misses a significant opportunity to determine the extent to which the performance of units and personnel in the college is in accord with existent policies and the best interests of the students. In many cases, complaints arise not so much from in-equity but from the student's inability to get a satisfactory explanation, or because of the insensitive treatment received when an attempt is made to do so. Most such complaints are resolved by sympathetic listening and an explanation. Other complaints justify and require action, and the dean should not hesitate to countermand a chairman's or faculty member's deci-sion when necessary, assuming always that this is done forth-rightly and after discussion with the individuals involved. The numerous appeal routes existing in colleges today are, in great part, due to the unwillingness of administrators to intervene in faculty matters.

Contacts with students will also provide the dean and associates with insight into the quality of teaching and advising. An accumulation of complaints about a particular teacher over time should certainly become the basis for a conference, direct-ly or indirectly through the chairman, with that individual. Fur-ther continuation of such complaints should weigh heavily in decisions about that individual's rewards and further association with the institution. Tenure is not intended to protect incompe-tency. Likewise, the information that accrues in a dean's office from the action or lack of action of advisers provides insight into both the functioning of the advising system and the flexi-bility and rigidity of the policies controlling it. When rules or policies are needlessly rigid and inflexible, the attitude of per-sonnel in the dean's office becomes a major factor in whether adjustments are made for students. A dean or a dean's secretary who makes it obvious that advisers' requests for waiver of a rule represent lack of support of institutional standards effectively destroys any significant role for advisers. Deans who insist that individually planned programs worked out by student and ad-viser must be reviewed in great depth by one or more adminis-trators and committees will effectively discourage all but the most determined students and advisers.

The dean has also the obligation of reviewing, grading, and evaluating practices across departments. Although chairmen should regularly review their departmental practices, they may hesitate to do so or they may do so with a conviction that their departments and disciplines require distinctive standards and grading policies. The suggestion here is not meant to indicate that there be complete uniformity (whatever this may mean) across departments. However, marked and unjustified disparity in grading and evaluation practices introduces factors into student program choice and student attrition that may not be equitable. Closely connected with this issue is a responsibility for reviewing changes in majors and withdrawals from the institution. When particular programs or departments become unduly identified with student program changes or dropouts, a further review of practices is indicated. In addition to these matters, a lengthy list of other items and relevant data (see Chapter Eight) should be reviewed by the dean or by a designated assistant or faculty member. In large institutions, some of the information related to the following items will be regularly supplied through studies from the office of institutional research. Even so, unless the information from these reports is followed up by the dean, in one manner or another, the institutional research reports are not likely to be useful.

1. The dean should be concerned about the scheduling of course offerings in the various departments. In many cases, the interrelationship of departments and student programs requires either a careful review by a knowledgeable individual or an a priori designation of hours and perhaps of places where certain courses or sections should be available.
2. The dean should be concerned about the adequacy and accuracy of information supplied by the departments in the catalogue and in informational materials provided to students and advisers.
3. The dean should be concerned that there be a reasonable correspondence between scheduled class hours of various types and the credit allocation to a course. Credit hour totals have significant implications for the departmental budget and for student and faculty load. They also point up unreasonable demands made by some departments without regard to the expectations of other departments.
4. The dean should have reports from various support services

indicating the extent to which a department makes use of these. Such reports may cover the use of educational technology, services assisting a department in the construction of examination or instructional materials, and the extent to which students are referred from the department to counseling and improvement services.

5. The dean should be aware of departmental program strengths and weaknesses as they relate to accrediting standards and should encourage departments to develop and maintain an acceptable position with regard to these standards. This may include ignoring such standards when they are unduly costly and are irrelevant to the institutional mission.

6. The dean should be aware of the practices of departments and advisers with respect to student career contemplation and planning. Departments vary greatly in their concern for student career development, and they also vary greatly in the direct career significance of the discipline involved. Hence observations from the dean's office become especially significant in directing the attention of faculty members to the importance of relating educational programs to career development.

7. From time to time, the dean should direct that careful analyses be made of the records of students majoring in various programs within the college. Such analyses will point to the extent to which the various departments and advisers involved are giving appropriate attention to breadth, ignoring or encouraging overspecialization, and supporting reasonable and appropriate individualization. Adherence to curriculum rules and program policies can also be determined by this record review.

Obviously, the dean who personally undertakes to do all of these things will fail to do most of them, and other responsibilities may be neglected. Hence the dean may need to delegate some of these tasks to assistants or appoint ad hoc committees for specific purposes. Some of the data collection and studies suggested may be viewed as providing essential information for the deliberations of standing committees. Even though an office of institutional research exists, the dean may wish to allocate *some* funds for support of curricular studies and encourage faculty members or students to engage in them. This latter possibility holds many opportunities for in-service training of faculty and students, even to the extent of regarding some of these assignments as internships for faculty or as credit assignments to students.

Although this volume is primarily focused upon undergraduate programs, a few comments are in order about the role of the graduate dean. This is especially true because departments generally have much greater autonomy with regard to graduate education. But departments with large graduate programs may become very lax in adherence to institution policies and may also carry over to the undergraduate program some of the practices and policies growing out of the graduate program. At one point particularly, the two become very closely interrelated. The department that uses teaching assistants as a means of recruiting graduate students and then assigns these individuals to handling laboratory or classroom requirements with minimal assistance may threaten the quality of undergraduate education in order to maintain the viability of the graduate program. The graduate dean can help this situation markedly by carefully monitoring the standards in admitting students and in building programs and by carefully reviewing the assignments of graduate assistants or fellows.

Although graduate programs tend to be much more specialized than undergraduate programs, there are master's and doctor's programs that draw upon several disciplines or departments. These programs present recurring problems with regard to graduate course offerings, definition of degree programs and requirements, adequacy of advising, and doctoral committee composition and functioning. For such programs, the graduate dean's responsibilities are similar to those of undergraduate college deans. Indeed, the activities and stance of the graduate dean can support the activities of undergraduate college deans. In particular, the monitoring of interdepartmental collaboration on graduate programs, completion of residency and other degree requirements, appropriateness of degree designations, and evaluation of the applicability and quality of theses and dissertations bear directly on the departmental standards and on the suitability of the graduate experience to the preparation of undergraduate teachers.

Role of the Academic Vice-President

All of the responsibilities and functions indicated for a college dean can appropriately be assigned also to the academic vice-president. In small institutions, one person may hold both titles. Like chairmen, deans will vary in their attention to curricular and program review. Unless the academic vice-president monitors college and departmental curriculum review and program practices, it is likely that there will be marked variation across the institution. As noted at the beginning of this chapter, professional colleges and the arts and science unit or units present somewhat different problems to the respective deans. Nevertheless, the interrelationship of the colleges and departments, and the possibility that the service role of departments in some undergraduate professional programs could be significantly enlarged for the purposes of career development, suggest that there is a considerable amount of common concern and a justification for developing and enforcing some uniform policies and practices across all undergraduate programs. Resource A—Principles for Program Development—and Resource B—Enrollment Standards for Program Development illustrate the nature and content of policy statements that might be appropriate at the institutional level.

Through accumulation and analysis of data on courses and program enrollments, the academic vice-president can be made aware of possibilities of collaboration and interaction among programs and courses that may not be readily apparent at the college level. It is also possible for the academic vice-president to note duplication in courses and programs across the university. Applied programs in vocational or professionally oriented colleges frequently attempt to develop their own courses in psychology, economics, accounting, mathematics, statistics, and various of the natural sciences. Departments are likely to become aware of such duplication and find some problems with it, but the general policy of minimal interference with the activities and programs of other units may not permit the raising of questions about these practices. Such duplication is not necessarily bad, and it may be very necessary and sound, but it should be known and justified. The academic vice-president should also be aware of program overlap and duplication with nearby universities. It is his or her responsibility, in cooperation with whatever deans are involved, to develop and maintain a statement that both recognizes the existence of such duplication and provides a sound rationale for maintaining or abandoning it.

It is the further responsibility of the academic vice-president to emphasize continually quality in teaching and advising and to develop and enforce policies regarding the essential information to be provided on course offerings and programs. In many institutions, the rotation of chairmen and of deans means that every few years a new individual appears who is still heavily oriented to a discipline, to a department, and often to graduate study and research. It usually takes at least a year for a new dean to develop some sensitivity to the problems of undergraduate education and an awareness that evocation and enforcement of some policies defining course specifications and program requirements are essential if advisers and students are to have some freedom in developing individualized programs. The academic vice-president position may also undergo some changes that complicate the role of that office in providing continuity in some of these matters. To the extent that these responsibilities and policies are spelled out in detail, individuals at that level can more readily understand and assume them. Regardless of their former discipline and departmental connection, they soon find that, in this position, they are relatively far removed from that departmental discipline and must look at every issue on a broad institutional basis. If an institution has a regular or recurrent review program for courses and programs, it should be directed from the vice-president's office. Full records on all reviews should be maintained there, and someone should be responsible for notifying colleges and departments as the date for the next review approaches. If comments, suggestions, and criticisms regarding programs and emanating from any source are filed in the context of these reports, any memorandum indicating an imminent review can also point out some of the issues that should be given specific attention. The designation and use of outside consultants in connection with a program review should be at the demand or option of the academic vice-president. Individuals at the program level who request outside consultants, intentionally or otherwise, tend to select those who are sympathetic to the present characteristics of that program. Consultants, in turn, tend to avoid antagonizing individuals who are responsible for their presence and for paying their honoraria.

Decisions about needed new programs, program elimination, and program cutback or expansion should, to the extent that the internal closure is involved, be made in the vice-president's office and be reinforced by academic budget decisions. External agencies may subvert or deny these internal actions. Like the dean, the academic vice-president will benefit from using advisory committees, assistants, and faculty members in various aspects of the curriculum review process. Reviews at the all-institutional level provide special opportunities for able individuals to rise above the limitations of their own disciplines and departments and develop broader insight and concerns.

The academic vice-president should be aware of and avoid the all too common tendency to assume that significant change will be brought about by some gimmick or by some inconsequential adjustment. For example, placing a great deal of emphasis on the elimination of one- and two-credit courses without elaborating on some of the issues of sound learning and quality involved may only lead (as I have seen) to a combination by two faculty members of two two-credit courses into a four-credit course. This course was still taught by the same individuals and evaluated in the same way up to the final stage of entering an average grade rather than a separate grade for each course. Calendar changes, at times, have been touted as a way to force faculty to review all course offerings. A calendar change may be beneficial if the calendar change in itself eliminates some problems or opens up educational and service opportunities not possible before. The problem with the calendar is that it divides the educational experience of students and the teaching activities of faculty members into arbitrary units, each complete in itself, thereby greatly complicating the essential concerns about continuity, sequence, coherence, unity, and integration of knowledge and practice. The academic vice-president will, in most cases, be heavily involved in budgetary allocation to colleges and departments. That officer should be cautious in tying either too much or too little to budgetary decisions. Either withdrawal of funds or the addition of funds can result in program units that bring about major changes in form without affecting either function or spirit. If every discussion of academic quality and innovation becomes an issue of costs and the impossibility of any additional dollars, it is likely that precious little creative innovation will appear.

Roles of the President and Board of Trustees

It is my view that the president and the board of trustees should not intervene in matters of course and program except as necessary to resolve internal disagreements or as opportunity exists for providing encouragement and support for restudy and change. A president who intervenes in curricular matters is likely to find an undue amount of time absorbed and some influence compromised. Inevitably, time must be spent with the academic vice-president and the deans to avoid countermanding or contradicting developments initiated at that level. The president who has strong convictions about the relationship of career education and liberal education or about some conception of general education may influence developments by internal and external statements, but curriculum and program changes do not come about by administrative direction or fiat. New programs, program elimination, and program renovation are almost certainly of concern to both the president and the board because these items generate the possibility of a new conception of the institution and subsequent public reactions, both good and bad. The board will benefit by occasional sessions in which the academic vice-president and the various deans talk about curriculum and program matters. Thereby, the board members can be more intelligent and insightful about the institution and respond more intelligently to anyone who has comments or questions about curriculum and program matters. In many cases, some of the more esoteric program statements introducing new curricular concepts with uncertain or abstruse meanings might have been avoided if they had first been discussed with a lay board and administrators. Both the board and the president should have a special concern for cooperation with other institutions and for fulfillment of their social responsibilities in regard to program need and duplication. The various statements in this book about curricular and program policies and practices become important not only to administrators within the institution and to faculty members developing programs but also to the board as indicative of the philosophy and framework within which the institution approaches its task of developing degree programs. It is not unlikely that an occasional discussion of such statements by board members will reveal possible interpretations and misinterpretations that the academic mind, so close to and so emotionally involved in the task, failed to note.

Summary

        This chapter has emphasized that successive levels of administration in a college or university must continually monitor what is going on in the curriculum and in the programs offered by the various units within the university. These programs and the degrees associated with them constitute the heart of the academic program for the largest segment of most universities— the undergraduates. In the past, faculty members have tended to assume that undergraduates lack commitment, insight, and experience in making judgments about programs and their relationship to later careers. The widespread interest in lifelong education for adults and the increasing number of adults pursuing degrees while holding full-time positions has made us all aware that some, if not all, students have insight and experience as well as aspirations, and that many are able to judge as well as or better than faculty members and advisers the relationship between academic courses and programs and careers. But experience and intelligence are not solely a matter of age, and a little reflection, coupled with experience as a teacher and adviser, indicates that many undergraduates of the traditional age are equally capable of doing planning for themselves. Furthermore, thoughtful educators in the present day are accepting the idea that the educational process itself should be a developmental experience for the person. Each educational experience is seen as having some relevance to life and career. Ultimate aspirations are regarded as appropriate considerations in developing individual programs. Such programs do not fall within narrow disciplinary lines or the rather limited scope of professional degree programs. No one can predict the new combinations of knowledge from various fields that may be found to be richly productive as new problems develop and are attacked in novel ways. Finally, the range of interests and talents of individuals, combined with their strengths and weaknesses, far transcends the possibility of arraying in any college or university all of the programs that may be appropriate for all students.

All colleges and universities should have a clear statement of policy and procedure with regard to program development. They need to arrange, through planning and administrative suggestion and direction, for continuing review and modification of programs and provide for the possibility that meaningful new programs can readily be developed for individual and recognized social needs. In so doing, the institution demonstrates a concern for quality education, an awareness of the relevance of that education to social needs, and a responsivity to society as the needs and problems of that society change. Administrators at all levels need to accept and support these concerns.

Suggestions for Further Reading

Foster, W. T. *Administration of the College Curriculum.* Boston: Houghton Mifflin, 1911.

Kieft, R. N., Armijo, F., and Bucklew, N. S. *A Handbook for Institutional Academic and Program Planning: From Idea to*

Implementation. Boulder, Colo.: National Center for Higher Education Management Systems, 1978.

Lenning, O. T. *The Outcomes Structure: An Overview and Procedures for Applying It in Postsecondary Education Institutions.* Boulder, Colo.: National Center for Higher Education Management Systems, 1977.

Lenning, O. T., and others. *A Structure for the Outcomes of Postsecondary Education.* Boulder, Colo.: National Center for Higher Education Management Systems, 1977.

Patterson, K. D. "The Administration of University Curriculum." *Journal of Higher Education,* 1967, *38,* 438-443.

 Resource A

Principles for
Program Development

 General

1. All undergraduate programs should provide a 25 percent institutionwide liberal or general education requirement. The courses acceptable for satisfying this requirement may vary with the student's program emphasis, the purpose being to extend the student's horizon to include concepts, principles, values, problems, or methods not a part of the major program emphasis.

2. All undergraduate programs should require an additional 30 percent of the initial 120 credit hours in courses generally accepted as included in the liberal arts and sciences, although the courses may not always be located in the college of arts and sciences.

Note: These principles are modified from a similar list in Paul L. Dressel, *The Undergraduate Curriculum in Higher Education* (Washington, D.C.: Center for Applied Research in Education, 1963), pp. 83-87.

3. All undergraduate vocational programs in a college should include a core of courses in that college amounting to about 10 percent of the basic 120 semester hours.

4. Each major or program should specify a common depth or specialization requirement.of 45 percent of the total 120 hours or approximately 60 percent of the credit requirements for a departmental major.

5. Approximately 10 percent of the initial 120 semester credit hours of the baccalaureate requirement should be reserved for an elective major component or for specialization directed toward subvocations in the field for which the college curriculum is preparatory.

6. All undergraduate programs should reserve at least 10 percent of the basic 120 credit hours for electives chosen by the student and adviser.

7. All programs should be screened to ensure that the objectives are reasonably attainable in a four-year program (or other specified period) and that the courses and other educational experiences required for this attainment are appropriate in content and outcomes to the college or university.

8. Any credit course should either develop or utilize a definable substantive body of content. Skills of a repetitive, how-to-do-it nature should be minimized as course objectives and relegated to the laboratory or to field experience, or simply specified as required demonstrable levels of competency for acceptance, continuation, or graduation in the field.

Majors

9. A department should generally offer only one major (although there must be obvious exceptions, as in a department of foreign languages). A few courses at the junior or senior level may be oriented to subspecialties, but otherwise specialization should be at the postgraduate level.

10. Departmental specialization beyond the common requirement should be in courses offered at the junior and senior levels and developed on the assumption that the common requirements are either prerequisites or taken concurrently.

11. Special courses or sections for majors in other fields should be resisted, unless the need for them can be demonstrated to be more fundamental than a matter of one or two credits or a slightly different selection or organization of content materials.

12. Introductory course offerings in the basic arts and sciences should be developed in relation to the needs of the total college or university rather than on narrow, specialized departmental concerns. Only thus is it possible to insist that each technical or professional curriculum use these basic courses in preference to developing its own. (See 11.)

13. With possibly a few exceptions, courses should be planned on a four- or five-credit basis. Class sessions, especially in courses beyond the freshman year, may be fewer than the number of credits.*

14. Laboratory requirements should be reduced to a minimum by carefully defining the objectives to be met and by developing evaluation procedures whereby student achievement can be determined.

15. Departments in disciplines attractive as general electives may appropriately offer an advanced course or two at the junior or senior level without prerequisites other than relevant courses of the general core requirement. Since these courses would not fall into the sequential course organization (if any exists) for majors, they could be excluded from satisfying the major requirements of the departments. The presence of such electives would permit and encourage students to broaden the scope of their education without forcing them into unreasonable competition with students better grounded in the area.

16. Departmental credit offerings in structured courses (see 18) should not exceed forty to fifty semester credit hours (excluding the offerings suggested in 11 and 15).

*If the four- or five-credit course pattern were adopted, requirements could be phrased in reference to courses. The four-credit pattern is sometimes regarded as inefficient in use of classroom space, but, if sessions are arranged on alternate days, five four-credit courses can be accommodated in four classrooms. Use of longer periods than the usual fifty minutes will permit a reduction to two or three class meetings.

17. At least half of the departmental major of thirty to forty hours should be a common requirement for all majors in the department.

18. One or more courses in each department should be designated as independent study, thereby permitting emphasis or specialization appropriate for individuals or small groups of students. Many of the advanced courses often listed in departments could be dropped and considered as one of the possible areas of independent study.

19. The maximum number of credits from any single department acceptable for a degree should be forty.

20. Every departmental major statement should include delineation of areas appropriate for supporting study, not so much in terms of specific courses as in terms of blocks of relevant knowledge, abilities, and skills.

21. The objectives or levels of competency required for enrollment in and credit in each course should be defined in sufficiently clear terms so that students may be properly placed and/or granted full credit for achievement, however attained.

Concentrations Other Than Departmental Majors

22. Some central purpose, some unifying or integrative element, should be specified.

23. Some sequential characteristics should be present, ensuring that depth rather than superficial contact with a series of related disciplines is achieved.

24. An identifiable core of organized knowledge and principles should be included.

25. The total credit hours required in the concentration should not exceed forty-eight.

26. Acceptable concentrations should not be restricted to those listed in the university catalogue. The attempt to list every acceptable concentration tends to encourage choice of a listed pattern rather than the planning of one suited to the student's needs and interests.

Planning Student Programs

27. A statement of the purposes of each major and a justification for all requirements and sequences should be available to advisers and to prospective majors.

28. Student programs should be planned to maintain as much flexibility in vocational choice as is consistent with preparation for activity in the vocation chosen. This can be accomplished by emphasizing liberal and general professional study rather than specialized work, and by organizing distinctive programs that prepare the student for several related jobs rather than for particular specialties.

29. Both liberal and technical or professional work, on the one hand, and breadth and depth, on the other, should be pursued throughout the entire program.

30. Early in the college career of each student, the entire college program should be tentatively mapped out by the student and adviser. This plan should include some attention to all relevant experiences, not solely to required course work. The existence of a plan is important to give direction to the student; it should, however, be subject to change if goals are changed.

31. Acceleration by year-round attendance or by comprehensive examinations should be considered. This has implications both for efficient use of space and for wise use of student time.

32. Wherever possible, students should be encouraged and assisted to engage in work or service related to their major or specialized study. Experience in assisting a professor by checking freshman papers would encourage review and increased understanding; it might also interest some students in college teaching. Other students might select experiences directly related to their vocational choice.

33. Students (especially those uncertain about their careers) should be encouraged to use their electives to explore unknown or unfamiliar areas.

34. Any full-time student should, upon authorization by his or her adviser, be permitted to visit any class (if space is

available) and be permitted to take an examination for credit thereafter.

35. Each student should be encouraged (when appropriate) to take a course offered by his or her adviser. Ultimately, the student should have an adviser in his or her field of interest.

36. The instructional methods and requirements of individual courses should be known to students and advisers so that the program planned for the student may include laboratory, writing, speaking, discussion, case method, and other learning experiences significant in attaining a broad liberal education.

37. All students should take at least one course that exposes them to points of view, values, and cultures very different from their own.

38. All students should enroll in the senior year in an integrative senior seminar. This seminar should be organized on either a universitywide or a collegewide basis. Limited to groups of not more than twenty-five students, the seminar should encourage them to review the summary implications of their university studies and experiences and the relationship of their past university activities to the role that they will shortly assume in society.

39. Faculty advisers would be expected to interpret these principles to students and to insist on the development of progress in conformity with them. Individual student programs should occasionally be reviewed to ascertain whether the spirit of these principles is being carefully followed.

 # Resource B

Enrollment Standards for Program Development

   The intent of these standards is to reduce small-enroll-
ment, high-cost instruction in all circumstances wherein such
patterns are not necessitated by the nature of the learning involved and the supervision required. In many courses, the interaction and collaboration among students and the feedback to
the instructor from them are essential in stimulating and assisting student learning and in inspiring and directing the activities
of the teacher. The designated enrollments are only illustrative
and may be modified as institutional norms of class size suggest.

Minimum Standards for Courses

Lower-Division Courses

1. A freshman or sophomore course offered only once
during the regular academic year that failed to enroll a total of

Note: These standards are modified from a policy statement long
used and frequently revised at Michigan State University.

thirty students in the last two times offered shall be dropped or given only in alternate years.

2. A course offered twice during the regular academic year that failed in the preceding year to enroll a total of thirty students shall be offered only once.

3. A course offered every quarter of the academic year that failed during the preceding year to enroll a total of thirty to fifty students shall be offered no more than two quarters. If fewer than thirty students are enrolled, the offering should be reduced to one quarter.

4. A proposed course offering that fails to enroll ten students shall be dropped, even if prior enrollment during the preceding year permits its listing under 1, 2, or 3.

Upper-Division Courses

5. A course offered only once in the regular academic year that failed to secure a total enrollment of ten students in the last two times offered shall be dropped or given only in alternate years.

6. A course offered twice in the regular academic year that failed in the preceding year to enroll at least twenty students shall be offered one term only.

7. A course offered in every quarter of the regular academic year that failed in the preceding year to enroll a total of twenty to forty students shall be offered only twice. If the total enrollment was under twenty, the offering should be reduced to one quarter.

8. If a proposed course offering fails to enroll five students, it shall be dropped for that term even if prior enrollment during the preceding year permits its listing under 5, 6, or 7.

9. Courses dropped under these rules may be reinstated only by following the procedures for the introduction of new courses. Enrollment estimates become crucial for reinstating such courses.

10. If certain courses require smaller classes than those herein provided, special exceptions may be requested of the appropriate administrators and committees.

11. Courses with a limited demand but essential to an

institutional program may be exempted from these regulations in whole or in part. Requests should be directed to the appropriate administrators and committees.

Minimum Standards for Number of Course Sections

12. If the total course enrollment in a particular term is fewer than twenty-five students, one section only shall be provided.

13. If the total course enrollment in a particular term is fewer than fifty but more than twenty-five students, not more than two sections shall be provided.

14. If the course enrollment for a particular term exceeds fifty students, the sections into which it is divided must be so formed that no section contains fewer than twenty students.

15. Where specialized methods of instruction are employed, the application of these rules may be modified by action of the appropriate administrators or committees.

~~ Bibliography

~~ The following section contains those references suggested after each chapter and many others relevant to the concerns of this volume. There are also numerous references dealing with aspects of the curriculum not discussed herein, for example, teaching and curriculum problems in the various disciplines.

Abercrombie, M. L. J. *Aims and Techniques of Group Teaching.* London: Society for Research into Higher Education, 1974.
Abrams, I., and Hatch, W. R. *Study Abroad.* New Dimensions in Higher Education, No. 6. Washington, D.C.: Office of Education, U.S. Department of Health, Education, and Welfare, 1960.
Adams, F. S., and Stephens, C. W. *College and University Work Programs: Implications and Implementations.* Carbondale: Southern Illinois University Press, 1970.
Ahearn, F. L., Jr., Bolan, R. S., and Burke, E. M. "A Social Action Approach for Planning Education." *Journal of Education for Social Work,* 1975, *11* (3), 5-10.
Ahmann, J. S. "Aspects of Curriculum Evaluation: A Synopsis." In R. W. Tyler, R. M. Gagne, and M. Scriven, *Perspectives of Curriculum Evaluation.* American Educational Re-

291

search Association Monograph Series on Curriculum Evaluation. Chicago: Rand McNally, 1967.

Albert, E. M. (Ed.). *The Teaching of Anthropology*. Berkeley:
University of California Press, 1963.

Aldridge, G., and McGrath, E. J. *Liberal Education and Social
Work*. New York: Teachers College Press, Columbia University, 1965.

Altman, R. A. *The Upper Division College*. San Francisco: Jossey-Bass, 1970.

American Society of Engineering Education. *Liberal Learning
for the Engineer*. Washington, D.C.: American Society of
Engineering Education, 1968.

Anderson, J. "The Teacher as Model." *American Scholar*, 1961,
30, 393-398.

Anderson, O. R. "The Effects of Varying Structure in Science
Content on the Acquisition of Science Knowledge." *Journal
of Research in Science Teaching*, 1968, *5*, 361-364.

Anderson, O. R. *The Quantitative Analysis of Structure in
Teaching*. New York: Teachers College Press, Columbia University, 1971.

Anderson, S. B., and Ball, S. *The Profession and Practice of Program Evaluation*. San Francisco: Jossey-Bass, 1978.

Askew, T. A. *The Small College: A Bibliographic Handbook*.
Washington, D.C.: Council for the Advancement of Small
Colleges, 1973.

Association of American Colleges. *Non-Western Studies in the
Liberal Arts College*. Washington, D.C.: American Council on
Education, 1964.

Astin, A. W. *The College Environment*. Washington, D.C.:
American Council on Education, 1968.

Astin, A. W. *Four Critical Years: Effects of College on Beliefs,
Attitudes, and Knowledge*. San Francisco: Jossey-Bass, 1977.

Axelrod, J. *The University Teacher as Artist: Toward an Aes-
thetics of Teaching with Emphasis on the Humanities*. San
Francisco: Jossey-Bass, 1973.

Axelrod, J., and others. *Search for Relevance: The Campus in
Crisis*. San Francisco: Jossey-Bass, 1969.

Babb, L. A., and others. *Education at Amherst Reconsidered.* Amherst, Mass.: Amherst College Press, 1978.

Baird, L. L. "Teaching Styles." *Journal of Educational Psychology,* 1973, *64* (1), 15-21.

Baker, J. J. W. (Ed.). *Biology in a Liberal Education.* Reports of the Colloquium on Biology in a Liberal Education, Stanford University, August 2-13, 1965. CUEBS Publication 15. Washington, D.C.: Commission on Undergraduate Education in the Biological Sciences, 1967.

Bardon, A. H. *Studying the Effects of College Education.* New Haven, Conn.: Edward W. Hazen Foundation, 1959.

Baskin, S., and others. *Innovation in Higher Education: Developments, Research and Priorities.* New York: McGraw-Hill, 1965.

Belknap, R. L., and Kuhns, R. *Tradition and Innovation: General Education and the Reintegration of the University.* New York: Columbia University Press, 1977.

Bell, D. *The Reforming of General Education.* New York: Columbia University Press, 1966.

Bellack, A. A. "The Structure of Knowledge and the Structure of the Curriculum." In D. Huebner (Ed.), *A Reassessment of the Curriculum.* New York: Bureau of Publications, Teachers College, Columbia University, 1964.

Benne, K. D., and Muntyan, B. *Human Relations in Curriculum Change.* New York: Dryden Press, 1951.

Bersi, R. M. *Restructuring the Baccalaureate: A Focus on Time-Shortened Degree Programs in the United States.* Washington, D.C.: American Association of State Colleges and Universities, 1973.

Bidwell, P. W. *Undergraduate Education in Foreign Affairs.* New York: Columbia University Press, 1962.

Blackburn, R., and others. *Changing Practices in Undergraduate Education.* Berkeley, Calif.: Carnegie Council on Policy Studies in Higher Education, 1976.

Bligh, D. *What's the Use of Lectures?* Harmondsworth, Middlesex, England: Penguin Books, 1972.

Bloom, B. S. (Ed.). *Taxonomy of Educational Objectives: The*

Classification of Educational Goals. Handbook 1: *Cognitive Domain.* New York: Longmans, Green, 1956.

Bonthius, R. H., and others. *The Independent Study Program in the United States.* Report on Undergraduate Instructional Method, Committee of Educational Inquiry, College of Wooster. New York: Columbia University Press, 1957.

Booth, W. C. (Ed.). *The Knowledge Most Worth Having.* Chicago: University of Chicago Press, 1967.

Bowen, H. R. *Investment in Learning: The Individual and Social Value of American Higher Education.* San Francisco: Jossey-Bass, 1977.

Boyer, E. L., and Kaplan, M. *Educating for Survival.* New Rochelle, N.Y.: Change Magazine Press, 1977.

Bragg, A. K. *The Socialization Process in Higher Education.* ERIC/Higher Education Research Report No. 7. Washington, D.C.: ERIC Clearinghouse on Higher Education, George Washington University, 1976.

Branscomb, H., Milton, O., Richardson, J., and Spivey, H. *The Competent College Student: An Essay on the Objectives and Quality of Higher Education.* Nashville: Tennessee Higher Education Commission, 1977.

Brick, M., and McGrath, E. J. *Innovations in Liberal Arts Colleges.* New York: Teachers College Press, Columbia University, 1969.

Briggs, L. J. *Handbook of Procedures for the Design of Instruction.* Pittsburgh: American Institutes for Research, 1970.

Brown, H. S., and Mayhew, L. B. *American Higher Education.* New York: Center for Applied Research in Education, 1965.

Brubacher, J. S., and Rudy, W. *Higher Education in Transition: A History of American Colleges, 1636-1968.* New York: Harper & Row, 1976.

Bruner, J. S. *The Process of Education.* Cambridge, Mass.: Harvard University Press, 1961.

Bruner, J. S. *Toward a Theory of Instruction.* Cambridge, Mass.: Belknap Press, Harvard University Press, 1966.

Butts, R. F. *The College Charts Its Course.* New York: McGraw-Hill, 1939.

Carnegie Foundation for the Advancement of Teaching. *Mis-*

sions of the College Curriculum: A Contemporary Review with Suggestions. San Francisco: Jossey-Bass, 1977.

Carpenter, P. *History Teaching: The Era Approach.* Cambridge, England: Cambridge University Press, 1964.

Cheit, E. *The Useful Arts and the Liberal Tradition.* New York: McGraw-Hill, 1975.

Chickering, A. W. *Education and Identity.* San Francisco: Jossey-Bass, 1969.

Chickering, A. W., and others. *Developing the College Curriculum: A Handbook for Faculty and Administrators.* Washington, D.C.: Council for the Advancement of Small Colleges, 1977.

Chisholm, R. *Theory of Knowledge.* Englewood Cliffs, N.J.: Prentice-Hall, 1966.

Claxton, C. S., and Ralston, Y. *Learning Styles: Their Impact on Teaching and Administration.* AAHE-ERIC/Higher Education Research Report No. 10. Washington, D.C.: American Association for Higher Education, 1978.

Cohen, A. *Objectives for College Courses.* Beverly Hills, Calif.: Glencoe Press, 1970.

Cohen, J. S. *The Superior Student in American Higher Education.* New York: McGraw-Hill, 1966.

Cole, C. C., Jr. *To Improve Instruction.* AAHE-ERIC/Higher Education Research Report No. 2. Washington, D.C.: American Association for Higher Education, 1978.

Cole, C. C., Jr., and Lewis, L. G. *Flexibility in the Undergraduate Curriculum.* New Dimensions in Higher Education No. 10. Washington, D.C.: U.S. Government Printing Office, 1966.

College Entrance Examination Board. *Curricular Change in the Foreign Languages.* 1963 Colloquium on Curricular Change. New York: College Entrance Examination Board, 1963.

Commager, H. S. *The Nature and Study of History.* Columbus, Ohio: Merrill, 1965.

Commission on International Understanding. *Non-Western Studies in the Liberal Arts College.* Washington, D.C.: Association of American Colleges, 1964.

Commission on Science Education. *An Evaluation Model and*

Its Application. Washington, D.C.: American Association for the Advancement of Science, 1965.

Commission on Undergraduate Education in the Biological Sciences. *Biology for the Non-Major.* Washington, D.C.: Commission on Undergraduate Education in the Biological Sciences, 1967.

Committee on the Student in Higher Education. *The Student in Higher Education.* ED 028 735. New Haven, Conn.: Edward W. Hazen Foundation, 1968.

Committee on the University Calendar. *The University Calendar.* American Association of Collegiate Registrars and Admissions Officers. Washington, D.C.: American Council on Education, 1961.

Connery, R. H. (Ed.). *Teaching Political Science.* Durham, N.C.: Duke University Press, 1965.

Council of Graduate Schools in the United States. *Assessment of Quality in Graduate Education: Summary of a Multidimensional Approach.* Washington, D.C.: Council of Graduate Schools in the United States, 1976.

Council on Education in Geological Sciences. *Audio-Tutorial Instruction: A Strategy for Teaching Introductory College Geology.* Washington, D.C.: Council on Education in Geological Sciences, 1970.

Cronbach, L. J. "The Psychological Background for Curriculum Experimentation." In P. C. Rosenbloom and P. S. Hillestad (Eds.), *Modern Viewpoints in the Curriculum.* New York: McGraw-Hill, 1964.

Cross, K. P. *The Integration of Learning and Earning: Cooperative Education and Nontraditional Study.* AAHE-ERIC/ Higher Education Research Report No. 4. Washington, D.C.: American Association for Higher Education, 1973.

Cross, K. P. *Accent on Learning: Improving Instruction and Reshaping the Curriculum.* San Francisco: Jossey-Bass, 1976.

Cunningham, W. F. *General Education and the Liberal College.* St. Louis, Mo.: Herder, 1953.

Darnell, R. M., and others. "Ecology and the Undergraduate Curriculum." *Bio Science,* 1970, *20* (13), 743-760.

Davis, J. R. *Teaching Strategies for the College Classroom.* Boulder, Colo.: Westview Press, 1976.

DeCarlo, C. R., and Robinson, O. W. *Education in Business and Industry.* Washington, D.C.: Center for Applied Research in Education, 1966.

Dennis, L. E., and Kauffman, J. F. *The College and the Student.* Washington, D.C.: American Council on Education, 1966.

Dressel, P. L. *The Undergraduate Curriculum in Higher Education.* Washington, D.C.: Center for Applied Research in Education, 1963.

Dressel, P. L. "A Look at New Curriculum Models for Undergraduate Education." *Journal of Higher Education,* 1965, *36* (2), 89-96.

Dressel, P. L. "Large Credit Blocks—Pro and Con." *Liberal Education,* 1965, *51,* 382-390.

Dressel, P. L. *College and University Curriculum.* (2nd ed.) Berkeley, Calif.: McCutchan, 1971.

Dressel, P. L. "Values Cognitive and Affective." *Journal of Higher Education,* 1971, *43,* 400-405.

Dressel, P. L., and Associates. *Evaluation in Higher Education.* Boston: Houghton Mifflin, 1961.

Dressel, P. L., and DeLisle, F. H. *Undergraduate Curriculum Trends.* Washington, D.C.: American Council on Education, 1969.

Dressel, P. L., and Mayhew, L. B. *General Education: Explorations in Evaluation.* Washington, D.C.: American Council on Education, 1954.

Dressel, P. L., and Thompson, M. M. *Independent Study: A New Interpretation of Concepts, Practices, and Problems.* San Francisco: Jossey-Bass, 1973.

Eble, K. E. *The Recognition and Evaluation of Teaching.* Project to Improve College Teaching and the Committee on Evaluation. Washington, D.C.: American Association of University Professors and Association of American Colleges, 1971.

Eble, K. E. *Professors as Teachers.* San Francisco: Jossey-Bass, 1972.

Eble, K. E. *The Craft of Teaching: A Guide to Mastering the Professor's Art.* San Francisco: Jossey-Bass, 1976.

Eble, K. E. *The Art of Administration: A Guide for Academic Administrators.* San Francisco: Jossey-Bass, 1978.

Eddy, E. W., Jr. *The College Influence on Student Character.* Washington, D.C.: American Council on Education, 1959.

Eiss, A. F., and Harbeck, M. B. *Behavioral Objectives in the Affective Domain.* Washington, D.C.: National Education Association, 1969.

Elam, S. (Ed.). *Education and the Structure of Knowledge.* Chicago: Rand McNally, 1964.

Elton, G. R. *The Practice of History.* New York: Crowell, 1967.

Eulau, H., and March, J. G. (Eds.). *Political Science.* Englewood Cliffs, N.J.: Prentice-Hall, 1969.

Feldman, K. A., and Newcomb, T. M. *The Impact of College on Students.* San Francisco: Jossey-Bass, 1969.

Flexner, A. *Medical Education in the United States.* Bulletin No. 4. New York: Carnegie Foundation for the Advancement of Teaching, 1910.

Ford, G. W., and Pugno, L. (Eds.). *The Structure of Knowledge and the Curriculum.* Chicago: Rand McNally, 1964.

Forrest, A., and Steele, J. *College Outcome Measures Project: Assessment of General Education Knowledge and Skills.* Iowa City, Iowa: American College Testing Program, 1977.

Foster, W. T. *Administration of the College Curriculum.* Boston: Houghton Mifflin, 1911.

Gagné, R. M. *The Conditions of Learning.* (2nd ed.) New York: Holt, Rinehart and Winston, 1970.

Gerhard, D. "The Emergence of the Credit System in American Education Considered as a Problem of Social and Intellectual History." *American Association of University Professors Bulletin,* 1955, *41,* 647-668.

Giddens, T. R., and Kenny, J. W. "Research Models for the Evaluation of Interim Programs." *Research in Higher Education,* 1975, *3* (4), 393-401.

Givens, P. R. *Student-Designed Curricula.* Research Currents, ED 061 917. Washington, D.C.: American Association for Higher Education, 1972.

Grant, M. K., and Hoeber, D. R. *Basic Skills Programs: Are They Working?* AAHE-ERIC/Higher Education Research Report No. 1. Washington, D.C.: American Association for Higher Education, 1978.

Green, T. F. "The Concept of Teaching." In D. Vandenberg (Ed.), *Teaching and Learning.* Urbana: University of Illinois Press, 1969.

Greene, T. *Liberal Education Reconsidered.* Cambridge, Mass.: Harvard University Press, 1953.

Greene, T., and others. *Liberal Education Reexamined: Its Role in a Democracy.* New York: Harper & Row, 1943.

Grose, R. F. "How Long Is a Credit? When Is a Course?" *College and University,* 1970, *46* (1), 20-32.

Handlin, O., and Handlin, M. F. *The American College and American Culture: Socialization as a Function of Higher Education.* New York: McGraw-Hill, 1970.

Harvard Committee. *General Education in a Free Society.* Report of the Harvard Committee. Cambridge, Mass.: Harvard University Press, 1945.

Harvey, J. *Reforming Undergraduate Curriculum: Problems and Proposals.* Washington, D.C.: ERIC Clearinghouse on Higher Education, George Washington University, 1971.

Haswell, H. A., and Lindquist, C. B. *Undergraduate Curriculum Patterns.* No. FS5, 256:56021. Washington, D.C.: U.S. Government Printing Office, 1965.

Hefferlin, J. L. *Dynamics of Academic Reform.* San Francisco: Jossey-Bass, 1969.

Heffernan, J. M. "The Credibility of the Credit Hour: The History, Use, and Shortcomings of the Credit System." *Journal of Higher Education,* 1973, *54* (1), 61-72.

Henderson, N. K. *University Teaching.* London: Oxford University Press, 1969.

Heywood, J. *Assessment in Higher Education.* New York: Wiley, 1977.

Heywood, J., and Montagu-Pollock, H. *Science for Arts Students: A Case Study in Curriculum Development.* Guildford, Surrey, England: Society for Research into Higher Education, 1977.

Hill, W. F. *Learning thru Discussion.* Beverly Hills, Calif.: Sage Publications, 1972.

Hodgkinson, H. L., Hurst, J., and Levine, H. *Improving and Assessing Performance: Evaluation in Higher Education.* Berkeley: Center for Research and Development in Higher Education, University of California, 1975.

Hofstadter, R., and Hardy, E. D. *The Development and Scope of Higher Education in the United States.* New York: Columbia University Press, 1952.

Hofstadter, R., and Smith, W. (Eds.). *American Higher Education.* Chicago: University of Chicago Press, 1961.

Hong, H. (Ed.). *Integration in the Christian Liberal Arts College.* Northfield, Minn.: St. Olaf College Press, 1955.

Hook, S., Kurtz, P., and Todorovich, M. (Eds.). *The Philosophy of the Curriculum: The Need for General Education.* Buffalo, N.Y.: Prometheus Books, 1975.

Hyman, R. T. *Ways of Teaching.* New York: Lippincott, 1970.

Katz, J., and Sanford, N. "The Curriculum in the Perspective of the Theory of Personality Development." In N. Sanford (Ed.), *The American College.* New York: Wiley, 1966.

Kaysen, C. (Ed.). *Content and Context: Essays on College Education.* New York: McGraw-Hill, 1973.

Kerr, J. F. (Ed.). *Changing the Curriculum.* London: University of London Press, 1968.

Kieft, R. N., Armijo, F., and Bucklew, N. S. *A Handbook for Institutional Academic and Program Planning: From Idea to Implementation.* Boulder, Colo.: National Center for Higher Education Management Systems, 1978.

King, A., and Brownell, J. *The Curriculum and the Disciplines of Knowledge.* New York: Wiley, 1966.

Kliebard, H. "The Tyler Rationale." In A. Bellack and H. Kliebard (Eds.), *Curriculum and Evaluation.* Berkeley, Calif.: McCutchan, 1977.

Krathwohl, D. R., and others. *Taxonomy of Educational Objectives: The Classification of Educational Goals.* Handbook 2: *Affective Domain.* New York: McKay, 1964.

Krislov, S. *A Laboratories Approach to Teaching Political Science.* Minneapolis: Department of Political Science, University of Minnesota, 1970.

Krug, M. M. *History and the Social Sciences: New Approaches to the Teaching of Social Studies.* Waltham, Mass.: Blaisdell Publishing Company, 1967.

Kruskal, W. *Mathematical Sciences and Social Sciences.* Englewood Cliffs, N.J.: Prentice-Hall, 1970.

LaFauci, H. M., and Richter, P. E. *Team Teaching at the College Level.* Elmsford, N.Y.: Pergamon Press, 1970.

Lauter, P., and Howe, F. *The Women's Movement: Impact on the Campus and Curriculum.* Current Issues in Higher Education, National Conference Series. Washington, D.C.: American Association for Higher Education, 1978.

Layton, D. (Ed.). *University Teaching in Transition.* Edinburgh: Oliver and Boyd, 1968.

Learned, W. S., and Wood, B. D. *The Student and His Knowledge.* Report to the Carnegie Foundation on the Results of the High School and College Examinations of 1928, 1930, and 1932. Bulletin No. 29. New York: The Carnegie Foundation for the Advancement of Teaching, 1938.

Lenning, O. T. *The Outcomes Structure: An Overview and Procedures for Applying It in Postsecondary Education Institutions.* Boulder, Colo.: National Center for Higher Education Management Systems, 1977.

Lenning, O. T., and others. *A Structure for the Outcomes of Postsecondary Education.* Boulder, Colo.: National Center for Higher Education Management Systems, 1977.

Levine, A. *Handbook on Undergraduate Curriculum.* San Francisco: Jossey-Bass, 1978.

Levine, A., and Weingart, J. *Reform of Undergraduate Education.* San Francisco: Jossey-Bass, 1973.

Lumsden, K. G. (Ed.). *Recent Research in Economics Education.* Englewood Cliffs, N.J.: Prentice-Hall, 1970.

Lydo, W. J. "A Suggested Conceptual System for Decision Making in Curriculum Development." *Educational Record,* 1960, *41,* 74-83.

Mager, R. *Preparing Instructional Objectives.* Belmont, Calif.: Fearon, 1962.

Mager, R. *Goal Analysis.* Belmont, Calif.: Fearon, 1972.

Mann, R. D. *The College Classroom: Conflict, Change and Learning.* New York: Wiley, 1970.

Mattfeld, J. A. "Toward a New Synthesis in Curricular Patterns of Undergraduate Education." *Liberal Education,* 1975, *61* (4), 531-547.

Mayhew, L. B. *The Collegiate Curriculum: An Approach to Analysis.* SREB Research Monograph No. 11. Atlanta, Ga.: Southern Regional Education Board, 1966.

Mayhew, L. B. *Colleges Today and Tomorrow.* San Francisco: Jossey-Bass, 1969.

Mayhew, L. B. *Contemporary College Students and the Curriculum.* SREB Research Monograph No. 14. Atlanta, Ga.: Southern Regional Education Board, 1969.

Mayville, W. V. *Interdisciplinarity: The Mutable Paradigm.* AAHE-ERIC/Higher Education Research Report No. 9. Washington, D.C.: American Association for Higher Education, 1978.

McAchan, H. H. *Writing Behavioral Objectives: A New Approach.* New York: Harper & Row, 1970.

McGrath, E. J. "The College Curriculum—An Academic Wasteland?" *Liberal Education,* 1963, *49,* 235-247.

McGrath, E. J. *Values and American Higher Education.* Topical Paper No. 2. Tucson: Higher Education Program, University of Arizona, 1976.

McKeachie, W. J. "Research on Teaching at the College and University Level." In N. G. Gage (Ed.), *Handbook of Research on Teaching.* Chicago: Rand McNally, 1963.

McKeachie, W. J. *Teaching Tips: A Guidebook for the Beginning College Teacher.* (7th ed.) Lexington, Mass.: Heath, 1978.

McLeish, J. *The Lecture Method.* Cambridge Monograph on Teaching Methods No. 1. Cambridge, England: Cambridge Institution of Education, 1968.

Meiklejohn, A. *The Liberal College.* New York: Arno Press and New York Times Press, 1969.

Meinert, C. W. *Time Shortened Degrees.* Research Report No. 8, ED 098 857. Washington, D.C.: American Association for Higher Education, 1974.

Miller, R. I. *The Assessment of College Performance: A Handbook of Techniques and Measures for Institutional Self-Evaluation.* San Francisco: Jossey-Bass, 1979.

Morrisett, I. (Ed.). *Concepts and Structure in the New Social Science Curricula.* West Lafayette, Ind.: Social Science Education Consortium, 1966.

National Society for the Study of Education. *The Integration of Educational Experiences.* Fifty-Seventh Yearbook, Part III. Chicago: University of Chicago Press, 1958.

Newcomb, T. M. *Personality and Social Change: Attitude Formation in a Student Community.* New York: Dryden Press, 1943.

Pace, C. R., and Stern, G. G. *A Criterion Study of College Environment.* Syracuse, N.Y.: Psychological Research Center, Syracuse University Research Institute, 1958.

Parker, J. C., and Rubin, L. J. *Process as Content: Curriculum Design and the Application of Knowledge.* Chicago: Rand McNally, 1966.

Parlett, M., and Dearden, G. (Eds.). *Introduction to Illuminative Evaluation: Studies in Higher Education.* Berkeley, Calif.: Pacific Soundings Press, 1977.

Patterson, F., and Longsworth, C. R. *The Making of a College.* Cambridge, Mass.: M.I.T. Press, 1966.

Patterson, K. D. "The Administration of University Curriculum." *Journal of Higher Education,* 1967, *38,* 438-443.

Payton, P. W. "Origins of the Terms 'Major' and 'Minor' in American Higher Education." *History of Education Quarterly,* 1961, *1* (2), 57-63.

Perkin, H. J. *Innovation in Higher Education: New Universities in the United Kingdom.* Paris: Organization for Economic Cooperation and Development, 1969.

Perry, W. G., Jr. *Forms of Intellectual and Ethical Development in the College Years: A Scheme.* New York: Holt, Rinehart and Winston, 1968.

Pfnister, A. O. *Planning for Higher Education: Background and Application.* Boulder, Colo.: Westview Press, 1976.

Phenix, P. H. *Realms of Meaning: A Philosophy of the Curriculum for General Education.* New York: McGraw-Hill, 1964.

Piaget, J. *To Understand Is to Invent.* New York: Grossman, 1973.

Porter, N. *The American Colleges and the American Public.* New York: Arno Press and New York Times Press, 1969.

Posner, G. J., and Strike, K. A. "A Categorization Scheme for Principles of Sequencing Content." *Review of Educational Research,* 1976, *46* (4), 665-690.

Puglisi, D. J. "The Concept of Structure Revisited." *The Social Studies,* 1975, *46* (5), 204-207.

Reiners, W. A., and Smallwood, F. (Eds.). *Undergraduate Education in Environmental Studies.* Hanover, N.H.: Public Affairs Center, Dartmouth College, 1970.

Richardson, L. P. *Undergraduate Curriculum Improvement: A Conceptual and Bibliographic Study.* NLHE Research Monograph No. 1. Durham, N.C.: National Laboratory for Higher Education, 1971.

Robinson, L. H. *Renovating the Freshman Year.* Research Currents. Washington, D.C.: ERIC Clearinghouse on Higher Education, George Washington University, 1972. ED 068 075

Robinson, L. H. *Women's Studies: Courses and Programs for Higher Education.* Research Report No. 1. Washington, D.C.: American Association for Higher Education, 1973. ED 074 097

Romney, L. *Measures of Institutional Goal Achievement.* Boulder, Colo.: National Center for Higher Education Management Systems, 1978.

Rosecrance, F. C. *The American College and Its Teachers.* New York: Macmillan, 1962.

Roucek, J. S. (Ed.). *The Study of Foreign Languages.* New York: Philosophical Library, 1968.

Rudolph, F. *The American College and University: A History.* New York: Vintage Books, 1962.

Rudolph, F. *Curriculum: A History of the American Undergraduate Course of Study Since 1636.* San Francisco: Jossey-Bass, 1977.

Rudy, W. *The Evolving Liberal Arts Curriculum: A Historical Review of Basic Themes.* New York: Bureau of Publications, Teachers College, Columbia University, 1960.

Ruml, B., and Morrison, D. H. *Memo to a College Trustee.* New York: McGraw-Hill, 1959.

Sandeen, A. *Undergraduate Education: Conflict and Change.* Lexington, Mass.: Heath, 1977.

Sanford, N. *Where Colleges Fail: A Study of the Student as a Person.* San Francisco: Jossey-Bass, 1967.

Schmidt, G. P. *The Liberal Arts College: A Chapter in American Cultural History.* New Brunswick, N.J.: Rutgers University Press, 1957.

Scriven, M. *Evaluating Educational Programs: The Need and Response.* Paris: Organization for Economic Cooperation and Development, 1976.

Sheffield, E. F. (Ed.). *Curricular Innovation in Arts and Science.* Report of a Canadian Universities Workshop. Toronto: Higher Education Group, University of Toronto, 1970.

Shoenfeld, J. D. *Student-Initiated Changes in the Academic Curriculum.* ED 065 105. Washington, D.C.: ERIC Clearinghouse on Higher Education, George Washington University, 1972.

Smith, A. H., and Fischer, J. L. (Eds.). *Anthropology.* Englewood Cliffs, N.J.: Prentice-Hall, 1970.

Snow, L. F. *The College Curriculum in the United States.* New York: Teachers College Press, Columbia University, 1907.

Snyder, B. R. *The Hidden Curriculum.* New York: Knopf, 1971.

Stark, J. S., and Marchese, T. J. "Auditing College Publications for Prospective Students." *Journal of Higher Education,* 1978, *49* (1), 82-92.

Suddarth, B. M. "An Investigation of General Education Requirements in College Curricula." *Research in Higher Education,* 1975, *3* (3), 197-204.

Taffe, E. J. *Geography.* Englewood Cliffs, N.J.: Prentice-Hall, 1970.

Tamminen, P. G. *A Guide to Resources for Undergraduate Academic Reform.* Washington, D.C.: American Council on Education, 1970.

Thwing, C. F. *A History of Higher Education in America.* New York: Appleton-Century-Crofts, 1906.

Trivett, D. A. *Competency Programs in Higher Education.* AAHE-ERIC/Higher Education Research Report No. 7. Washington, D.C.: American Association for Higher Education, 1975.

Tussman, J. *Experiment at Berkeley*. London: Oxford University Press, 1969.

Tyler, R. W. *Basic Principles of Curriculum and Instruction*. Chicago: University of Chicago Press, 1949.

Tyler, R. W., Gagné, R. M., and Scriven, M. *Perspectives of Curriculum Evaluation*. American Educational Research Association Monograph Series on Curriculum Evaluation. Chicago: Rand McNally, 1967.

University of Chicago, Members of the Faculty. *The Idea and Practice of General Education*. Chicago: University of Chicago Press, 1950.

University of London Teaching Methods Unit. *Improving Teaching in Higher Education*. Leicester, England: Cavendish Press, 1976.

Walker, R. H. *American Studies in the United States: A Survey of College Programs*. Baton Rouge: Louisiana State University Press, 1958.

Weiss, C. *Evaluation Research: Methods of Assessing Program Effectiveness*. Englewood Cliffs, N.J.: Prentice-Hall, 1972.

Whitehead, A. N. *The Aims of Education*. New York: Macmillan, 1929.

Whitehead, A. N. *Modes of Thought*. New York: Macmillan, 1938.

Wilson, J. W., and Lyons, E. H. *Work-Study College Programs: Appraisal and Report of the Study of Cooperative Education*. New York: Harper & Row, 1961.

Withey, S. B. (Ed.). *A Degree and What Else?* New York: McGraw-Hill, 1971.

Wood, L., and Davis, B. G. *Designing and Evaluating Higher Education Curricula*. AAHE-ERIC/Higher Education Research Report No. 8. Washington, D.C.: American Association for Higher Education, 1978.

Wynne, J. P. *General Education in Theory and Practice*. New York: Bookman, 1952.

 Index

307